THE GOSPEL DAY;

OR,

THE LIGHT OF CHRISTIANITY.

By CHARLES E. ORR.

The light of Christianity
Now sheds its peaceful ray,
To light us on our journey home
To an eternal day.

The Gospel Day
By C. E. Orr

First Published by the Gospel Trumpet Company
Copyright © 2008 Reformation Publishers

All rights reserved. No part of this publication may be reproduced, stored in a retrieval system, or transmitted in any form or by any means--electronic, mechanical, photocopy, recording, or any other—except for brief quotations in printed reviews, without the prior permission of the copyright holder.

Softcover
ISBN 978-1-60416-157-1

Hardcover
ISBN 978-1-93330-429-8

Printed on Demand

Reformation Publishers, Inc.
14 S. Queen Street, Mt. Sterling, Kentucky 40353, USA
www.reformationpublishers.com
Email rpublisher@aol.com
Orders 1-800-765-2464
Information 859-520-3757
Text 606-359-2064
Fax 859-520-3357
Printed and bound in the United States of America

PREFACE.

Our task is finished. It has not been a disagreeable, unpleasant one, but joyous. Many times our soul was blessed and lifted up as the Spirit set before our mind the wondrous beauty of Christianity. In our soul we experience a deep sense of gratitude to God for his aid and guidance in this work. Many were the prayers we offered unto him for the aid of the Holy Spirit in the prosecution of this work. He has heard and answered our prayer, and we are satisfied. Praises be unto God! We lay no claims to literary ability; we have not studied to display such talent in this volume. We have only endeavored to give simple, plain truth respecting a holy life. We have endeavored to lift up true Christianity to its proper plane and to remove as far as possible, the clouds of error that have long obscured its beautiful, pellucid light. How far we have succeeded we leave to the reader.

This work would not be much of a production for some minds, but for ours it is quite an achievement. It is much more original than we at first intended it to be: however, we have selected from the *Gospel Trumpet* the following subjects: "Woman's Freedom," "Eating of Meat," and "The Sin Against the Holy Ghost," which were written by Geo. L. Cole, Russel Austin, and A. L. Byers, respectively. All other selections are, we believe, properly acknowledged where they appear.

6   PREFACE.

Seventy-six pages of the original manuscript were lost in the mail. This, at first, presented itself as a discouragement, but we at once remembered that all things work together for good to them that love the Lord, consequently we concluded that the Lord wanted some truth brought out that was not contained in the first writings; so we set to our task of reproducing the lost pages with a will, and God has crowned our efforts with a much greater satisfaction to ourselves. We now feel we have done what we could, and as this manuscript leaves our hand it shall be with a prayer that God will make it a rich blessing to many hearts.

Should this book be the means of lifting up some weary, despondent soul, or succeed in turning some sinner from the error of his way, or helping some deceived one out of his deception, or inspiring some fallen one to a truer, nobler life, I shall be many, many times repaid for my labor, and shall indeed give God the glory. If some one detects an error in this work do not be hasty in condemning me, but write me, thus giving me opportunity of explaining the supposed error, or of humbly confessing my fault. With deep affection in my soul, I pray the God of heaven to bless every reader of this book, and kindly ask all who pray to pray that I may do all the good I can in this world and gain an eternity in the blissful fields of heaven.   Yours in **Christian love,**
    Chas. E. Orr, Federalsburg, Md.

CONTENTS.

	PAGE
INTRODUCTION	9

PART I.

THE MORNING; OR, CHRISTIANITY IN THE FIRST CENTURIES OF THIS GOSPEL AGE AS REVEALED IN THE LIFE AND TEACHING OF CHRIST AND THE APOSTLES.

CHAPTER I.—CHRISTIANITY A LIGHT	30
CHAPTER II.—THE HOLY SCRIPTURES	44
CHAPTER III.—SIN	52
CHAPTER IV.—SALVATION	56
CHAPTER V.—THE WAY FROM SIN TO PERFECT SALVATION	63
CHAPTER VI.—FRUITS AND THE TWO WORKS	101
CHAPTER VII.—THE CHURCH OF GOD	130
CHAPTER VIII.—THE ORDINANCES OF THE NEW TESTAMENT	152
CHAPTER IX.—DIVINE HEALING	174
CHAPTER X.—THE SOUL	181
CHAPTER XI.—SPIRITUAL CULTURE	192
CHAPTER XII.—THE COURSE OF THE WORLD	221
CHAPTER XIII.—THE DOMESTIC RELATION	240
CHAPTER XIV.—EVIL HABITS AND INJURIOUS INDULGENCES	287

CONTENTS.

CHAPTER XV.—THE TRINITY 307
CHAPTER XVI.—MISCELLANEOUS SUBJECTS...319

PART II

THE NOONDAY; OR, THE DOCTRINES OF AN APOSTATE RELIGION OBSCURING THE GOSPEL LIGHT.

CHAPTER I.—THE DATE OF THE BEGINNING OF THE NOONDAY....................... 371
CHAPTER II.—SCRIPTURAL PREDICTIONS OF AN APOSTASY 383
CHAPTER III.—FALSE TEACHING OF THE APOSTASY 434

PART III.

THE EVENING; OR, CHRISTIANITY IN THE CLOSING DAYS OF THIS GOSPEL ERA.

CHAPTER I.—THE APOSTASY IN TWO DAYS... 455
CHAPTER II.—THE TIME OF THE EVENING... 460

THE GOSPEL DAY;

OR, THE LIGHT OF CHRISTIANITY.

INTRODUCTION.

IN Jesus' name we are here to unveil before the reader the picture of a beautiful virgin, whom we shall call Christianity. Never was there a character seen upon the earth half so beautiful as she. In her loveliness she has won the heart of many. The proud and noble have been brought down to worship at her feet. The lowly have been lifted up to admire her gracious charms. Peasants have invited her into their humble homes, where she reigned as a queen of light and peace. Gloom and darkness is driven away by her sweet angelic smile. She has lifted the despondent out of the vortex of despair, and by her animating presence encouraged them to bright hopes and a happy life. The bitter lot of the poor she has sweetened, and the burden and care of riches takes wings and flies away at her approach. She has been brought into the presence of kings and almost won their hearts. Men have sacrificed the world to gain her love. She is a ray of heavenly light in this dark world.

The words of finite man are inadequate to describe the true character of Christianity. In our description we shall exalt her only by the words contained in the book sent down from heaven. That alone is worthy to eulogize her name. When the reader has followed our delineation to the close, and inspected every feature of this virtuous queen, we trust the decision of his heart will be yet deeper than his who said, "Almost thou persuadest me to be a Christian."

Christianity should be full of interest to all mankind, She not only cools the heated brow, cheers the drooping heart, and strews life's pathway with flowers of peace, but she deals with man's eternal destiny. She will smooth the rough places all along his journey of life, and when he has come down to the end, it is she that will bear him across the valley and welcome him to the home prepared for his eternal inhabitancy.

Since the day of her nativity she has had a bitter obstinate foe, Satan, and wicked men have combined to bespoil her white robes and mar her fair form. They have struggled long and hard to bring her low. They have endeavored to extinguish her radiant light and defame her true character. We have only to take a stroll through the halls of denominationalism to learn how far they have succeeded. To many pews and pulpits our virgin has no excellence or beauty. In the pulpit orator's exposition of her she is not exalted one whit above the coarse, vulgar world. Satan has succeeded in veiling her fair form and true virtues from the hearts of many. In the opinions of many she is reduced to a mere nothing. Angels weep to see her fair robes trailed in the dust. Those who pretend to love her have brought her to shame. The low, degrading opinions entertained regarding her throughout the realms of sectarianism grieves the souls of her true admirers. They have brought her down from her pure, high throne and mingled her with the lives of ordinary sinful men. They have stripped her of her clean, white garments and covered her with a cloak of many colors. They have robbed her of her virtues and have stained her fair name until to-day all that is seen of Christianity in the aristocratic circles of Christendom is a maiden weeping over her stained vesture, lost virginity and reproached name. Thank God, such is true only in appearance. True Christianity is seen by her few devoted followers to-day the same pure, spotless virgin, the same queen of peace and light, as when she crowned the brow of the lowly Nazarene and his immediate followers. She has lost none of her virtuous charms. She is true. She reigns a lovely queen, glorious in power, pure in principle, "Clear as the sun, fair as the moon, and terrible as an army with banners."

Satan has robed a harlot and named her Christianity and succeeded in imposing her upon many in the world. They are fondling with her. She indulges them in sensuality, while encouraging them to hope in a peaceful immortality. The kings of the earth have committed fornication with her. They are reveling, feasting and banqueting with her, crazed by her seductive charms. She has neither purity, peace, nor power. Her robes are defiled by sin. She scoffs at pure Christianity and calls her old-fashioned. This strange young woman is using every device to allure souls into her wanton chamber. She is most subtle of heart. She "flattereth with her words. In the twilight, in the evening, in the black and dark night, she walketh in the streets, and lieth wait at every corner, that she might catch and kiss him who is void of understanding." With a beguiling, impudent face she says to him: "I have peace offerings with me; I have decked my bed with tapestry, with carved works, with fine linen of Egypt. I have perfumed my bed with myrrh, aloes, and cinnamon. Come let us take our fill of love until the morning: let us solace ourselves with love."

Such is the gay, fast, frivolous Christianity of the popular present day religions of our honored land. The generality of denominational membership (we speak in love) desire a Christianity that will go with them to the halls of pleasure; that will dine with them at the banquets; that will smile on them as they walk in the ways of sin and worldliness, calming their fears with her flattering words and peace offerings. Primitive Christianity, they consider, was good enough for primitive days, but she would be a horrid enough old maid in these days of progress. In this fast driving age the Christianity that crowned the life of the holy apostles is altogether too antiquated. She drew men from the world, she crucified their lust, she taught them to practise self-denial and keep their body in subjection; she brought them in humility at her feet; she led them in the paths of virtue and honor; she upbraided them for sin, and told them of the vengeance and wrath of God against every evil.

The world to-day, in general, is saying, "Away with such an old-time Christianity; she has no charms for us. She is too common and plain, too grave and sober. We will not walk with her; give us the gay and dashing young harlot that we may walk with her amid the pleasures of the world, and with her gratify our lusts. She never chides us for sin, nor troubles us about the anger of God nor the torments of hell. She invites us into her bosom and gives us a sweet opiate draught of 'stolen waters and the bread of secrecies, and bids us take our 'fill of love.'"

Dear reader, "go not after her." "Let not thine heart decline to her ways, go not astray in her paths. For she hath cast down many wounded: yea, many strong men have been slain by her. Her house is the way to hell, going down to the chambers of death."

The mission of this volume is to exalt true Christianity to her proper plane and reveal her true character by relating to the reader the teachings of Christ —her beloved consort—and the experience and teachings of his inspired followers, and thus tear off the sacrilegious robes of the harlot of false religions and expose her shame to the gaze of every honest soul.

Christianity is not a mere profession, but a principle. Every being is possessed with a principle. Satan has a principle, which might properly be termed devilanity; Christ has a principle which is termed Christianity. When this Christ principle is instilled into man's soul by the Spirit of God he becomes a Christian. He possesses the Christ-life, nature, or principle. Now Christ was the truth. Then the Christ nature or principle is according to the truth, whether it be in Christ or man. We have only then to lift up the whole truth, which by the wisdom and grace of God we shall do in this work, which will reveal true Christianity and expose every imposition. Christ is the vine; Christians are the branches. The vine and the branches are of the same nature. The branches retain life by abiding in the vine. They who abide in Christ walk (or live) even as Christ walked (or lived); that is, the vine and the branches bear the same kind of fruit. This is the philosophy of true Christianity. Anything bearing fruit in nature contrary to the truth or Christ principle is not Christianity, but is devilanity. "Ye are of your father the devil, and the lusts of your father will ye do;" or sinful fruit ye will bear.

CHRISTIAN POWER.

Christianity—stately queen,
Virgin—loveliest ever seen,
Fairest art thou upon the earth,
And of a higher, nobler birth.
When king Agrippa heard thy name,
And how abroad was spread thy fame,
And saw thee lovely as thou art,
Thou almost won his heathen heart.
When in the midnight's gloomy hour,
The Romish jailer saw thy power,
When thund'ring tones his ear did greet,
He trembling worshiped at thy feet.
When kneeling down beside the dead,
In sacred, solemn tones, thou said,
"Dorcas, in Jesus' name arise,"
And opened were the woman's eyes.
When man four days in death had lain,
Thou gavest him back his life again.
When woman did her sin deplore,
Thou whispered, "Go, and sin no more."
When wicked Simon saw thy power
He strove to win thee with a dower;
Within his sinful heart he thought
Thy power with money could be bought;
Thou spurned his offer and made bold,
To bid him perish with his gold.
They lied to thee and lost their life,
Both Ananias and his wife.
Such was thy power in days of yore,
And such 'twill be forevermore.

CHRISTIAN PURITY.

Fairest art thou among the fair,
Thy graces none but thee can wear;
In trailing robes of snowy white,
Thou art on earth a gleam of light;
Thy cheeks are comely as the rose,
Thy neck as white as winter snows;
Thy lips are like a scarlet thread,
Thy locks like silver on thy head.
To him who with thee is in love,
Thou'rt meek and gentle as the dove;
Virgin, so pure and bold and free,
No spot is found at all in thee.
Such was thy purity of yore
And such 'twill be forevermore.

THE GOSPEL DAY SEEN IN PROPHECY.

Upon reading the account of man's creation in the first chapters of Genesis we conclude that he enjoyed perfect peace and happiness. From the beautiful description given there of the garden of Eden—man's abode—we understand that God was interested in his felicity. In the nature of created things he could retain this happiness only by obedience to the Creator's laws. By a subtle foe he was induced to transgress those laws and thus became acquainted with sin and sorrow. After the transgression he hid himself among the trees of the garden from the presence of the Lord because a fear rested upon his conscious being.

> Man in sweet felicity was made,
> But sorrowed when God he disobeyed.

The man was turned out upon the world to earn his support by labor. The ground was cursed for his sake. It brought forth thorns and thistles, and in sorrow he must eat of it all the days of his life. Cherubims and a flaming sword prevented his return to the tree of life, which stood in the midst of the garden. The apostle John in his revelations beheld this sad scene. He saw the book of life—tree of life— to be sealed with seven seals, and he saw a strong angel proclaiming with a loud voice, "Who is worthy to open the book, and to loose the seals thereof? And no man in heaven, nor in earth, neither under the earth, was able to open the book, neither to look thereon," and he wept much. Rev. 5:1-4. How sad the scene! Man was created in holiness and happiness. He dwelt in the garden of Eden and had access to the tree of life, the very source of peace. But sin entered his heart. He was driven away to be in sorrow all his days. No man in heaven nor earth could secure his return. God saw his wretchedness and that his "wickedness was great in the earth" and "it grieved him at his heart." Gen. 6:5, 6. Sin swayed its scepter over the heart of man and he groaned beneath its tyrannical power, but God's mercy was not "clean gone forever." They cried unto the Lord because of the oppressors and he promised to send them a "Savior, and a great one," to deliver them. Isa. 19: 20. Man was encaged in the prison-house of sin, but God promised to send a deliverer "to proclaim liberty to the captives, and the opening of the prison to them that are bound." Isa. 61: 1.

The beloved apostle John, in the vision before mentioned, wept because no man was found worthy to open the book; but one of the elders said unto him, "Weep not: behold, the Lion of the tribe of Juda, the Root of David, hath prevailed to open the book, and to loose the seven seals thereof." Praise God! John in his vision saw the man fall from his pure and happy state into sin and the book of life becoming sealed. He also saw that no man in heaven nor earth was able to restore him to his original place and holiness, and it caused him to weep. But in his vision there appeared one who prevailed to open the book and "redeem us unto God out of every kindred and tongue and people and nation."

In the prophetic days of ancient Israel men who walked with God and trusted in his promises were permitted a visionary look down through the centuries to behold the dawning of a day glorious in the effulgency of its light and the greatness of its power. Even in those dim, remote days the wondrous glory of a day when the "Prince of Peace" should come was foreseen by the prophets, who break forth in beautiful strains of music, expressing their joy and admiration. Isaiah in speaking of that expected day says, "Arise, shine; for thy light is come, and the glory of the Lord is risen upon thee. For, behold, the darkness shall cover the earth, and gross darkness the people: but the Lord shall arise upon thee, and his glory shall be seen upon thee. And the Gentiles shall come to thy light, and kings to the brightness of thy rising." Isa. 60: 1-3.

It is a day of wonderful light. When the prophet speaks of the Gentiles coming to the light the reader begins to understand the time of the dawning. He further says, "Violence shall no more be heard in thy land, wasting nor destruction within thy borders; but thou shalt call thy walls Salvation, and thy gates Praise. The sun shall be no more thy light by day; neither for brightness shall the moon give light unto thee: but the Lord shall be unto thee an everlasting light, and thy God thy glory. Thy sun shall no more go down; neither shall thy moon withdraw itself: for the Lord shall be thine everlasting light, and the days of thy mourning shall be ended." Isa. 60: 18-20.

The prophet by a long stretch of faith passed through the gates of Praise to within the walls of Salvation and beheld a light above the brightness of the sun and the softness of the moon. We quote these texts, and the following, to impress the reader's mind and heart with the greatness of the light and the wonders of that coming day as seen in expectation by those ancient holy men. After a while we will come to the dawning, then the noontide, then the evening of this great day, and we will find the glory and the wonders to be as the prophets foresaw and described.

What can the holy seer mean by saying, "Violence shall no more be heard in thy land, wasting nor destruction within thy borders"? We have only to turn to the eleventh chapter, where we have this clearly explained. Let us read: "And there shall come forth a rod out of the stem of Jesse, and a Branch shall grow out of his roots: and the spirit of the Lord shall rest upon him, the spirit of wisdom and understanding, the spirit of counsel and might, the spirit of knowledge and of the fear of the Lord; and shall make him of quick understanding in the fear of the Lord: and he shall not judge after the sight of his eyes, neither reprove after the hearing of his ears; but with righteousness shall he judge the poor, and reprove with equity for the meek of the earth: and he shall smite the earth with the rod of his mouth, and with the breath of his lips shall he slay the wicked. And righteousness shall be the girdle of his loins, and faithfulness the girdle of his reigns. The wolf also shall dwell with the lamb, and the leopard shall lie down with the kid; and the calf and the young lion and the fatling together; and a little child shall lead them. And the cow and the bear shall feed; their young ones shall lie down together: and the lion shall eat straw like the ox. And the sucking child shall play on the hole of the asp, and the weaned child shall put his hand on the cockatrice' den. They shall not hurt nor destroy in all my holy mountain: for the earth shall be full of the knowledge of the Lord, as the waters cover the sea. And in that day there shall be a root of Jesse, which shall stand for an ensign of the people; to it shall the Gentiles seek: and his rest shall be glorious."

Who does not know who is referred to by the words "the Root of Jesse," whom the Gentiles shall seek, "and his rest shall be glorious"? We hear of one saying in the New Testament, "Come unto me, all ye that labor and are heavy-laden, and I will give you rest." "Violence shall no more be heard in thy land." "The wolf shall dwell with the lamb" in the day when the Gentiles shall seek rest in the Root of Jesse. This prophecy will never have a literal fulfilment, as some erroneously teach. It only exalts the salvation of the Branch of Jesse to deliver men from the wolf and lion disposition. It is the peacefulness of Christianity. In the day the prophet is speaking of there shall be peace on the earth. Man can find deliverance from sin and obtain a peaceful rest—not being disturbed by evil and ill dispositions.

Isaiah in again beholding this glorious rest-day discovers a way which is called the way of holiness. He says, "The unclean shall not pass over it; . . . no lion shall be there, nor any ravenous beast shall go up thereon, it shall not be found there; but the redeemed shall walk there: and the ransomed of the Lord shall return, and come to Zion with songs and everlasting joy upon their heads: they shall obtain joy and gladness, and sorrow and sighing shall flee away." Isa. 35:8-10. Any one can understand that a literal beast is not meant here when he speaks of a lion, but that wicked, unclean men can not walk in the way of holiness—only the redeemed can walk there.

Earlier in this chapter he speaks of the eyes of the blind being opened, and the ears of the deaf being unstopped, and the lame being made to leap as a hart, and the tongue of the dumb being made to sing. We have only to read the New Testament to learn of the fulfilment of this prophecy. In that day men of unclean, ravenous, and lion-like natures shall find deliverance and be made gentle, lowly and humble—"The wolf and the lamb shall dwell together." What a wonder and expectation must have filled the hearts of those devout men in those days of darkness and gloom, as they looked forward to that time when the blind should see, the deaf hear, and the lame walk; when there should be no more violence nor destruction nor wasting, but there should be songs of everlasting joy, and sorrow and sighing would flee away.

"In that day shall this song be sung in the land of Judah; we have a strong city; salvation will God appoint for walls and bulwarks." Isa. 26:1. In that day salvation's walls shall surround the people of God. In the time of this prophet it was stone walls that surrounded their city, but he looked forward to a time when the walls of salvation would surround the city of God. Salvation means deliverance. In that day the people of God should find a deliverance or cleansing from sin. It is the gospel day when Christ should offer a sacrifice for the whole world. The people cried unto God because of their oppressors, and he sent them a Savior, and a strong one, to deliver them. Isa. 19:20.

Were we to turn to the first chapter of the gospel by Luke we would there learn who this deliverer was. There we read: "Blessed be the Lord God of Israel: for he hath visited and redeemed his people, and hath raised up a horn of salvation for us in the house of his servant David; as he spake by the mouth of his holy prophets, which have been since the world began: that we should be saved from our enemies, and from the hand of all that hate us; to perform the mercy promised to our fathers, and to remember his holy covenant; the oath which he sware to our father Abraham, that he would grant unto us, that we being delivered out of the hand of our enemies might serve him without fear, in holiness and righteousness before him all the days of our life."

By reading the whole of this chapter you will learn that this horn of salvation, this deliverer, was the child Christ Jesus. This deliverer was to appear in that day. The most simple will at once understand that the day foreseen and foretold by the holy seers was the Christian dispensation, or the day of "grace and truth."

The prophet again exclaims: "And in that day thou shalt say, O Lord, I will praise thee: though thou wast angry with me, thine anger is turned away, and thou comfortedst me. Behold, God is my salvation; I will trust, and not be afraid: for the Lord Jehovah is my strength and my song; he also is become my salvation. Therefore with joy shall ye draw water out of the wells of salvation. And in that day shall ye say, Praise the Lord." Isa. 12:1-4. "In that day shall the branch of the Lord be beautiful and glorious, and the fruit of the earth shall be excellent and comely for them that are escaped of Israel. And it shall come to pass, that he that is left in Zion, and he that remaineth in Jerusalem, shall be called holy." Isa. 4:2, 3.

The prophet Joel in contemplation of that day of great blessings says: "And it shall come to pass in that day, that the mountains shall drop down new wine, and the hills shall flow with milk, and all the rivers of Judah shall flow with waters, and a fountain shall come forth of the house of the Lord, and shall water the valley of Shittim." Joel 3:18.

Zechariah in beholding this fountain exclaims: "In that day there shall be a fountain opened to the house of David and to the inhabitants of Jerusalem for sin and for uncleanness." Zech. 13:1.

> Wonderful Fountain of cleansing,
> The prophet did foresee,
> Deep Fountain of peace and glory
> Opened to all shall be.

The prophet again in beholding the glory and purity of that day says: "In that day shall there be upon the bells of the horses, HOLINESS UNTO THE LORD." Zech. 14:20.

> The prophet did foretell a day,
> Through which extends a holy way,
> Where walk the ramsomed of the Lord,
> Made pure in heart, through Jesus' blood.

Another man of God is permitted to look down through the darkness and see the glory of this day of cleansing. "But who may abide the day of his coming? and who shall stand when he appeareth? for he is like a refiner's fire, and like fullers' soap: and he shall sit as a refiner and purifier of silver: and he shall purify the sons of Levi, and purge them as gold and silver, that they may offer unto the Lord an offering in righteousness." Mal. 3:2, 3. In that day there shall be a fountain of cleansing, or a fire of refining, when hearts shall be made pure as gold and silver is refined and made pure. It is the day in which Isaiah says, "Though your sins be as scarlet, they shall be as white as snow; though they be red like crimson, they shall be as wool." Isa. 1:18.

The day foretold by this holy train of Old Testament prophets was spoken of as a day of "peace and rest"; a day of "praise and salvation"; a day of "refining"; a day when a "cleansing fountain shall be opened"; a day when "scarlet stains shall be made white as snow"; a day when "the lame man shall leap as a hart, and the tongue of the dumb shall sing," and the deaf ears shall hear, and blind eyes be made to see; a day when the ransomed of the Lord shall return and come unto Zion with songs and everlasting joy upon their heads; a day when "the desert shall blossom as the rose"; a day when the wolf and the lamb shall dwell together; a day when the "Branch of the Lord shall be beautiful and glorious." Praise God!

That day seen so far away by those righteous men awakened songs of praise in their hearts. They were not speaking of the eternal day in the glory world; neither of a supposed millennial age, but of this present glorious dispensation of grace and salvation. It requires only two texts to clearly prove this. The first is Isa. 49:8: "Thus saith the Lord, In an acceptable time have I heard thee, and in a day of salvation have I helped thee." The second is found in 2 Cor. 6:2. Paul here quotes this promise the Lord made, and then says, "Behold now is the accepted time; behold, now is the day of salvation." Again in Rom. 13:12 the apostle speaks of his having arrived at that day. He says, "The night is far spent, the day is at hand, let us therefore cast off the works of darkness, and let us put on the armor of light." How beautiful! The Christian's armor in the "day of salvation" is one of light, the darkness is flown away. The Old Testament writer said that in that day God would send a Savior. In the New Testament it is recorded that "unto you is born this day in the city of David a Savior, which is Christ the Lord." The Savior God had promised was the Christ, and the day was now come.

> All hail the glad gospel day,
> Peace and good will to men;
> The darkness has flown away,
> And grace has conquered sin.

By many a prophetic Old Testament text that day of wonderful light and glory was spoken of as a day when God's salvation should appear. In the second chapter of Luke it is recorded that there lived in Jerusalem a just and devout man, who knowing those prophetic sayings concerning that great day of consolation, waited for its dawning. It was revealed unto him by the Holy Spirit that he should not see death, before he had seen the Lord's Christ. He came by the Spirit into the temple: and when the parents brought in the child Jesus, to do for him after the custom of the law, then took he him up in his arms, and blessed God, and said, "Lord, now lettest thou thy servant depart in peace, according to thy word: for mine eyes have seen thy salvation." Simeon, as he looked upon this young child, saw the salvation the ancient prophets saw only by faith. The day of which they prophesied the Holy Spirit witnessed to his heart he should live to see, and he saw it. It was the dawning of the day of Christian power and purity, in which we shall find came to pass all the prophetic wonders of salvation. You need not look forward to some marvelous coming age in which to find a fulfilment of these prophecies, but "to-day if ye will hear his voice, harden not your hearts." "How shall we escape if we neglect so great salvation?"

For convenience and clearness we have thought best to divide this work into three parts. Part first to consist of the revealing of Christianity as seen in the life and teaching of Christ and the teaching and lives of his followers during the first few centuries of this Christian era, which is termed the morning of the gospel day. Part second will consist of the apostolic prophecies with possibly a few Old Testament prophecies concerning an apostasy during the middle centuries, or, the noontide of the gospel day; also showing that these prophecies find an exact fulfilment in the customs and doings of the popular religious denominations of this present time. Part third will consist of the prophecies relating to the restoration of the glorious truths of Christianity, or a return of God's people to the apostolic plane of Christian faith and power and teaching in the evening of this day of salvation. With this introduction we feel confident the reader understands the plan of this work and will readily comprehend its teachings. "Consider what I say; and the Lord give thee understanding," is my prayer.

PART I.
THE MORNING;
(Isa. 21:11, 12.)

or,

CHRISTIANITY IN THE FIRST CENTURIES OF THIS GOSPEL AGE AS REVEALED IN THE LIFE AND TEACHING OF CHRIST AND THE APOSTLES.

In this division of this work we desire to set forth in a clear, comprehensive manner the true character and principles of Christianity as seen in the teachings of the Holy Scriptures. The Bible is our only source of knowledge respecting the true nature of a Christian life. Man may presume, but the Scriptural declarations are in verity. The New Testament sets forth in such clearness the nature of a Christian heart and the conduct that naturally issues from such a heart that none need be deceived as to their spiritual standing. Christianity is in absolute and perfect accord with the Holy Scriptures. This is a fact that all must concede. No matter what may be the philosophy and theory of man, Christianity is just what the Bible plainly declares it to be. A life that is out of harmony with the sacred truth can not be a Christian life. For this reason we desire to set forth the principal teachings of the New Testament respecting practical Christianity.

CHAPTER I.

CHRISTIANITY A LIGHT.

Throughout the Scriptures Christianity is spoken of as a light. The Christian era is referred to as a day. A day is when the light shineth. In speaking of the beautiful dawning of the Star of Christianity the prophet says: "And the Gentiles shall come to thy light, and kings to the brightness of thy rising." "Arise, shine; for thy light is come." "The sun shall be no more thy light by day; neither for brightness shall the moon give light unto thee: but the Lord shall be unto thee an everlasting light, and thy God thy glory." Isa. 60. It is not meant to say here that Christians have no need of the light of the sun or the moon, but to teach that the light of the sun and the brightness of the moon is not to be compared to the transcendent light of Christianity. Whose heart has not been touched with a feeling of admiration as they beheld the bright dawning of the round, red sun, or the beautiful rising of a full moon? These are not to be compared with the "brightness of the rising" of the gospel day. "To them which sat in the region and shadow of death light is sprung up." Mat. 4: 16. "Through the tender mercy of our God, whereby the dayspring [sun rising—margin] from on high hath visited us, to give light to them that sit in darkness and in the shadow of death, to guide our feet into the way of peace." Luke 1: 78, 79.

Jesus says of himself, "I am the root and the offspring of David, and the bright and morning star." Rev. 22: 16. Christ speaking to the church at Thyatira, says to those that overcome and keep his works unto the end, that he will give them the morning star. Rev. 2: 28. He will give them the true light and glory of Christianity, or his own light and nature. All will do well to take heed to do his works "until the day dawn and the day star arise in their hearts."

In the natural world there is a literal solar system consisting of the sun, moon and planets. The sun is the center around which all the planets revolve, and from which they receive their light. The moon borrows its light from the sun. When some object interposes between the moon and the sun the moon is left in darkness. In the spiritual world there is a spiritual solar system consisting of sun, moon and stars. As in the literal system, the moon and stars revolve around the Sun and borrow their light therefrom.

THE SPIRITUAL SUN OR LIGHT.

It is not difficult to glean from the Scriptures the knowledge of the true center of this spiritual solar system, or the true source of light. The last writer of the Old Testament Scriptures, in his last chapter says: "But unto you that fear my name shall the Sun of righteousness arise with healing in his wings." All understand this text to refer to the Lord Jesus. His visitation to this world, through the mercy of God, is termed, "The sun-rising." Luke 1: 78, margin. Christ is the Sun and true source of light of the gospel day. The church of God collectively is the moon of this spiritual solar system, and its individual members are the stars. In the Savior's prophecy as recorded in Mark 13: 24, 25, the term "sun" is a metaphor, signifying Christ; the "moon," the church, as a whole; the "stars," Christians, or especially the ministry.

This darkening of the sun and moon and the falling of the stars we will clearly explain in part second of this work. The church of God receives its light from Jesus. He is "the light of the world." In the language of Isa. 60: 1 the church is addressed: "Arise, shine; for thy light is come." Christ is her light. The church shines by the light of Christ, as the moon shines by the light of the sun. "Out of Zion [the church of God], the perfection of beauty, God hath shined." The church as a whole is a brilliant reflector to reflect the light of Christ to this universe. Every Christian is a bright spot in this luminous reflector. Amen. "Let your light so shine."

A few years ago, one beautiful Sunday summer evening, as we were on our way to an appointed meeting, we observed the moon rising in the splendor of its fulness. It shed its soft, peaceful rays over the earth in marked beauty. After a short time we became aware of a gathering darkness. On looking up we saw a dark object gathering over the moon. Slowly, but surely the dark object crept on until all was darkened. Not one ray of light fell from the moon. The sun had ceased to shine upon her. We understood that the world had come in between the sun and the moon and obstructed the sun's rays. The same is true of the spiritual moon, the church. In the first few centuries of this Christian day it shone with the light and glory of God, but the time came when the "moon [church] ceased to give her light," and all because, as we will learn, the world came between it and the Sun (Christ).

CHRISTIAN POWER AND PURITY.

Christianity is a light in this world because of the greatness of its power and the excellence of its purity. John, who is denominated the forerunner of Jesus, or the heralding star of Christianity, said that "he was not that Light, but was sent to bear witness of that Light. That was the true Light, which lighteth every man that cometh into the world." John 1: 8, 9. Of whom speaketh the prophet then? The Son of God will answer this question in these words: "I am the light of the world: he that followeth me shall not walk in darkness, but shall have the light of life." John 8: 12. Jesus was the light of the world because of his power and purity. All power was given unto him in heaven and in earth. Mat. 28:18.

He was holy, harmless and undefiled. Heb. 7:26. The Lord Jesus lived a pure and holy life. "He did no sin, neither was guile found in his mouth." He had power to open the blind eyes, to unstop the deaf ears, to loose the dumb tongue, to make the lame man leap as a hart, and to heal all manner of diseases, and to raise the dead. There is no sin in heaven; there is no sickness there. He brought the light of heaven to this world in displaying his power over sin and disease. Glory to his name!

We wish to impress this fact upon the reader's mind that he was a light because of his purity and power, and because he was the "Truth." And now if you will but believe it, that is the true light of Christianity. The Lord Jesus was only a visitant. His stay on earth was transient. He came from heaven, and heaven soon again received him. Referring to his departure he said to his disciples: "Yet a little while is the light with you. Walk while ye have the light; . . . while ye have light, believe in the light, that ye may be the children of light." John 12:35, 36.

Again he says, "As long as I am in the world, I am the light of the world." John 9:5. We learn the sad story of his crucifixion, then the glad news of his resurrection, and then his ascension in a cloud to the glory, from whence he came. Is the light of Christianity gone from the world? Is this world left again in darkness? No; thank God! Jesus now says to his devoted followers: "Ye are the light of the world. A city that is set on a hill can not be hid." Mat. 5:14. It is the "city of Zion, the perfection of beauty," out of which God doth shine. "The glory of God is risen upon her." Jesus told them to believe in the light while they had the light, that they might be the children of light. Paul, in exhorting Christians to a holy life, said: "That ye may be blameless and harmless, the sons of God, without rebuke, in the midst of a crooked and perverse nation, among whom ye shine as lights in the world." Phil. 2:15. "For ye were sometimes darkness, but now are ye light in the Lord: walk as children of light." Eph. 5:8. "Ye are all the children of light, and the children of the day: we are not of the night, nor of darkness." 1 Thes. 5:5.

This is the spiritual moon reflecting the light of the Sun. It is "God that shineth in thee." They are "light in the Lord," and they are commanded to "let their light shine, that God might be glorified." This is beautiful. Oh, what a privilege

> To be a vessel transparent,
> Clear as the crystal sea,
> Letting the glorious light of heaven
> Brilliantly shine through thee.

Beloved saints, take heed that there be not one spot in thee to obstruct the light of God. 'Let it shine.'

Submissively place thyself in the crucible and there be polished and refined and purged and cleansed until thou art "purer than snow, and whiter than milk, and more ruddy than rubies."

How can the Lord now, since his ascension, shine through his church? The Scriptures make this very plain. Jesus told his own that he would not long be with them, but said, "I will pray the Father, and he shall give you another Comforter, that he may abide with you forever; even the Spirit of truth; whom the world can not receive, because it seeth him not, neither knoweth him: but ye know him for he dwelleth with you, and shall be in you. I will not leave you comfortless: I will come to you." John 14: 16-18.

In verse twenty-six he tells us the Comforter is the Holy Ghost. In the second chapter of Acts we have the account of the Holy Spirit's coming. If you will again look over the quotation from John 14: 16-18 you will notice he uses "Comforter" and "I" interchangeably. He will give you another Comforter. "I will not leave you comfortless: I will come to you." The Holy Spirit's coming on Pentecost was Christ in another personage. Christ in the Spirit has now come to dwell in the midst of his people, and to be a light in them. Jesus was here in the body on a mission of mercy. He tasted death for every man. He comes again in the Spirit to "reprove the world of righteousness, of sin, and of judgment." In Heb. 10: 5 Jesus says, "A body hast thou prepared me." A body in which to offer a sacrifice for the sins of the world. He now has a body in which he dwells in the Spirit. Christians are "a holy temple in the Lord, in whom they are builded together for a habitation of God through the Spirit." Thus God inhabits his people, "dwells in them, and walks in them." The church of God is now the body of Christ. He is the "head over all things to the church, which is his body." Eph. 1:22, 23; see also Col. 1:18.

In speaking of saints in 1 Cor. 12:27 the apostle says, "Now ye are the body of Christ and members in particular." He was the light of the world in his incarnation, and now the church, his body, is the light of the world. Incarnate he was a light because of his purity and power, and he lives the same pure life and manifests the same marvelous power in his body, the church, as when here in his personal ministry. He healed the sick, cast out devils, opened blinded eyes, unstopped deaf ears, and raised the dead. After the Holy Spirit's coming he performs the same wondrous works in his body, the church. Through the apostle Peter he healed a lame man, restored to life a dead woman, etc. He is "the very same Jesus." When he was here in the flesh he could be seen and his marvelous works witnessed by the natural eye. The Holy Spirit is imperceptible to the natural eye, and therefore can only reveal himself to the world as he works in the midst of his people. It is thus that Christians reflect the light of Christ.

In the sixteenth of Mark the Lord commanded his disciples to go "into all the world, and preach the gospel to every creature. He that believeth and is baptized shall be saved; but he that believeth not shall be damned. And these signs shall follow them that believe; in my name shall they cast out devils; they shall speak with new tongues; they shall take up serpents; and if they drink any deadly thing, it shall not hurt them; they shall lay hands on the sick, and they shall recover. So then after the Lord had spoken unto them, he was received up into heaven, and sat on the right hand of God." ver. 15-19.

In verse nineteen it is said the Lord was received up into heaven and sat on the right hand of God. In verse twenty it is said, "They [the disciples] went forth and preached everywhere, the Lord working with them, and confirming the word with signs following." The Lord worked with them; then he must have returned. He did in the manner we have told you. He returned to be a light in the midst of his people by confirming the truth wherever it is lifted up. He did do it, and he now does it. God bears witness to his truth, both with signs and wonders, and divers miracles, and gifts of the Holy Ghost. Heb. 2:4. For Christianity to be a light there must be the performance of signs and wonders and divers miracles. Such is true Christianity, and such is her light, a queen swaying her scepter over the works of Satan, setting at liberty the captives, breaking the bands of Satan asunder, healing the diseased, and scattering peace and bright hopes in the hearts of men. Glory to God forevermore!

THE BEAUTIES OF CHRISTIAN CHARACTER.

Not only does the Lord dwell in the midst of his people to perform deeds and signs of wonder, but he dwells in them in all the beauty of his holiness. In their hearts he rules a "King of peace" and purity. Those in whom he dwells "walk even as he walked," and "as he is, so are they in this world."

A certain writer speaks thus of the beauties of Christian character: "Live as we may, age dims the luster of the eye, and pales the flush of the cheek, while infirmity mars the human form divine. But while this is true, dim as the eye is, pallid and sunken as may be the face of beauty, frail and feeble that once strong, erect and symmetrical form, the immortal soul, just fledging its wings for heaven, may look out through those faded windows, as beautiful as a dewdrop on a summer's morning, as melting as the tears that glisten in affection's eye, by growing kindly, by cultivating sympathy with all mankind, by cherishing forbearance toward the follies and fribbles of our race, and feeding day by day on that love of God and man which lifts us from the brute and makes us akin to angels."

Christian character is the same whether it be in Christians or in Christ. The character of the Savior is also the character of those in whom he dwells. Their nature is the same, and their outward life is the same. This is what is meant when it is said: "We should walk even as he walked." For the clear proof of these few assertions we will arrange in parallel columns a few texts of Scripture describing the character of Jesus and a few describing the character of Christians, and we will find that not anything more is said of tne Savior with respect to a holy life than is said of his devoted followers.

CHARACTER OF CHRIST.	CHARACTER OF CHRISTIANS.
LOVELY.	
"His mouth is most sweet: yea, he is altogether lovely." S. of Sol. 5: 16.	"Behold, thou art fair, my love; behold, thou art fair;... thou art all fair, my love; there is no spot in thee." S. of Sol. 4: 1, 7.
LOWLY.	
"Take my yoke upon you, and learn of me; for I am meek and lowly in heart." Mat. 11: 29.	"Better it is to be of a humble spirit with the lowly, than to divide the spoil with the proud." Prov. 16: 19.
OBEDIENT.	
"For as by one man's disobedience many were made sinners, so by the obedience of one shall many be made righteous." Rom. 5: 19.	"Wherefore gird up the loins of your mind, be sober, and hope to the end for the grace that is to be brought unto you at the revelation of Jesus Christ; as obedient children." 1 Pet. 1: 13, 14.

COMPASSIONATE.

"But when he saw the multitudes, he was moved with compassion on them, because they fainted and were scattered abroad as sheep having no shepherd." Mat. 9: 36.

"Finally, be ye all of one mind, having compassion one of another, love as brethren, be pitiful, be courteous." 1 Pet. 3: 8.

FAITHFULNESS.

"Faithful is he that calleth you, who also will do it." 1 Thes. 5: 24.

"And the things that thou hast heard of me among many witnesses, the same commit thou to faithful men, who shall be able to teach others also." 2 Tim. 2: 2.

FORBEARANCE.

"Whom God hath set forth to be a propitiation through faith in his blood, to declare his righteousness for the remission of sins that are past, through the forbearance of God." Rom. 3: 25.

"Forbearing one another, and forgiving one another." Col. 3: 13.

MEEKNESS.

"Take my yoke upon you, and learn of me; for I am meek and lowly in heart." Mat. 11: 29.

"But let it be the hidden man of the heart, in that which is not corruptible, even the ornament of a meek and quiet spirit, which is in the sight of God of great price." 1 Pet. 3: 4.

LONG-SUFFERING.

"And account that the long-suffering of our Lord is salvation." 2 Pet. 3: 15.

"With all lowliness and meekness, with long-suffering, forbearing one another in love." Eph. 4: 2.

HUMBLENESS.

"And being found in fashion as a man, he humbled himself, and became obedient unto death, even the death of the cross." Phil. 2: 8.

"Likewise, ye younger, submit yourselves unto the elder. Yea, all of you be subject one to another, and be clothed with humility: for God resisteth the proud, and giveth grace to the humble." 1 Pet. 5: 5.

SPOTLESSNESS.

"But with the precious blood of Christ, as of a lamb without blemish and without spot." 1 Pet. 1: 19.

"Pure religion and undefiled before God and the Father is this, To visit the fatherless and widows in their affliction, and to keep himself unspotted from the world." Jas. 1: 27.

MERCIFULNESS.

"The Lord is merciful and gracious, slow to anger, and plenteous in mercy." Psa. 103: 8.

"Blessed are the merciful: for they shall obtain mercy." Mat. 5: 7.

HARMLESSNESS.

"For such an high priest became us, who is holy, harmless, undefiled, separate from sinners, and made higher than the heavens." Heb. 7: 26.

"That ye may be blameless and harmless, the sons of God, without rebuke, in the midst of a crooked and perverse nation, among whom ye shine as lights in the world." Phil. 2: 15.

GUILELESSNESS.

"Who did no sin, neither was guile found in his mouth." 1 Pet. 2: 22.

"Jesus saw Nathanael coming to him, and saith of him, Behold an Israelite indeed, in whom is no guile!" John 1: 47.

SINLESSNESS.

"For we have not an high priest which can not be touched with the feeling of our infirmities; but was in all points tempted like as we are, yet without sin." Heb. 4: 15.

"Whosoever is born of God doth not commit sin; for his seed remaineth in him: and he can not sin, because he is born of God." 1 John 3: 9.

Thus we could go on to a much greater length, showing by the Scriptures that the character of a Christian, or his nature or life is the same as the life or character of Christ. Christianity is Christ in us. The life of a true Christian is one of great beauty. It is a light in this world. It is far above the ways of sin and worldliness. It is the Christ-life in man. The self-life of man has ceased, is crucified; nevertheless he lives, yet not he, but it is Christ that liveth in him. The Christian life is inspiring, ennobling, clothed in humility. It points the way to Christ and heaven. It is a brilliant ornament, which in the sight of God is of great price. God places great value upon a Christian life. It is worth more than ten thousand worlds. Is it not a shame that it is trifled with as it is? Thousands are taking the name of Christian, when it is impossible to distinguish them from the world; they emit not one ray of light.

Esthetics is the science of the beautiful, and treats of the feelings produced through the senses by objects of beauty. The most vile and dishonest admire honesty in others; thus gentleness, kindness, meekness, produce pleasant feelings and are called beautiful. God is the source of meekness, gentleness, and love. He is the source of the beautiful. Christianity is God in man, exhibiting his beauty. "Lord, let thy beauty be upon us." The dewdrop sparkles like a diamond as the sun's rays fall upon it. The life of man sparkles with an unsurpassed beauty as the rays of light and salvation fall upon it from the throne. As we behold the beauty of God assimilated into the life of man and thus revealed we think what a pity that all in the world are not Christians.

> Christian, oh, may thy tribe increase,
> Thy light and glory ne'er decrease;
> Shine on and magnify the Word,
> And point the world to Christ and God.

CHAPTER II.
THE HOLY SCRIPTURES.

We have said before that Christianity is in perfect accord with the Bible. The Word of God reveals Christianity to us. It is an infallible expression of its doctrines and duties. Jesus is the way to everlasting rest; the Bible is the guide. Some one has said, "Both are equally certain, equally divine. Let us be thankful for such unspeakable gifts. Next to the mercy of a Savior, able and ready to save to the uttermost all who come unto God by him, is the book of inspiration of God, which as a lamp to our feet, and a light to our path, conducts us to such a Friend, and teaches us the way of salvation."

The Word of God is a lamp and a light to guide to everlasting bliss. "The entrance of thy word giveth light." The word is written in the Christian's heart. In his conduct he adorns the doctrine of God our Savior and thus reveals the light of the gospel. Christianity is therefore a light, because it is a product of the truth. We can understand at once then that anything that is in opposition to the Scriptures can not be a light. The nearer the life accords with the whole truth the greater the light. The Scriptures contain all that is necessary for the formation of a perfect Christian. Whosoever submits heart and life to the Word of God and walks in obedience to its commands will be transformed into the glorious image of the Son of God and made ready for that better land. The apostle says, "All scripture is given by inspiration of God, and is profitable for doctrine, for reproof, for correction, for instruction in righteousness: that the man of God may be perfect [a perfect Christian], thoroughly furnished unto all good works." 2 Tim. 3:16, 17.

Tradition is unnecessary for the production of a true Christian character. The Scriptures contain all the doctrine, reproof, correction and instruction needful. The Scriptures have but one true interpreter, and but one interpretation. All who rightly understand the Bible understand it alike. We are aware this is contrary to much of the present day teaching. Many are now saying that "we can not understand the Word of God the same, therefore just as we understand it so it is unto us." This is very loose and robs the "two-edged sword" of all its sharpness and power. It leaves man to interpret it in a manner that will not condemn his sinful life A class of grammar students, if allowed to analyze sentences and parse words each according to his understanding, would never become perfect grammarians. One may parse a word as a "verb," another the same word as an "adverb," another as a "participle," and if each were right according to his understanding, how could we have any fixed rules of grammar? All would be confusion and no one would know what is proper speech. Students to become efficient scholars must understand mathematics, astronomy, botany, etc., alike. Every volume written by man if understood rightly must be understood alike by all.

To allow every man his own private interpretation of Scripture, or every religious society its interpretation is to admit of no certain, no fixed rules governing a Christian life. We can illustrate it better in this way. A certain rich man has a number of circulars printed. These circulars he distributes among the poor of a certain neighborhood. On these circulars he tells them that at the end of twelve months he will give one thousand dollars to each one complying with the conditions given below. The conditions are these: You must not steal. "Lie not one to another." Do not render evil for evil. Love your enemies, and pray for those who despitefully use you. "If thine enemy hunger, feed him; and if he thirst, give him drink." "Speak evil of no man." "Return good for evil." "As ye would that others should do to you, do ye even so to them." If a man smite you upon the right cheek, turn to him the other also. Prefer others before yourself. "Do all things without murmuring." Do not wear gold or pearls or costly array. Pray when you are afflicted. Do not jest or talk foolishly, but have a sound speech. Greet one another with a kiss. Wash one another's feet. You must all speak the same thing. You must be of one mind. If ye do these things you shall receive the inheritance, but he that offends in one is guilty of all.

Now who of a sound mind could not understand as plain and simple language as this? But suppose one man or woman does not want to lay off their gold and pearls, so they decide he meant that for women of ancient times and not for us. Another thinks the command to greet with a kiss means to shake hands. Another thinks to visit my neighbor when he is sick is washing his feet. To pray when we are afflicted is meant for the people of olden time. One man whose heart is full of hatred against a neighbor decides no man can love his enemy, therefore this command does not mean what it says, so he will go on hating his enemy, but expects to get his inheritance. One man decides one command means one thing, another that it means something else, each one making each command to mean that which is most pleasing to do. Who would receive the one thousand dollars at the time appointed? You can at once see the folly of their entertaining hopes of receiving the inheritance.

Thousands are thus treating the Word of God, saying this and that commandment does not mean what it says, but means thus and so, or, it was for a people of some other time, etc. At this present day there are many who are taking the traditions of men and customs of some religious society for their rule of life and duty.

Recently while passing through a strange part of the country we stopped at a farmhouse to inquire our way. It became convenient to tell the lady, who came to answer our inquiry, that we had come into her neighborhood to hold a few religious meetings. She invited us into her house to see her four weeks' old baby which was sick. While talking with her she said that she became afraid that her child was going to die, so she sent for the minister and had it christened. I asked her if she believed that if the babe had died without being christened that it would have gone to hell. "No," she said, "I do not believe that, but I believe that it would have gone to heaven." I then asked her, Do you not believe that if your little child lives that it will go into sin and some day will have to repent and be converted in order to get to heaven just the same as if it never had been christened? She said that she believed it would. I then asked her what good the christening had done her child. She answered, "I do not know." I then asked her to give me one commandment in the Bible obligating her to christen her child. She said, "I know of none." I then asked her why she had her babe christened. She said, "Because most all the people do around here."

She like thousands of others was taking the custom of the neighborhood, or religious order, and never searched the Scriptures to know what are the commandments of God. We need to be doers only of the Word of God. "Not every one that saith, Lord, Lord, shall enter into the kingdom of heaven; but he that doeth the will of my Father which is in heaven." The God of heaven has given laws and fixed rules and recorded them in the Holy Scriptures to govern our daily life. These laws we are positively commanded to obey. To disobey is a sin. 1 John 3:4. Sinners do not go to heaven. There is not one text in the whole Bible encouraging us to hope of going to heaven if we are knowingly disobeying any commandment of God. In this present day a mighty concourse of people are passing on down the way to an eternity, professing to be children of God, but living careless and negligent, doing many things they should not do, and failing to do a great many things they should do.

This greatly reminds me of the way the people regarded a certain stock law that was passed by the legislature of our district in my boyhood days. This law forbade the running at large of cattle, hogs, sheep, etc. Now there was in our neighborhood much of what was called "commons." It was unfenced land, and was used as a common pasture land for all. Consequently the enacting of such a law was obnoxious to nearly all of the citizens of this neighborhood, and it was almost unanimously violated; and because it was violated by so many it was never enforced. Cattle, sheep, and hogs continued to run at large the same as if there was no law prohibiting the same. After a time most people had forgotten there was such a law.

The same is true respecting the Word of God. People have gone on in their own ways, violating those holy laws until many are doing things, and do not know there is a law of God forbidding it. God's laws are not held in the high esteem they should be. They are his power unto salvation to all that believe. They are able to save the soul. They are to be kept in remembrance, to be kept in the heart, to be obeyed. They are to search, to meditate upon, to trust in, to rejoice in, to delight in, to taste, to long after, to stand in awe of, to esteem as a light, and to be let dwell richly within us. It is the Word of God that shall judge us in that great judgment-day. They that love God and keep his words, "against such there is no law;" consequently they will "have boldness in that day." God's law is eternal; it shall never pass away. The Lord Jesus says, "Heaven and earth shall pass away, but my words shall never pass away." "The word of God which liveth and abideth forever." 1 Pet. 1:23.

The earth and all that therein is shall pass away,
But God's pure Word shall live and stand for aye and aye:
Man runs his race of life, then, passing from the scene,
Returns to dust, and is as though he ne'er had been—
This is not spoken of the inner man, the soul—
This, says the Word, shall live while ceaseless ages roll.
The city with its walls and towers of granite stone,
Shall be to dissolution brought by rain and sun;
The ships which round the world on crested wave have flown,
Go down amid the storm, and never more are known;
The daring mountain peak, all covered o'er with snow,
Shall mid terrific blast descend to depths below;
The proud empire whose scepter sways o'er land and sea,
Shall fall and pass away ere dawns eternity;
And haughty finite sovereign power no more shall be,
The stars in firmament above shall quit their place;
The waning moon shall cease her still nocturnal race,
And earth no more sail through immensity of space.
Because of sin all these shall pass fore'er away,
Shall melt with fervent heat in that avenging day,
But God's pure Word shall live and stand for aye and aye.

CHAPTER III.
SIN.

The time was when there was no sin in this world. At that time it was an Eden. By man transgressing God's holy law sin entered this world. "Wherefore, as by one man sin entered into the world, and death by sin; and so death passed upon all men, for that all have sinned." Rom. 5:12. This is the origin of sin in this world and the awful consequence. God's design was that his creation be sinless and pure, but by disobedience sin has marred the scene of God's creative purity. The following texts will acquaint the reader with the characteristics or nature of sin.

1. *Sin is defiling.* "There is a generation that are pure in their own eyes, and yet is not washed from their filthiness." Prov. 30:12. "Though your sins be as scarlet, they shall be as white as snow; though they be red like crimson, they shall be as wool." Isa. 1:18. Here we see the defiling nature of sin. It stains the soul as with scarlet. White is the emblem of purity. The pure soul is spoken of as being clothed in "fine linen, clean and white." Sin stains those robes with crimson, or scarlet spots. Though you wash with niter, or with much soap, those deep-dyed marks of iniquity can not be thus cleansed away.

2. *Sin is deceiving.* "But exhort one another daily, while it is called to-day; lest any of you be hardened

through the deceitfulness of sin." Heb. 3:13. One sin has opened the gate or way to many more. There is a kind of opiate power in sin that renders its victim unconscious of its awful magnitude, thus its deceitfulness.

3 *Sin is reproachful.* "Righteousness exalteth a nation: but sin is a reproach to any people." Prov. 14:34. We can not enable you to see that sin is a reproach in any better way than by placing two pictures before you. One picture is that of a community where all the citizens, old and young, love and fear God. They live together in peace and love; there are no quarrelings or contentions, envyings or unkindnesses among neighbors, neither in home life. There is no stealing, lying, cheating, swearing, drunkenness, fightings, backbitings, vulgarisms, unholy revelries, etc. Such manner of life exalts that community, and all good people are desirous of making their homes there.

The second picture is that of a community where neighbors are quarreling, hating and lawing with each other. In home life there are angry words and bitter feelings and estrangements. There are lewd revelries and wanton pleasures. There are stealings and lyings, cheatings, fightings, swearings, drinking, chewing and smoking, slang phrases, etc. Such is a reproach, and thus we learn how righteousness exalts a nation and sin becomes a reproach to any people.

4. *Sin gives death its horror.* "The sting of death is sin." 1 Cor. 15:56. Many a thing in this world carries a sting by which it inflicts pain. Death and the thoughts of death are painful and cause a shudder and fear because death has a sting. It is sin.

5. *Sin excludes the soul from heaven.* "Then said Jesus again unto them, I go my way, and ye shall seek me, and shall die in your sins: whither I go, ye can not come." John 8:21. Heaven is a pure and holy place. No sin will ever enter there. If we die in our sins heaven is lost unto us forever.

WHAT IS SIN?

Many people have become confused concerning a sinless life because they did not understand what sin was. A temptation or trial is not a sin, but it is the yielding to temptation that is a sin. "All unrighteousness is sin." 1 John 5:17. All that is wrong is sinful. There are but few people that will not confess that we should live right in this world. To live right in every way is the fruit of righteousness. James says, "Therefore to him that knoweth to do good, and doeth it not, to him it is sin." 4:17. To refuse to do a good thing known unto us when we have opportunity is wrong and displeasing to God. Solomon says, "The thought of foolishness is sin." "In a multitude of words there wanteth not sin." The apostle John clearly and positively defines sin in these words: "Whosoever committeth sin transgresseth also the law: for sin is the transgression of the law." 1 John 3:4.

To transgress or violate any known law of God is sin. This is clear and comprehensive. For instance, a man knows it is wrong to steal, therefore if he steals it is a sin. A man knows it is wrong to tell a falsehood, therefore if he speaks falsely he commits a sin. A man knows it is wrong to become intoxicated, and yet he does become so; he has violated a known law of right and wrong, and has therefore committed a sin. Who is the man of common sense that does not know it is wrong to lie, steal, swindle, defraud, curse, drink, get angry and cross; to refuse to help a needy neighbor when he can, to talk foolishly, to tell unseemly tales, to backbite, slander, commit adultery, hold enmity against another, or to be proud and vain, etc.?

All these, and many more, the Bible says are wrong, and man knows them to be wrong; therefore to do them is a sin. Sin brings man into bondage. John 8:34. Man is unable to liberate himself from sin, but God has sent a Deliverer. Praise his name! "If the Son therefore shall make you free, ye shall be free indeed." John 8:36. Of this glorious deliverance we shall speak in the following chapter.

CHAPTER IV.
SALVATION.

Salvation is the song that was to be sung by the redeemed in that day. "Behold now is the day." Our salvation has come. "Glory to God in the highest, and on earth, peace, good will toward men." Salvation means deliverance. A prophecy concerning the Christ—our salvation—says: "He hath sent me to bind up the broken-hearted, to proclaim liberty to the captives, and the opening of the prison to them that are bound." Isa. 61:1. Christ our Savior came to deliver us from the prison-house of sin.

In the preceding chapter we learned that sin left its crimson and scarlet stains upon the soul. Salvation cleanses the soul, removing the stains, making it as white as snow. Washing in "niter and much soap" will not prove effectual, but the blood of Jesus will remove every stain. Sin reproaches, but the salvation of Jesus exalts. It lifts man up from the coarse, degrading, shameful life of sin, and exalts him to integrity, nobility, and purity. It removes the discontentments, uneasiness, condemnations and fears, and brings joy, peace and rest. Salvation breaks the strong fetters of sin and man rejoices in the beautiful light and liberty of this gospel day. The scepter is wrested from the cruel tyrant, sin, and righteousness in quietness and peace sways the scepter, and man rejoices. Sin is dethroned and Christ is crowned King of glory, and his triumphant reign is in the heart and life of man. Sin no longer has dominion. Christ hath made us free.

> O God, thy vict'ries I extol
> With all the freedom of my soul.

Salvation removes the awful sting of death and allows man to approach the last hour

> "Like one who wraps the drapery of his couch
> About him and lies down to pleasant dreams."

A PRESENT SALVATION.

"Behold, now is the accepted time; behold, now is the day of salvation." 2 Cor. 6:2. The present dispensation, or gospel day, is the salvation age. It is the accepted time, or the time which God has accepted for the salvation of man. That there is another dispensation of time beyond this present Christian era in which man can be saved is Satan's falsehood to cause man to neglect salvation in this "accepted time," beyond which he knows there is no escape. "How shall we escape if we neglect so great salvation?" "To-day if ye will hear his voice harden not your hearts."

The apostle Paul says, "The grace of God that bringeth salvation hath appeared to all men." Titus 2:11. It "hath appeared." This is the time when salvation has appeared unto all men, and all men must accept it in this time or lose it forever. In Titus 3:5, Eph. 2:5, Rom. 6:22, Jude 1, 1 Cor. 1:2, and many other texts, salvation is spoken of as having been received. Beyond controversy salvation is a present attainment.

SALVATION BY GRACE AND NOT BY WORKS.

Salvation from sin is by the grace of God. The word "grace" is defined by lexicographers as favor or mercy. Grace is a characteristic in the nature of God which offers mercy or favor though wholly unmerited by the recipient. Man is an offender against God. Through repentance he finds favor or grace in God's sight without any worthiness, excellence or meritoriousness in himself, but because of the merciful nature of the Lord. "For by grace are ye saved through faith." Eph. 2:8. "By grace ye are saved." ver. 5. "Who hath saved us, and called us with a holy calling, not according to our works, but according to his own purpose and grace, which was given us in Christ Jesus before the world began." 2 Tim. 1:9. "Being justified freely by his grace." Rom. 3:24.

If man could attain to salvation by works, then he could plead his own merits; but we are taught that we can only plead the mercy of God. The apostle says that salvation is "not of works, lest any man should boast." Eph. 2:9. If it were by works man would have some cause for boasting; but because it is wholly by grace, he has nothing of self in which to boast. Again he says, "Not by works of righteousness which we have done, but according to his mercy he saved us, by the washing of regeneration, and renewing of the Holy Ghost." Titus 3:5.

SALVATION PERFECT.

There is no weakness nor incompleteness in God's salvation. It saves to "the uttermost." Heb. 7:25. Salvation is so complete that man requires no additional cleansing or purifying to fit him for heaven.

The salvation to which the apostle had attained made him "ready to be offered." There is no cleansing beyond the gates of death, but in this life we are commanded to make ready. "Though your sins be as scarlet, they shall be as white as snow." This text proves the efficacy of the blood or the completeness of salvation.

Also the following texts magnify the preciousness and perfectness of redemption: "Then will I sprinkle clean water upon you, and ye shall be clean: from all your filthiness, and from all your idols, will I cleanse you." Ezek. 36:25. "Purge me with hyssop, and I shall be clean: wash me, and I shall be whiter than snow." Psa. 51:7. "Ye are complete in him." Col. 2:10. "The blood of Jesus Christ his Son cleanseth us from all sin." 1 John 1:7. "If we confess our sins, he is faithful and just to forgive us our sins and to cleanse us from all unrighteousness." 1 John 1:9. It is sin that excludes us from heaven. It is salvation that saves us from sin, therefore we, when saved, are ready for that better land.

FUTURE SALVATION.

There are a few texts of Scripture which teach a salvation yet in the future. "And ye shall be hated of all men for my name's sake: but he that endureth to the end shall be saved." Mat. 10:22. "Wherefore, my beloved, as ye have always obeyed, not as in my presence only, but now much more in my absence, work out your own salvation with fear and trembling." Phil. 2:12. These texts do not prove that there is no salvation only at the end of human life, else what could be the meaning of the many texts that speak of a present salvation? These two texts are very easily harmonized with those teaching a present experience of saving grace.

As long as we are in this world it is possible for us to lose our salvation. Though we are now saved from sin by grace it is possible for us to be overtaken in some way and lose this experience. As long as we are here we must endure temptation. But if we endure unto the end when this mortality puts on immortality we pass beyond the possibility of losing salvation, hence, we are saved eternally. By resisting temptation, by praying and watching, we "work out our salvation." The time comes when there are no more temptations to resist, and we are safe and saved forever.

I am saved now from all sin, but to keep this experience I must watch, pray, work, resist and endure unto the end of my life, and then my salvation receives the seal of eternity—saved in glory forever. Amen.

WONDERS OF SALVATION.

When man the wonders of creation
Beholds in deepest contemplation,
Adores not the Almighty One,
Must have indeed a heart of stone.

Thou mortal! seest not the sun
His daily course so proudly run?
The moon in her nocturnal race,
With sweet and tender, smiling face?
The stars in pale but beauteous light,
Twinkling, shining all the night?
Stupendous ocean, wild and free,
Bold image of eternity?
The mountain cliff that checks the storm,
And sheds its tears on valley farm?
Poor soul twice dead indeed must be,
And plucked up like uprooted tree,
Or dulled by sensuality,
Or lured by prodigality,
Which does not bound with admiration,
Or feel a warmth of true devotion
Upon beholding this creation.

All nature smiling sweet and tender,
Sun, moon and stars in wondrous splendor,
And mortal man, a bit of sod,
Reveals the handiwork of God.
Howe'er there is one work divine,
Excels all others of my rhyme,
The making of a world like this,
Sent circling through so vast a space;
Bright worlds above in glory streaming,
Can not compare with this remaining.
It claims all Heaven's admiration,
It moves all Hell to disputation,
Excels the glorious translation
Of Enoch from his brief probation
To higher plane of situation.
All that's been done in whole creation
Is naught, compared with man's salvation;
Saved from the scarlet stains of sin,
By power of God been born again;
Then by the Holy Spirit's power
Made pure in instantaneous hour.

Oh, new and wonderful creation,
Exceeds by far the old formation;
Sun, moon and stars and mountain's plane,
The dark and deep blue ocean's main,
Do not God's power so much display
As when he takes man's sins away.
Old things are gone, all things are new,
All heaven by faith is now in view;
And peace, sweet peace fills all the soul,
And rest, though stormy billows roll;
Such is man's happy situation
In this most wonderful salvation.

CHAPTER V.

THE WAY FROM SIN TO PERFECT SALVATION.

We have learned that sin entered this world and that all mankind have sinned. We have also learned that Jesus came to save man from his sins. Now the question may arise in the mind of some, what must I do to be saved? We hope in this chapter to quote such scriptures as will plainly teach you the way of salvation, or how to be fully saved, and also the scriptures describing each experience.

REPENTANCE.

The first step for the sinner is to repent. When on Pentecost men were pricked in their hearts and cried, "What shall we do?" Peter answered, "Repent." It is in accordance with God's plan of redemption, also with nature and reason, that man should repent of his sins in order to receive pardon. Repentance was the theme on which John preached in the wilderness of Judea. It seems also to have been the first subject on which the Lord preached. Mark 1:15. It is the will of God that men should repent of their sins. "The Lord is not slack concerning his promise, as some men count slackness; but is long-suffering to usward, not willing that any should perish, but that all should come to repentance." 2 Pet. 3:9.

It is here implied if man does not repent he shall perish. Jesus says, "Except ye repent, ye shall all likewise perish,"even as did those whose blood Pilate mingled with their sacrifices, and those eighteen on whom the tower of Siloam fell.

The first round in the ladder that reaches to eternal rest is repentance. If man never takes this step upon the way he can never reach that happy end. Because repentance includes so much, many men would gladly overstep this first round and begin their Christian life on some round higher up. This they can not do; they must take this first step, or perish. And should they strive to climb up some other way they are dishonest, and the Savior calls them "thieves and robbers."

When the Pharisees and Sadducees came to the baptism of John he said unto them, "Bring forth therefore fruits meet for repentance." Mat. 3:8. There are fruits of repentance. The tree is known by its fruits. When man really repents of his sins, by his fruits or manner of life it will be made known. One of the fruits of repentance is sorrow. We might have said that repentance is sorrow, for "godly sorrow worketh repentance to salvation not to be repented of; but the sorrow of the world worketh death."

A well known politician became an embezzler of the county fund, and was sentenced to a few years in the state's prison. After having received his sentence he, in the sheriff's charge, passed out of the court-room, and with tears flowing from his eyes said, "My reputation is gone forever." That was a sorrow of the world and is not the way to salvation. Had the tears been flowing because he had sinned against God, who loved him, it would have been sorrow that "worketh repentance."

The apostle says in 2 Cor. 7:11, "Behold this self-same thing, that ye sorrowed after a godly sort, what carefulness it wrought in you, yea, what clearing of yourselves, yea, what indignation, yea, what fear, yea, what vehement desire, yea, what zeal, yea, what revenge!" These are the fruits of repentance. The first here mentioned is "carefulness." The impenitent lives a reckless, careless life; but a watchfulness comes into the heart of the penitent. He becomes mindful of his acts and carefully avoids the ways of sin. He turns away from sin. Oh, what carefulness it works in him. He complies with the commandment of God, "Let the wicked forsake his way." The marginal reading of Mat. 3:8 is "bring forth fruit answerable to the amendment of life." The penitent carefully turns away from sin, and there is therefore an amendment of life.

The second fruit of repentance mentioned in 2 Cor. 7:11 is "clearing of yourselves." Men usually in their sinful life do many a wrong deed. When they have a godly sorrow they are very willing to do all they can to "clear away," or right the wrongs they have done. For instance, a man has in conversation with one neighbor spoken evil of another neighbor and injured his character. When he repents of his sins he will acknowledge to his neighbor that he spoke falsely, and will do what he can to repair the injury he has done. Debts he has long neglected he will pay when he repents of his sins, if it is possible. Wherein he has stolen or defrauded in any way he will restore as far as he is able. Zacchæus, when he came down from the sycamore tree, had a penitent heart, and said: "The half of my goods I give to the poor; and if I have taken anything from any man by false accusation, I restore him fourfold." Luke 19:8. God does not command a fourfold restoration, but he does demand a restoring of an equal amount of what has been taken. If the penitent is unable to do this he can, no doubt, make confession, and promise to restore as soon as possible.

It is very consistent and reasonable that God makes such demands of the penitent. No man can rightly object to such requirements. It establishes confidence in the hearts of unbelievers. They see a beauty in the Christian religion. It not only saves a man from doing wrong deeds in his future life, but calls upon him to repair as far as possible the wrongs and injuries he has done in his past life. In talking about two of the leading members of a certain religious denomination an unbeliever recently remarked: "If these men would pay me what they owe me I would have more confidence in Christianity." We saw then how consistent it was that God requires man to correct his past life as far as he can. It forces confidence in the hearts of the unsaved and gains their attention. This is the "clearing of yourselves."

The penitent gladly turns away or forsakes his evil ways. He abhors sin. Ah, what "vehement desire" to be free; what zeal! He gladly does all he can to repair the injuries he has done. When he has defrauded man of money he will confess it and restore it. When he has contracted debts and long neglected them he will confess his negligence and strive to pay them. Where he has misrepresented any one and thereby done him an injury he will make confession. And wherein man has wronged him and he has hatred in his heart against him, he will freely forgive. Jesus says, "If ye forgive not men their trespasses, neither will your Father forgive your trespasses." Mat. 6:15.

When the penitent has met all the requirements of the Scriptures, and confesses all. to God, he has promised to forgive him. "If we confess our sins, he is faithful and just to forgive us our sins." 1 John 1:9. After the forsaking of sins and the restitution of wrongs and the forgiveness of injuries, and confession to God, there remains yet for man to

BELIEVE.

A prison-keeper inquired of Paul and Silas: "Sirs,

what must I do to be saved?" And they said, "Believe on the Lord Jesus Christ and thou shalt be saved." Acts 16:30, 31. At this point Satan has succeeded in confusing many an honest soul. They have forsaken all to follow Jesus, but have not that perfect confidence that God forgives and accepts them. Satan will allow them to believe that God will save them in some future time, but struggles hard to prevent their believing that Jesus saves them now. The apostle says, "By grace are ye saved through faith." Eph. 2:8. "Whosoever believeth that Jesus is the Christ is born of God." 1 John 5:1. "But as many as received him, to them gave he power to become the sons of God, even to them that believe on his name." John 1:12. "Therefore being justified by faith, we have peace with God." Rom. 5:1. It is not by enthusiasm or excitement that we are saved, but "by grace through faith."

Jesus on one occasion said, "Which of you intending to build a tower, sitteth not down first, and counteth the cost, whether he have sufficient to finish it." Luke 14:28. He uses this illustration to teach us the manner in which we should come to him. The cost is "a death to sin and the world." The prize is heaven and eternal glory. When you have carefully counted the cost and deliberately decided in your soul to follow Jesus, then believe on his name, "and thou shalt be saved."

JUSTIFICATION.

The term justification is used both in the Old Testament and the New. There is a difference between the justification under the law and the justification by grace. The one was obtained by the blood of animals and the other by the blood of Jesus. Since we are writing upon the glorious themes of the New Testament we shall say but little of the justification by the sacrifices of animals.

Justification implies a forgiveness of sins. The sense of guilt resulting from a transgression of God's law is removed. The justified therefore experience a safety, a peace and rest. Fears and uncertainties are banished, and the soul is filled with confidence and hope. "Therefore being justified by faith, we have peace with God." Rom. 5: 1. Peace is the natural result of justification. It is sin that destroys the happiness of man. Before sin entered into this world man lived in a delightful Eden. His heart was open and frank before God, and he rejoiced in his presence. Sin brought a sense of shame and guilt, and he hid from the presence of God. All men admire the innocency of childhood. The peaceful countenance of an infant, its freedom from care, anxieties and unrest but remind us of the peacefulness of pardon.

There was a justification by the law, but the law day has passed away. We have come to the gospel day in which no flesh shall be justified by the works of the law, but by "the faith of Jesus Christ." Gal. 2:

16; 3:11. The Bible promises nothing more in justification than a full pardon of all transgression and restoration to childhood innocency. "And Jesus called a little child unto him and set him in the midst of them and said, Verily I say unto you, except ye be converted and become as little children, ye shall not enter into the kingdom of heaven." Mat. 18:2, 3. A justified man is as innocent and free from transgression as a little child. Is it not a just cause of surprise that men will teach the forgiveness of sins necessary to the experience of justification, and yet teach that the justified commit sin? "O Consistency, thou art a jewel."

It occurs to our mind that if men would use consideration, mingled with reason and judgment, they would see the inconsistency of the above teaching. Should a man who had used abusive language to you come and penitently ask your forgiveness, you would forgive, but that does not give him liberty to continue his abuse. When the penitent comes to God he will pardon, but this does not give him liberty to continue in sin. God created man with an intelligence, a reason and common sense. The ravages of sin have greatly impaired these qualities of the mind that believes that justification necessitates a forgiveness of sins, yet the experience can be retained while committing sin. A sound writer has said, "Common sense is a quality of mind not so common as the words imply. Many claim it who have no right to its possession. It is a high standard of mental worth. The brain coin that bears its imprint has a par value wherever man is governed by pure reason." No true Christian believes he can live in sin and be a Christian. Even those who are governed by pure reason do not believe such. By the blood of Jesus "all that believe are justified from all things." Acts 13:39.

REGENERATION.

Justification by grace through faith in Jesus does not end with a forgiveness of past transgressions only, but includes the impartation of the divine, or eternal life to the soul. The blood of animals offered for sins in the Jewish economy was unable to impart this life to the offerer of the sacrifice. Jesus says, "I am come that ye might have life." "Whosoever believeth in him shall not perish, but have everlasting life." "He that hath the Son hath life, and he that hath not the Son of God hath not life." "God hath given to us eternal life, and this life is in his Son."

The process by which man enters the natural life is termed a birth or generation. The process by which man enters the spiritual life is expressed by the words, "being born again," or "regeneration." With the words "being born again" we naturally associate life. When Nicodemus heard the words he thought the process of bringing into physical life was to be repeated. The Savior told him, "That which is born of the flesh is flesh; and that which is born of the Spirit is spirit.'' John 3:6. In life there is activity and power. Not only are the transgressions forgiven, but by regeneration life and power come into the soul, which gives man strength to resist sin. The Israelite only hoped for a forgiveness of his past sin through his offering. That beautiful hope of constant victory over sin was not his to enjoy. He knew the power of sin and the weakness of his offering; consequently he expected naught else but to offer his sacrifices over and over, day by day, and year by year continually. He who to-day comes to God pleading for forgiveness of his sins through the offering of the eternal Son and expects to still continue in sin enjoys no better hope than a Jew. He dishonors the great sacrifice of God's Son by counting it no more than the sacrifice of animals.

In regeneration the holy, pure, divine life comes into the soul. Man passes from "death unto life." The dominion of sin has come to an end. Sin is dethroned and its kingdom destroyed. Regenerated man is crowned a king. The royal robes of white enshroud him. The scepter of righteousness he sways triumphantly and reigns a mighty conqueror, "a king and priest unto God." Praise and honor to his name!

This new life within man's soul finds expression in a new life without. Since the new life within is holy and pure the new life without is holy and pure.

"Make the inside of the cup and platter clean and the outside will be clean also." The apostle John tells us the manner of life that follows "being born again." "We know that whosoever is born of God sinneth not, but he that is begotten of God keepeth himself, and that wicked one toucheth him not." 1 John 5:18. "Whosoever is born of God doth not commit sin, for his seed remaineth in him: and he can not sin, because he is born of God." 1 John 3:9. This text does not teach the impossibility of committing sin as some have supposed, but the impossibility of committing sin and retaining the spiritual birth. In 1 John 2:29 we are clearly taught that righteousness of life succeeds the regeneration of man. Sin belongs only to Satan and sinners. It is not found in the life of God, nor of the angels, nor of Christ, nor of the Christians.

ADOPTION.

The term "adoption" is a few times used in the New Testament. It is that part of justification which places us in the family of God. In the apostolic days the Romans were accustomed to adopting the children of some other family into their own. The law on these occasions demanded a full surrender of the child with all his possessions to his new governor or father. The father received the child as an heir to all his possessions, equal with his own children.

So we in justification give ourselves to God with

all our talents and possessions, and he receives us into his family, and we become joint-heirs with his Son. This is true, and very precious because it is true. The apostle in speaking of adoption says, "For ye have not received the spirit of bondage again to fear; but ye have received the Spirit of adoption, whereby we cry, Abba, Father." Rom. 8:15. We are here taught that it is in adoption that we look upon God as our Father. We are taught the same in Gal. 4:5, 6. By the Spirit of adoption we look unto God as our Father and consider ourselves his own children. As members in the family of God we yield ourselves unto his service and "our members as instruments of righteousness unto him." This prohibits sin. To live impure, or to commit more or less sin, and have the yoke of Christ upon us, or to be a joint-heir with him is indeed very disparaging.

CONVERSION.

Since the word conversion is used in connection with justification we will give it only brief notice. Jesus said, "Except ye be converted and become as little children," etc. Peter said, "Repent and be converted." Justification properly implies a pardon or forgiveness of our transgressions or sins. Regeneration implies a bringing into the spiritual life. Adoption implies the reception of the new-born child into the family of God. Conversion, the turning about, or a change in life. Any one of these terms include all the others. These are all accomplished in what is known as the first work of grace, and is most frequently and properly termed justification.

SANCTIFICATION.

Sanctification is one among the clear and positive doctrines of the New Testament. Justification, regeneration, adoption, and conversion are terms used to signify the same work of grace, or the same experience in the Christian life. Sanctification has reference to a higher work of grace, or higher life. It is an experience obtained subsequent to justification. The Savior in praying to the Father for his disciples said: "Sanctify them through thy truth: thy word is truth." John 17:17. Before making this petition he told the Father of their separation from the world and of their persecution by the world, which are certain evidences of justification.

Sanctification is defined thus in Webster's Unabridged Dictionary:

1. Sanctification is the act of God's grace by which the affections of men are purified or alienated from sin and the world and exalted to a supreme love of God; also the state of being thus purified or sanctified. 2. Sanctifier. One who sanctifies or makes holy, specially the Holy Ghost. 3. Sanctify. To set apart to a holy or religious use; to make holy or free from sin; to cleanse from moral corruption or pollution; to make holy.

Sanctification is the destruction of the body of sin or depraved nature. The work of sanctification, or the sanctifying process, is expressed as a cleansing or purging or refining. It is the restoration of the soul to its original purity or holiness by the removing of the depraved nature incurred by the transgression in Eden. We will conclude this subject by a Bible lesson.

1. Sanctification is the will of God. "For this is the will of God, even your sanctification." 1 Thes. 4:3.

2. Sanctification is effected by God. "And the very God of peace sanctify you wholly; and I pray God your whole spirit and soul and body be preserved blameless unto the coming of our Lord Jesus Christ." 1 Thes. 5:23. "Jude, the servant of Jesus Christ, and brother of James, to them that are sanctified by God the Father, preserved in Jesus Christ, and called." Jude 1.

3. Sanctification is effected by the Lord Jesus. "For both he that sanctifieth and they who are sanctified are all of one: for which cause he is not ashamed to call them brethren." Heb. 2:11.

4. Sanctification is effected by the Holy Spirit. "And such were some of you: but ye are washed, but ye are sanctified, but ye are justified in the name of the Lord Jesus, and by the Spirit of our God." 1 Cor. 6:11.

5. Sanctification is through the Word of God.

"Sanctify them through thy truth: thy word is truth." John 17:17.

6. Sanctification is through the atonement of Christ. "Wherefore Jesus also, that he might sanctify the people with his own blood, suffered without the gate." Heb. 13:12.

7. Sanctification is perfect salvation. "But we are bound to give thanks alway to God for you, brethren beloved of the Lord, because God hath from the beginning chosen you to salvation through sanctification of the Spirit and belief of the truth." 2 Thes. 2:13.

8. Sanctification as a cleansing removes spots, wrinkles, and blemishes from the church. "Husbands, love your wives, even as Christ also loved the church, and gave himself for it; that he might sanctify and cleanse it with the washing of water by the word, that he might present it to himself a glorious church, not having spot, or wrinkle, or any such thing; but that it should be holy and without blemish." Eph. 5: 25-27.

9. Sanctification prepares men for the service of God. "But in a great house there are not only vessels of gold and of silver, but also of wood and of earth; and some to honor, and some to dishonor. If a man therefore purge himself from these, he shall be a vessel unto honor, sanctified, and meet for the Master's use, and prepared unto every good work." 2 Tim. 2:20, 21.

Because this text is very generally misunderstood

we feel like giving an explanation of it. It was long misunderstood by us. Only very recently the Holy Spirit interpreted it to our heart. One evening we asked God to give us an understanding of this difficult passage of Scripture, and the next morning we fully understood it. It is very simple. In a great house there are vessels of gold and silver, wood and earth, some to honor and some to dishonor. This house represents man in his natural state. There are some good traits of character in most every unregenerated man, and also some evil traits. He has some honorable dispositions and some dishonorable. Full salvation, which includes both justification and sanctification, will save and purge him from every dishonorable inclination and evil trait of character, and fit him for the Master's use. He will be used only to the glory of God. All his fruits will be holy unto the Lord.

10. Sanctification prepares man for heaven. We have quoted from 1 Cor. 6:11. By reading the two preceding verses we learn that sanctification is necessary to the entrance of heaven.

HOLINESS.

There is a sweet melody in the word "holiness." We associate it with everything that is heavenly. It is frequently used synonymously with sanctification, yet not always with all the forms of the word sanctification. On the whole there is a slight difference in the meaning of the two terms. Holiness is the consummation of the work of sanctification. By transposing a few words in Heb. 12:14 we would have it read, "Without holiness no man shall see the Lord." Holiness is here a noun objective to the preposition without. In some translations this sentence would read, "Without sanctification no man shall see the Lord." Sanctification is here a noun, the object of the preposition without. As nouns these words are used interchangeably.

In Jude, first verse, we have this sentence, "To them that are sanctified by God the Father." The word "sanctified" is here used as a predicate adjective, and describes the people addressed. It would not alter the meaning of the text were we to translate it thus: "To them that are made holy by God the Father." The word holy is here used as a predicate adjective, and describes the people addressed. In the sentence, "Sanctify them through thy truth" (John 17:17), the word "sanctify" is a verb, denoting action, of which we have no form of the word holiness. The word holiness can not be used as a verb. The word sanctification frequently expresses action; the word holiness never. They are synonymous when they express the pure state of man. Sanctification is the act that brings man into a holy state, which is also the sanctified state. Sanctification may be applied to the holy state, and also to the action that brings us into that state. Since the word sanctification contains action it is positive proof there is a cleansing in it.

Now we desire by a few Scriptural texts and a few suggestions to deepen the reader's conception of the state of holiness. Everything in the realm of Christianity, or the kingdom of God, from heaven to earth is holy. Let us here give you a brief Bible lesson, kindly asking you to carefully read each text.

1. God is holy. "In the year that king Uzziah died I saw also the Lord sitting upon a throne, high and lifted up, and his train filled the temple. Above it stood the seraphims: each one had six wings; with twain he covered his face, and with twain he covered his feet, and with twain he did fly. And one cried unto another, and said, Holy, holy, holy, is the Lord of hosts: the whole earth is full of his glory." Isa. 6: 1-3.

If the reader here obtains a just conception of the holy character of God it will give him an understanding of the true nature of Christianity and the manner of life of a Christian. A gentleman once asked me if it was wrong or unbecoming to a Christian to attend the present day street carnivals. We replied in about these words: "If you gain a true conception of the holiness of the Almighty you will not need to ask me such a question."

2. Heaven is holy. "Now know I that the Lord saveth his anointed; he will hear him from his holy heaven with the saving strength of his right hand." Psa. 20: 6.

3. Christ is holy. "For such an high priest became us, who is holy, harmless, undefiled, separate from sinners." Heb. 7: 26.

4. The angels are holy. "When the Son of man shall come in his glory, and all the holy angels with him, then shall he sit upon the throne of his glory." Mat. 25: 31.

5. God's commandments are holy. "Wherefore the law is holy, and the commandment holy, and just, and good." Rom. 7: 12.

6. God's arm is holy. "The Lord hath made bare his holy arm in the eyes of all the nations; and all the ends of the earth shall see the salvation of our God." Isa. 52: 10.

7. God's mountains are holy. "And it shall come to pass in that day, that the great trumpet shall be blown, and they shall come which were ready to perish in the land of Assyria, and the outcasts in the land of Egypt, and shall worship the Lord in the holy mount at Jerusalem." Isa. 27: 13.

8. God's hill is holy. "Lord, who shall abide in thy tabernacle? who shall dwell in thy holy hill?" Psa. 15: 1.

9. God's name is holy. "My mouth shall speak the praise of the Lord; and let all flesh bless his holy name forever and ever." Psa. 145: 21.

10. God's works are holy. "The Lord is righteous in all his ways, and holy in all his works." Psa. 145: 17.

11. God's people are holy. "For thou art a holy people unto the Lord thy God: the Lord thy God hath chosen thee to be a special people unto himself, above all people that are upon the face of the earth." Deut. 7:6. Read Eph. 1:4; Col. 1:22; 1 Pet. 1:15; 2 Pet. 3:11.

12. God's people are his holy temple. "If any man defile the temple of God, him shall God destroy; for the temple of God is holy, which temple ye are." 1 Cor. 3:17.

13. God's church is a holy church. "Husbands, love your wives, even as Christ also loved the church, and gave himself for it; that he might sanctify and cleanse it with the washing of water by the word; that he might present it to himself a glorious church, not having spot, or wrinkle, or any such thing; but that it should be holy and without blemish." Eph. 5:25-27.

14. The way to heaven is a holy way. "And an highway shall be there, and a way, and it shall be called the way of holiness; . . . the redeemed shall walk there." Isa. 35:8, 9.

Let us repeat: God is holy; heaven is holy; the angels are holy; Christ is holy; the Spirit is holy; God's Word is holy; the way to heaven is holy. Reader, we want you to picture before you a holy heaven and the holy way that leads to heaven. Read this text: "Follow peace with all men, and holiness without which no man shall see the Lord." Heb. 12:14.

Looking into the Word of the Lord we find that man was chosen to holiness. Eph. 1:4. That God calls him to holiness. 1 Thes. 4:7. That God designed that man should serve him in holiness. Luke 1:75. That God chastens man in order that he might be partaker of his holiness. Heb. 12:10. That God purposes that man shall be saved from his sin and bear fruit unto holiness. Rom. 6:22. That God commands him to be holy in all manner of conduct. 2 Pet. 3:11. God commands him to be holy because he is holy. 1 Pet. 1:15, 16. Looking unto God's great and holy plan in redeeming man, and the holiness of heaven, and God sitting on his holy throne, and Christ the Holy One at his right hand, and the holy angels shouting praises, how can you entertain a hope of ever entering that glorious land without holiness?

PERFECTION.

Many have stumbled at the command to be perfect. That finite man may be perfect in this sinful world sounds ridiculous to many unregenerated hearts. This is because they do not understand God nor his power to deliver man from sin. With the many exhortations and commands to perfection contained in the Holy Scriptures is it not singular that man will yet say, "We can not be perfect in this life"? Many people who oppose the doctrine of Christian perfection do not at all understand it. They consider it to be an end of all growth, consequently they do not understand its nature. There is a perfection of celestial beings not to be experienced by mortal man; but there is a perfection unmistakably taught in the Scriptures which Christians are privileged to experience and enjoy in this life.

Christian perfection relates to right desires and actions and purity of affections. Paul in closing his epistle to the church at Corinth says: "Finally, brethren, farewell. Be perfect, be of good comfort, be of one mind, live in peace; and the God of love and peace shall be with you." Surely every one must concede that there is a perfection to which Christians can attain. When Christians are exhorted to be perfect is it not folly to say, "They can not be perfect"? Could we not with equal propriety say, "We can not be of good comfort"? "We can not live in peace"? "The God of love and peace will not be with us"? etc.

The apostle in writing to the Philippian brethren uses language which clearly implies that some of them had attained to the experience of perfection. He says, "Let us therefore, as many as be perfect, be thus minded." Phil. 3:15. Some of them certainly were perfect. In verse twelve he does speak of a perfection to which he had not attained. This he expected to attain in the glory world. Christian perfection is a life that accords with the Holy Scriptures. Whosoever receives the correction, and reproving and the instructions in righteousness contained in the Scripture will become a perfect Christian. 2 Tim. 3:16.

Whosoever lives as the Word of God says that Christians should live, the same is a perfect man. Paul prays that God would make the Hebrews perfect. Heb. 13:20, 21. Peter petitions the God of all grace, who hath called us unto his eternal glory by Christ Jesus, after we have suffered a while to make us perfect, stablish, strengthen, settle us. 1 Pet. 5:10.

Jesus was made perfect through suffering. God chastens us that we might be partakers of his holiness. The gold and silver to be made pure and perfect must be refined in the crucible. We to reflect the beauty and glory of God must, too, pass through the refiner's fire. The apostle Paul in writing his first epistle to the church at Corinth says: "Howbeit we speak wisdom among them that are perfect." 2:6. Certainly there were perfect Christians in the church at that place. To the Ephesian brethren he says that God "gave some, apostles; and some prophets; and some evangelists; and some, pastors and teachers; for the perfecting of the saints." 4:11, 12. Now we at once know that this work of instruction and perfection is to be accomplished in this life.

He further says, "Till we all come in the unity of the faith, and of the knowledge of the Son of God, unto a perfect man, unto the measure of the stature of the fulness of Christ." ver. 13. By stature is meant the height of any one. Christ is the stature or height of perfection, and we are to measure up to it. This accords with what the Savior himself said:

"The disciple is not above his master: but every one that is perfect shall be as his master." Luke 6:40. To the church at Colosse the apostle says: "Whom [Christ] we preach, warning every man, and teaching every man in all wisdom; that we may present every man perfect in Christ Jesus." Col. 1:28. Again he says, "Epaphras who is one of you, a servant of Christ, saluteth you, always laboring fervently for you in prayers, that ye may stand perfect and complete in all the will of God." 4:12.

WHAT IS CHRISTIAN PERFECTION?

As we have before said, There is a perfection only attainable after the resurrection, but there is a perfection attainable in this life, and it is the nature of this perfection that we wish to understand. It is holiness of nature, right desires and actions and purity of affections toward God and man. It implies an entire consecration to God. A young man came to Jesus inquiring what he should do to inherit eternal life. Jesus said unto him, "If thou wilt be perfect, go and sell that thou hast, and give to the poor, and thou shalt have treasure in heaven: and come and follow me." Mat. 19:21. This teaches a resignation of all to God, which is necessary that we might be refined and polished to such a brilliancy that will make us a light in the world. Christians are termed jewels in the Scriptures. "And they shall be mine, saith the Lord of hosts, in that day when I make up my jewels."

> Oh, to be a brilliant jewel,
> Sparkling, shining for the Lord,
> Polished by the great Refiner,
> Washed and winnowed through the blood.

Christian perfection includes soundness and inoffensiveness of speech. "If any man offend not in word, the same is a perfect man, and able also to bridle the whole body." Jas. 3:2. We consider this a very strong text, and an abundance of grace is required to enable us to perfectly fulfil it.

GOD'S PERFECTION IS THE STANDARD OF CHRISTIAN PERFECTION.

"Be ye therefore perfect, even as your Father which is in heaven is perfect." Mat. 5:48. The perfection which God designs that Christians shall have equal with his own relates to the purity of his nature and affection. In the immediate preceding verses the Savior commands Christians to love their enemies, bless them that curse them, do good to them that hate them, and pray for them which despitefully use them and persecute them. As Christians this is our nature. We will not "render evil for evil." We will befriend our persecutors, feed our enemy when he hungers, and give him drink when he thirsts. In verse forty-five the Savior tells us of the Father's behavior toward his enemies: "He maketh his sun to rise on the evil and on the good, and sendeth rain on the just and on the unjust." Here we behold the merciful nature of God and how he does good for evil. If we love only those who love us and do good only to those who do good to us (ver. 46, 47) we are not in the nature of God; we are no more than publicans and sinners. But if we love our enemies and do good to those who hate us, we are reflecting the character of God. In this respect he would have us to be "perfect, even as he is perfect." O beloved, see that you entertain right feelings toward all men. Do good to your enemies; love them, pray for them, and convince them that you are more than the ordinary sinful man, and God will bless you now and eternally.

In the parable of the sower and its explanation the Savior said the seed which fell among thorns are they which hear the word and go forth and are choked by the cares and riches and pleasures of life, and bring no fruit to perfection. Luke 8:14. Christian fruit is loving our enemies, doing them good, doing good unto all men, speaking evil of none, manifesting love, faith, meekness, gentleness, joy, etc. This is Christian fruit, and may God help every reader to bring it forth to the highest degree of perfection.

PURITY.

"Keep thyself pure." 1 Tim. 5:22. In such commands there is something animating and ennobling. To enable us to have some conception of purity we have only to think of heaven and of the angels. This world has been betimes visited by celestial beings. They are spoken of as being clothed in white and having countenances shining as the light. Mat. 28:3; Mark 16:5; John 20:12; Acts 1:9, 10. White is an emblem of purity. These transient visitors from above robed in white raiment represent the purity of heaven. Purity is not ascribed alone to heavenly beings, but it is a characteristic of the redeemed upon the earth. Purity is effected through the atoning blood. The sweet singer David said: "Purge me with hyssop, and I shall be clean: wash me, and I shall be whiter than snow."

The beloved John in a vision saw "a pure river of water of life, clear as crystal, proceeding out of the throne of God and the Lamb." Rev. 22:1. This "river of water of life" is the cleansing stream of God's salvation. "Whosoever will, let him take the water of life freely." Rev. 22:17. This means salvation. "I will give unto him that is athirst of the fountain of the water of life freely." Rev. 21:6. This is the cleansing fountain of salvation. This stream is pure. It flows from the throne of God. It is as pure as its source. Whosoever enters this crystal stream will be made as pure as its waters.

> Though the soul be stained with scarlet stains,
>   It shall be white as snow;
> Though the soul be stained with crimson stains,
>   It shall be white as wool.

The prophet Isaiah in speaking of the cleansing fountain of salvation in that day, said: "And I will turn my hand upon thee, and purely purge away thy dross, and take away all thy tin." Isa. 1:25. The cleansing stream will remove all the dross and leave the soul pure. These are garments of salvation. This is not literal, but the cleansing away of sin and the infusion of righteousness is represented by the taking away of filthy rags and being clothed in the garments of salvation. The Lamb's wife, which is his church— which is his people— was "arrayed in fine linen, clean and white: for the fine linen is the righteousness of saints." Rev. 19:8.

We will now give a Bible lesson describing the purity of man through the blood of Jesus.

A pure soul. "Seeing ye have purified your souls in obeying the truth through the Spirit unto unfeigned love of the brethren, see that ye love one another with a pure heart fervently." 1 Pet. 1:22.

A pure heart. "Blessed are the pure in heart: for they shall see God." Mat. 5:8.

A pure mind. "This second epistle, beloved, I now write unto you, in both which I stir up your pure minds by way of remembrance." 2 Pet. 3:1.

A pure conscience. "I thank God whom I serve from my forefathers with pure conscience." 2 Tim. 1:3.

A pure language. "For then will I turn to the people a pure language, that they may all call upon the name of the Lord, to serve him with one consent." Zeph. 3:9.

Pure thoughts. "Finally, brethren, whatsoever things are true, whatsoever things are honest, whatsoever things are just, whatsoever things are pure, whatsoever things are lovely, whatsoever things are of good report; if there be any virtue, and if there be any praise, think on these things." Phil. 4:8.

A pure religion. "Pure religion and undefiled before God and the Father is this, To visit the fatherless and widows in their affliction, and to keep himself unspotted from the world." Jas. 1:27.

When man is made thus pure in all the faculties of his being he is said to be pure even as Christ is pure (1 John 3:3), and is then a perfect example of purity to the world. 1 Tim. 4:12.

The question is asked, "Who shall ascend into the hill of the Lord? or who shall stand in his holy place?" Psa. 24:3. The answer is, "He that hath clean hands and a pure heart." Purity is a requisite for heaven. "Blessed are the pure in heart, for they shall see God." In this language there is indubitably implied the impossibility of seeing God without purity of heart. God is pure, and heaven is a pure place, and without purity of soul and heart and life you can never enter heaven nor see God.

RIGHTEOUSNESS.

This is one of the terms used in the Scriptures describing the character of God and his people. "The

Lord is righteous," and the source of all righteousness. Man can not possess righteousness independent of God. It is beautiful to contemplate the righteous character of the Almighty as revealed in the holy Scriptures. It enables us to better understand our own nature when we are "filled with all the fulness of God." The Savior in his prayer addresses God as "righteous Father." John 17:25. The Revelator in his vision heard an angel proclaiming, "Thou art righteous, O Lord." Rev. 16:5. The Psalmist in exalting the righteousness of the Lord said: "Thy righteousness also, O God, is very high." Psa. 71:19. It is far above the ways and life of natural man: "For as the heavens are higher than the earth, so are my ways higher than your ways, and my thoughts than your thoughts." Isa. 55:9. All of God's ways are in righteousness: "The Lord is righteous in all his ways." Psa. 145:17. God's acts are done in righteousness: "Now therefore stand still, that I may reason with you before the Lord of all the righteous acts of the Lord which he did to you and your fathers."

Oh, the sublimity of the righteous character of God! How lofty and high. How far above the ways and acts of natural man. Man in his natural state does not possess any of the righteous principles of God: "There is none righteous, no not one." But God in the incarnation of his Son is both God and man, and through this means the righteousness of God is delegated unto man. In Jesus Christ we have the combining of man and God— the righteousness of God and humanity of man. Through the death of the man Christ Jesus and his resurrection the way was prepared for mankind to receive the righteousness of God. "For he hath made him to be sin for us, who knew no sin: that we might be made the righteousness of God in him." 2 Cor. 5:21. Jesus in his innocency and righteousness bore the sins of the guilty, so that in him we can experience a cleansing "from all unrighteousness" and receive instead "the righteousness of God."

Jesus likens himself and his people to a vine and its branches. He says, "I am the vine, ye are the branches." It is through the vine that the branches receive substance and strength and life from the soil. It is through Jesus that we receive righteousness, grace, and strength from God. It is only in Jesus' name that we receive anything from the Father The branches bear the fruit. Receiving the righteousness of God through Jesus we bear the fruit of righteousness. The more of this fruit we bear the more we show forth the praise of God. When there is a large yield of grain we conclude it was sown in good soil, and thus the soil gets the praise. We "being filled with the fruits of righteousness which are by Jesus Christ" do show forth "the glory and praise of God." Phil. 1:11. "Herein is my Father glorified, that ye bear much fruit." John 15:8. Though the grain be planted in good soil, cultivation is necessary to a bountiful harvest. Though we be planted in Christ cultivation is necessary to the production of rich fruit. "And every branch that beareth fruit, he purgeth it, that it may bring forth more fruit." John 15:2. Sin—all sin must be purged or cleansed away in order to bear fruits of righteousness.

"A tree is known by its fruits." Should there be a tree bearing promiscuously throughout apples, pears, peaches, plums, grapes, etc., who could tell what kind of a tree it was? Should it bear apples alone we at once know the kind of tree. All sin is therefore purged away from the heart of a Christian that he may be "filled with the fruits of righteousness," and be known as a light in the world. Sin and righteousness do not grow upon the same tree. How clearly and plainly this is taught in the sixth chapter of Romans. Except they be blinded by prejudice and false teaching all the world must understand this. Verse eighteen says, "Being then made free from sin, ye became the servants of righteousness." There are two things plainly taught in this text that we wish to call your attention to. First, to become **a servant** of righteousness necessitates a freedom from sin. "Ye can not serve two masters." Second, this experience of being made free from sin and becoming servants of righteousness the Roman brethren had received some time in the past. "Ye became the servants of righteousness." ver. 20. "For when [some time in their past life] ye were the servants of sin ye were free from righteousness."

In the face of these two texts how can man be so daring and proud and self-conceited as to teach the impossibility of Christians living a pure and sinless life in this world? Surely, there is no fear of God before their eyes. Verse eighteen declares that to become servants of righteousness necessitates freedom from sin; and verse twenty declares that to be a "servant of sin" necessitates freedom from righteousness. "What fruit had ye then in those things whereof ye are now ashamed?" ver. 21. Of the things of sin they once engaged in they are now ashamed. "What fruit had they then?" Ans.—"No fruit of righteousness." "But now being made free from sin, and become servants to God, ye have your fruit unto holiness." ver. 22. Praise God! You must be made free from sin to be capable of bearing fruit unto holiness or righteousness. The fruit of the righteous is to the praise and glory of God. The Lord makes use of the fruit of the righteous to induce sinners to seek him. In this way the fruit of the righteous is a tree of life. How blessed and noble to be a tree planted by the river of waters richly laden with righteous fruit. Amen.

REDEMPTION.

The authors of the dictionaries define the word *redemption* as "the act of deliverance, release, repurchase," etc. The redemption through Christ is the deliverance or repurchase of man. Man in his original, primeval state enjoyed unity and an affinity with God. Because of transgression on the part of man this natural agreement between God and man was destroyed. All creation—herb, and tree, beast and fowl, and man—was pronounced very good by the Creator as he beheld it in review after creation. Gen. 1: 29-31.

But because of Eden's sin the very nature of all things became changed. The ground became cursed, and thorns and thistles sprang up. Gen. 3: 17, 18. The nature of the beast creation, no doubt, became affected by man's transgression. Gen. 6: 7, 11-13. The transgression in Eden was the entrance of sin into this world. Rom. 5: 12. Previous to this, all in the world was sinless harmony, and the earth itself uncursed by thorns and thistles. By the entrance of sin man's nature became changed. and since the nature of man became depraved there has not been a single individual born of the flesh but has possessed a depraved nature, except the child conceived by the Holy Spirit. The Psalmist says: "Behold, I was shapen in iniquity, and in sin did my mother conceive me." Psa. 51: 5.

This same is true of every child. The nature of the child in its formation in the womb is depraved. The moral condition of the parents may modify to an extent, but never wholly change that nature. The child does not inherit a depraved nature from its parents. It is not because the parents are depraved that the child is conceived in sin, but because nature is depraved. It required a supernatural conception to beget a pure child, everything in nature being depraved. The child does not inherit either physical or moral image directly from its parents. It is true, the child generally bears a marked resemblance to the parent, both physically and morally, but on the whole it is born in the image of Adam, morally and physically. It is generally the case that if a parent have three arms, or possess but one, his offspring will have two, receiving its physical image from the first created man. Should the parents be holy, the child will possess a carnal nature, because it is the nature of all the race.

How holy parents beget children depraved in nature is a puzzling problem to some minds, especially to those who are busying themselves about the intricate matters of God. This need be no more puzzling than a deformed parent begetting perfectly formed children. Nature, in embryo, begins its work of forming both the physical and moral image of the child, which is after the similitude of the original parents and not the immediate ones. While justification, which is the forgiveness of actual transgression, the inevitable result of a depraved nature, is a wonderful and glorious achievement of grace, it is but a very small part of the redemption of Christ. The supernatural overthrow of the depraved nature by the power of the Holy Spirit is the principal and real redemptive work. The pardon of committed sins is the clearing away of the rubbish, or preparation work, for the Third Person in the Holy Trinity to effect a revolution in the nature of man. Halleluiah to God! This change in nature is more wonderful than the revolting of nature at the command of Joshua. Man now, instead of being depraved in nature, is restored to his original holy nature.

This destruction of the carnal nature and the restoration of the original nature is accomplished by the Holy Spirit at the moment of his reception as an indwelling Comforter. Peter teaches this truth when he says: "God, which knoweth the hearts [or nature], bare them witness, giving them the Holy Ghost, even as he did unto us [at Pentecost]; and put no difference between us and them [Gentiles], purifying their hearts by faith." Acts 15: 8, 9. Purifying the heart is the purification of man's affections, or nature. This is accomplished at the time of the giving of the Holy Ghost as declared in the last text; and this purifying of the hearts of the Gentiles at the giving of the Holy Ghost, is just what was done for the apostles at Pentecost. This is a plain, undeniable fact taught in this text. To turn to philosophizing upon how we can be conceived with a carnal nature, or how we can be converted and yet be depraved in nature is to soon become spoiled through vain deceit after the rudiments of the world and not after Christ. Col. 2:8. In the very nature of things, and according to the Word of God, pardon of sins necessarily precedes the destruction of the carnal, depraved nature by the Holy Spirit. In the fall of man there was the act of transgression and also a change in man's moral image. In his restoration there must be a pardon of transgression and subsequently a change in nature.

It is a law of God that the redemption of man be accomplished through faith, by his grace. Our faith can not reach beyond our knowledge. By knowledge we mean a real soul-consciousness or conviction and not an intellectual knowledge. At this point many a dear soul has erred from the truth. They have endeavored to bring their faith up to their intellectual knowledge, which ends in presumption. True Bible faith is grounded in the soul. It results from a soul-knowledge, or conviction. To accept pardon of sins or healing of the body with only an intellectual knowledge of these blessings and not a real heart-conviction is mere presumption, and ends in failure and disgrace. To follow the comprehensions of the intellect, and not the enlightenment of the Holy Spirit upon the soul, concerning the mysteries of God's salvation is to be led into error, because the intellect can not fathom the things of God. We do now emphatically say, according to God's established law, that no unregenerated heart can have a comprehension or conviction of a corrupt moral nature and its purification. Why? Because transgression stands between it and purity. The awakened guilty soul knows nothing but its guilt, and for forgiveness only does it plead. After being pardoned, the soul gains a knowledge of carnality, and it is then convicted for the second cleansing.

Those who believe that purity of heart is attained in pardon take as a basis of such belief the language of Paul in 2 Cor. 5:17; Rom. 8:1-7; and similar texts. Now the apostle often speaks of full salvation, or complete redemption of the soul, in a general way. He says that "salvation is by the grace of God through faith." By this he does not mean justification only, but sanctification as well. He has not specified the two works, but has spoken of full salvation in a general way of being by grace through faith. Thus Eph. 2:8-10 includes full salvation. In 2 Cor. 5:17 he again speaks of full salvation in a general way. It is true we are in Christ when converted, but we are none the less in him when sanctified. To say that Paul is referring to the justified only in this text is an error. By the two preceding verses we have reason to believe he is referring to those who are wholly sanctified. This then is no proof text that carnality is destroyed in justification, because you can not prove that he is referring to those who are only justified. In conclusion we would say that Christ came to redeem man only. Beast and bird have no part in the redemption. They shall perish. The earth is not redeemable, but being under the curse—spotted by sin—it shall be destroyed.

CHAPTER VI.
FRUITS AND THE TWO WORKS.

FRUITS OF THE SPIRIT.

Men are likened unto trees in some Scriptural texts. The righteous are termed good trees, and the wicked evil trees. Now the "tree is known by its fruit." The fruits of the flesh are borne upon the evil tree, while the fruits of the Spirit are borne upon the good tree. The fruits of the Spirit are enumerated in Gal. 5:22, 23: "But the fruit of the Spirit is love, joy, peace, long-suffering, gentleness, goodness, faith, meekness, temperance: against such there is no law." We shall describe these fruits separately by the word of truth, as briefly as possible.

LOVE.

This is the sweetest theme in the Scriptures and the greatest thing in earth or heaven. "God is love," and because he is love he sought to rescue, through the sacrifice of his Son, his fallen creatures. It was love that prompted God to make so great a sacrifice for man. It is love that prompts man to sacrifice all for God. When man loves God he loves everything in God's creation. No man can love God and hate his brother; no man can love God and hate his enemies. God loves his enemies. It is the nature of the love of God. When man possesses the love of God in his heart he will love his enemies. To love those who love us and despise those who despise us, is not a love that is a fruit of the Spirit. When man possesses the love of God he does not love the world. 1 John 2: 15-17. Everything in our service to God if acceptable must be actuated by love. Supernatural gifts are nothing without love. 1 Cor. 13: 1, 2. The greatest deeds of sacrifice profit us nothing without they are done in love. ver. 3. In the following verses of this chapter the nature of love is beautifully and obviously portrayed.

1. Charity suffereth long. By long-suffering is meant to patiently bear with the failings and foibles of our brother, "With all lowliness and meekness, with long-suffering, forbearing one another in love." Eph. 4: 2. There is a beautiful thought in 1 Tim. 1: 16. That Jesus might show his long-suffering through us as a pattern for all who may in any way know of our life.

2. Charity is kind. Where love is there is kindness. The greater the love the greater the kindness. The lioness in all the fierceness of her nature strokes her whelp in tenderness and kindness. Thus kindness is a product of love. Love will put a tenderness in our

looks, a gentleness in our speech, and a kindness in our acts. If you are not as kind as you know you should be, seek God for more of his love.

3. Charity envieth not. How impossible to envy those we love. The more fortunate they are the more we rejoice. The more they are praised and honored the deeper is our joy. With those we love, we weep when they weep and rejoice when they rejoice. If there is a secret envy in your heart because of the praise and prosperity of others, the love of God is wanting. "Let not thine heart envy sinners." Prov. 23:17.

4. Charity vaunteth not itself. We can only love God at the sacrifice of all self-love. When man possesses the love of God there is no self-praise, nor seeking of honor; there is no setting self forward, but the lowliest seat is the most desirable.

5. Charity is not puffed up. There are no feelings of self-importance in the heart when the love of God is abounding. We love him so devotedly we desire him to receive all the praise. Should God make some use of you it will be natural to give him all the praise.

6. Charity doth not behave itself unseemly. There is a becomingness in all the actions of pure and holy love. There is a beautiful consistency in the worship of God when all is actuated by pure love. There is nothing unseemly in our behavior toward God or our fellow man, even to the most cultured minds, when influenced by love. It is noble and sublime, elevating

and pleasing to pure hearts. Praise is comely when flowing from a heart full of love, but a wild hurrahing is unseemly. All unseemly conduct in modes and forms of worship—such as tossing the head to and fro, swaying the body, the loud stamping of feet, rolling on the floor, lying stiff and rigid, shouting until the face reddens and veins distend and exhaustion overcomes, are disgracing to God and disgusting to refined ears and pure hearts.

7. Charity seeketh not her own. When man possesses the love of God he does not seek his own pleasure and happiness but is interested in the welfare and happiness of others; 'He looks not upon his own things but upon the things of others.' We seek opportunities to do good to those we love.

8. Charity is not easily provoked. There is a weightiness in the love of God. It balances all our actions. We are not hasty under provocations; we are not excited or vexed at every trivial occurrence.

9. Charity thinketh no evil. The meditations of a heart of pure love are holy. A holy man's thoughts are upon pure and true subjects. He thinketh no evil.

10. Charity rejoiceth not in iniquity. Sin saddens and grieves the heart of love. Should there be a secret rejoicing in your heart because some brother has fallen into sin, you are proud and an abomination unto God.

11. Charity rejoiceth in the truth. Where the truth

is accepted it causes the heart of love to rejoice. Should God use some other individual in setting the truth before people which causes them to rejoice, if you love God and the truth you will rejoice with them.

12. Charity beareth all things. Amid adversities, afflictions, persecutions, temptations and trials, when storms gather, and breakers threaten, when friends prove false, and the way grows weary, love looks trustingly up to God and says, "Thou doeth all things well, blessed be thy name."

13. Charity believeth all things. Those who love are ever ready to believe the best of everything and everybody. They see all the good qualities of man before they see his faults. They are ready to believe all the good they hear of any one and slow to believe evil. They rejoice to put confidence in man, and when man's evil ways break that confidence they still hope for something good.

14. Charity hopeth all things. It is very difficult to discourage the heart that is full of love. When love waxes cold then disappointments may cause a murmur. Love hopes for the very best outcome for good of everything.

15. Charity endureth all things. The same might be said of this as that "charity beareth all things." Whatever darkness may arise to-day, Love hopes for sunshine to-morrow and patiently endures.

16. Charity never fails. Thank God! Pretended

friends may fail you; the world may fail you; wealth and honor may fail you; but love will never fail. It will bear you over the rough places in life's pathway. It will drive away the clouds. It will kiss the chastening rod. It will sweeten the bitter cup. It will soften the hardest pillow, and when you are brought down into the shadow of death Love looks across to the golden glories and sings as the cords are being severed—Love never fails.

> "Fairest and foremost of the trains that wait
> On man's most dignified and happiest state,
> Whether we name thee Charity or Love,
> Chief grace below, and all in all above."—*Cowper.*

JOY.

The second mentioned fruit of the Spirit is joy. God is glorified by our fruit-bearing. To be filled with joy is honoring God. Not rejoicing only when the world is smiling upon you and prosperity extends her jeweled hand. At these times the ungodly can rejoice. But when the world frowns and prosperity hides her face, when trials and temptations are divers, to then rejoice is a golden fruit for God. Tribulations may come, but, when filled with the Spirit, we glory in them. Rom. 5:3. O beloved, look upward to God and rejoice. Trust in his promise and count everything joy, no matter what may be the circumstances of life. Trials, temptations, discouragements, afflictions, imprisonments, persecutions, destruction, and poverty—know that nothing can separate you from the love of God; so go on your way rejoicing.

PEACE.

Jesus sets up his throne of peace in the hearts of the righteous and there he reigns a king. Peace he gives unto us, not as this world gives, but a peace that flows like a river—a peace that is abiding. "Acquaint thyself with God and be at peace." Listen to what the Word of God says about the peace of the righteous. "Great peace have they;" "Thou wilt keep him in perfect peace;" "Peace like a river;" "Filled with all peace and joy."

A precious fruit, which the Christian should develop by placing greater confidence in God.

LONG-SUFFERING.

"With all lowliness and meekness, with long-suffering, forbearing one another in love." Eph. 4:2. When we put on Christ, we put on his nature and characteristics. He was long-suffering; and we are commanded to put on as the elect of God "bowels of mercies, kindness, humbleness of mind, meekness, long-suffering." Col. 3:12.

GENTLENESS.

The apostle speaks of his gentleness on one occasion in these words: "But we were gentle among you, even as a nurse cherisheth her children." 1 Thes.

2:7. "The servant of the Lord must not strive; but be gentle unto all men." 2 Tim. 2:24. "To speak evil of no man, to be no brawlers, but gentle, showing all meekness unto all men." Tit. 3:2. That wisdom which is from above is gentle. Jas. 3:17. Cultivate the grace of gentleness and thus glorify God.

GOODNESS.

"For the fruit of the Spirit is in all goodness and righteousness and truth." Eph. 5:9. "Doing good unto all men as we have opportunity" is the command of God: "See that none render evil for evil unto any man; but ever follow that which is good, both among yourselves, and to all men." 1 Thes. 5:15. Let goodness fill our actions toward all. Be good.

FAITH.

If you have faith in God prove it by your works. Your works are the fruit. Why are you discouraged and cast down if you have faith? Why do you seek protection from the world if you have faith in God? Why do you fear and tremble if you have faith? Faith has subdued kingdoms, stopped the mouths of lions, quenched the violence of fire, caused the sun to stand still, escaped the edge of the sword, waxed valiant in fight, and turned to flight the armies of the aliens. Faith overcomes the world and pleases God. Show your faith by your works and thus honor the name of Jesus.

MEEKNESS.

This is a beautiful fruit of the Spirit. It is almost synonymous with humility. Christ was meek and lowly. We are to be like him. "Show all meekness unto all men." God will "beautify the meek with salvation." We are commanded to put on meekness. Col. 3:12, 13. Wear it constantly, long usage will not impair it. We are to manifest meekness in our whole conduct. Jas. 3:13. We must instruct those who oppose us, in meekness. 2 Tim. 2:24, 25. Meekness is necessary to a Christian walk. Eph. 4:1, 2. With it we are to restore the erring. Gal. 6:1. It is precious in the sight of God. 1 Pet. 3:4.

TEMPERANCE.

To be temperate in our whole life is truly exemplary. In all the things God has given us for use we are to be temperate; in eating, drinking, sleeping, laboring, be temperate.

These are the fruits of the Spirit, against which there is no law. Bear them in profusion and there will be no law against you in that final day. Amen.

FRUITS OF THE FLESH.

Since we have given an exposition of the fruits of a Christian, which have their origin in heaven, as expressed by the apostle, we deem it necessary to set before the reader in a true Bible light the fruits of the flesh, which have their origin in an evil nature. While we are aware that many are deceived as to their spiritual condition, as saith the Scriptures, yet none need to be. The Word of God so carefully enumerates the fruits of a Christian heart and the fruits of an evil heart, that all may know by impartial examination what manner of tree they are. "The tree is known by his fruits." "Know thyself." "Now the works of the flesh are manifest, which are these; adultery, fornication, uncleanness, lasciviousness, idolatry, witchcraft, hatred, variance, emulation, wrath, strife, seditions, heresies, envyings, murders, drunkenness, revelings, and such like: of the which I tell you before, as I have also told you in time past, that they which do such things shall not inherit the kingdom of God." Gal. 5: 19-21.

1. Adultery and fornication. "But I say unto you, That whosoever looketh on a woman to lust after her hath committed adultery with her already in his heart." Mat. 5: 28. "Whosoever putteth away his wife, and marrieth another, committeth adultery: and whosoever marrieth her that is put away from her husband committeth adultery." Luke 16: 18. This is clear and plain language and all can understand it without comment.

2. Uncleanness. This may include filthy habits, but especially impure thoughts and conversation, unholy practises and desires.

3. Lasciviousness. All lewdness and wantonness.

4. Idolatry. Covetousness is idolatry. Col. 3: 5.

Covetousness—A desire to gain money, goods, honor, or praise, even at the expense of another.

5. Witchcraft. Enchantments and spells, such as healing by hypnotism, and sciences. Omens, signs and superstitions, so frightfully common.

6. Hatred. A feeling of ill-will against any one or anything. "Whosoever hateth his brother is a murderer." 1 John 3:15. Feelings of hatred are opposed to feelings of love.

7. Variance. When hatred in the hearts of two individuals develops into open acts, it is variance.

8. Emulation. This is a disposition to strive to excel others, even at their expense—exaltedness.

9. Wrath. An outburst of hatred.

10. Strife. Contentions, janglings, disputings.

11. Seditions. Divisions, parties, factions, or sects.

12. Heresies. Erroneous teachings and beliefs, forming sects and factions.

13. Envyings. A feeling of jealousy at the success of others. "Let us walk honestly as in the day; not in rioting and drunkenness, not in chambering and wantonness, not in strife and envying." Rom. 13:13. See also 1 Cor. 3:3; 2 Cor. 12:20; Jas 3:14, 16.

14. Murders. To hate a brother is to become a murderer. See hatred.

15. Drunkenness. An effect produced by drinking fermented wines, or inebriating drinks of any kind.

16. Revelings. Worldly amusements of any kind: theater-going, dancing, picnics, suppers, fairs, socials,

Christmas festivities, etc. They which do such things shall not inherit the kingdom of God.

You will notice that the fruits of the flesh are directly opposed to the fruits of the Spirit. By careful and prayerful study of this catalogue of evil fruits and an examination of your actions, thoughts, and inclinations, you can unmistakably know whether you are prepared or not for heaven. Make your calling and election sure. Never be contented if there is any fruit in your life of the nature of the above. I have been asked the question, "Will a Christian ever attend the present day church entertainments?" A Christian, largely ignorant of the vast separation from the world salvation makes, may, through the persuasion of friends, or some other similar cause, attend such a place of revelry, but he will not enjoy the hour. He will be uneasy and long for the last act that he may get away to commune with God. Whoever has a heart to enter into such worldliness with enjoyment has a heart unfit for heaven. He is not a Christian.

TWO WORKS OF GRACE.

Many treat with scorn the doctrine of "two works of grace," but that can never make it unscriptural. It is very unwise to disbelieve a truth merely because we have been taught and always believed to the contrary. An early education has a great influence upon the mind. Through the teachings of a relative we embraced an error in our youth. In after years when the subject was read and thought upon it was difficult to comprehend and believe the plain truths of history. It is wisdom therefore to always carefully and prayerfully examine a doctrine before condemning and rejecting it. "Why does not God fully redeem the soul in one instantaneous work of grace?" many ask. What right have we to question God concerning his plan of redemption? Was not the whole scheme in his hand? What part has man performed in the arrangement of the affair? Then why should he question? It only remains for us to humbly bow our hearts and accept the plan as God has devised it, else we can never have a part in it.

Why did God require Naaman to dip seven times in Jordan? Why did Jesus put his hands the second time upon the blind man of Bethsaida before he saw clearly? Why does God redeem a soul by two works of grace? These questions are equally absurd. But you say, God does the thing most reasonable. That he does, and redemption by two works of grace is the very most reasonable and natural way to restore the soul to its normal condition. Man was holy in his nature in creation. By sin he became possessed of an evil nature. The Psalmist says, "I was shapen in iniquity; and in sin did my mother conceive me." Psa. 51:5. The apostle declares he was by nature a child of wrath. Eph. 2:3. Other texts could be quoted, but these together with the knowledge of a child's disposition is sufficient to convince any candid mind. Children naturally learn evil things, while good traits more often have to be forced upon them by training. It comes natural for them to get angry, to be selfish, to tell falsehoods, to fight, to be proud, etc.; not in all to the same degree, but such disposition is largely predominant in the generality of children, and exists to a certain degree in all.

Children are not responsible for this evil nature as we have previously spoken. They are not responsible for their wrong acts, because they have no knowledge of right and wrong. They may tell falsehoods before they have strength of intellect to comprehend wrong, and it is no sin to them; but when the child reaches such maturity of mind as to know right and wrong, a falsehood then told makes him a transgressor and he feels the guilt of sin upon his soul, which he never felt unto that hour. The evil nature that influenced him to speak falsely did not condemn him, it is the yielding to such a nature that brought the condemnation. God commands him to repent. Of what? Not of the evil inclined disposition, but of the sin of lying. Suppose the child after a year, or a few years does repent of his sins; he repents of all, even to his first, but his repentance goes no farther; he is no farther responsible, and it is impossible for man to repent of that for which he is not responsible. God forgives him, and the forgiveness extends just as far as the repentance.

Man is not pardoned or forgiven of that for which

he is wholly irresponsible. Every committed sin is forgiven, even to the first, and he is as innocent and free from sin and guilt as when a babe in his mother's arms. This is the first work of grace. He is justified, he is born again, or reborn—brought back to the state of his babyhood. "Except ye be converted, and become as little children, ye shall not enter into the kingdom of heaven." Mat. 18:3. Conversion or the first work of grace restores us to the happy innocency of childhood. The evil nature still remains to be removed in sanctification, the second work of grace. This is not an act of forgiveness or pardon, but a cleansing. It is not through repentance, but consecration.

The Jewish economy contains types and shadows of this twofold salvation. Egyptian bondage is typical of sin. Crossing the Red Sea is typical of justification. Crossing the Jordan, that of sanctification. The Jewish tabernacle consisting of the holy and most holy place is a shadow of the spiritual tabernacle of God—the church. The disciples were saved men before Pentecost. That was the date of their sanctification. In reading the eighth chapter of Acts we learn at the fifth verse that Philip went down to Samaria and preached Christ, and many believed. Evil spirits were cast out and the palsied and lame were healed. They certainly were Christians. Reading on to the fourteenth verse we learn that Peter and John went down and prayed for them and they received the Holy Ghost. The Holy Ghost is the sanctifier. Rom. 15:16. Cornelius was a devout Christian man, fearing God, giving much alms to the people, and praying to God always. He was directed in a vision by an angel of God to send to Joppa for Peter. When Peter was come he preached unto them, and as he spoke the Holy Ghost fell on all them which heard the word. Acts 10th chapter. He with his household were devout Christians before they received the Holy Spirit—the sanctifier.

We will now quote a few texts of Scripture teaching two works of grace. "Therefore being justified by faith, we have peace with God through our Lord Jesus Christ: by whom also we have access by faith into this grace [sanctification] wherein we stand, and rejoice in hope of the glory of God." Rom. 5:1, 2. Paul says to the Gentiles that he was sent unto them "to open their eyes, and to turn them from darkness to light, and from the power of Satan unto God, that they may receive forgiveness of sins, and inheritance among them which are sanctified by faith that is in me." Acts 26:18. "Not by works of righteousness which we have done, but according to his mercy he saved us, by the washing of regeneration, and renewing of the Holy Ghost." Titus 3:5.

The Thessalonian brethren were abounding in faith and love and patience of hope in Jesus; however Paul tells them that God wills their sanctification. 1 Thes. 4:3. The apostle exhorts the Roman church to a perfect consecration of life and all to God that they might prove what is that good and acceptable and perfect will of God." Rom. 12:1, 2. This "perfect will" is sanctification. These texts we consider sufficient to give light unto the teachable, and any number perhaps would be without force or effect unto the unteachable.

The two works of grace are very generally misunderstood, especially the grace of sanctification. We believe God will help us here to make it clear to many a reader. Justification, the first work of grace, is a full pardon of every transgression, a removal of guilt. A justified life is one wholly free from transgression. The justified do not commit sin. Sanctification is a destruction of the depraved nature, or a cleansing of inherited sin from the soul. This grace fully prepares the soul for heaven. The soul is as pure in this grace as it will be in heaven. All elements and dispositions contrary to the nature of heaven are dethroned. All pride, levity, lust, and impatience proceeding from an evil nature are perfectly cleansed away. To have pride in a pure heart is impossible. To have lust or lightness or impatience in a pure heart is equally impossible.

We might ask the question, Will not the sanctified under any circumstance have the slightest yieldings to exaltation, levity and impatience? and, if the sanctified speak a word in lightness or impatience does he forfeit the experience? We will answer these questions in the fear of God. Many who have claimed the experience of sanctification have found discouraging trouble at this point. In the company of flatterers they yielded to the spirit of exaltation. In the company of the frivolous they have yielded to the spirit of levity. Under a severe trial they have spoken words of impatience, and are then almost in despair.

Man is a twofold being, an inward spiritual man, and an outward physical man. In sanctification the inward man is possessed only by God. The physical members are to be used by the soul to the praise of God. Satan will bring his force to bear against the outward man to influence to evil and thus destroy the life of the soul. Thus the physical being becomes the battle ground between God in the soul and Satan. Early in the experience of sanctification when there has been but little time for development there may be slight triumphs of Satan without forfeiting the experience of sanctification, but the soul is awakened to greater activity and earnestness to control every action and word to the praise of God. The Lord is sought in earnest prayer for more of his power, for more of his grace, that they may be more deeply fortified in the life divine. The slight victories of the evil one become slighter and less frequent. The individual thus increases in faith, in humility, in gentleness, in kindness, in love according to the additions required to make our calling and election sure. 2 Pet. 1. By giving diligence the soul ere long will gain such power in God as to authoritatively command the perfect obedience of every member of the physical being. The body will be kept under subjection and every member used as an instrument of righteousness unto God.

Any diseased condition of the outward man is an advantage to Satan. Shattered nerves strengthen his temptations to impatience and discouragements. That Satan may have no advantage over us, God in his plan of redemption made provision for the healing of the body. If the soul through prosperity or otherwise becomes slothful, disease may be permitted to attack the body, or other afflictions may come to awaken to greater watchfulness. To become more hasty of speech, to become less grave, to become less humble and meek, less patient, is to be correspondingly losing the power of God, and is called backsliding. There are those to-day who have been claiming to be sanctified for some years, and they are no more patient nor sober-minded nor sound in speech, no more humble, nor have more faith than they had the first year of their experience. In all probability they are backslidden and have naught but an empty form. By diligence, careful watching and incessant prayer, the soul can reign triumphant. Every look, every action, every word, and thought will be under the direct influence of the divine life, and soul, body, and spirit be preserved blameless until the coming of the Lord.

We wish to give in parallel columns nine scriptures, describing man raised to the plane of justification, and nine describing the state of the wholly sanctified. Also a few texts expressing God's will to the sinner, and parallel texts to the justified. And in conclusion a few texts showing the provisions God has made for the justification of the sinner and the sanctification of the justified.

STATE OF THE JUSTIFIED.

1. *In Christ.* "For we are his workmanship, created in Christ Jesus unto good works, which God hath before ordained that we should walk in them." Eph. 2: 10.

2. *Obtained grace.* "For by grace are ye saved through faith; and that not of yourselves: it is the gift of God." Eph. 2: 8.

3. *Justified.* "And by him all that believe are justified from all things, from which ye could not be justified by the law of Moses." Acts 13: 39.

4. *Have light.* "I am the light of the world: he that followeth me shall not walk in darkness, but shall have the light of life." John 8: 12. "Awake thou that sleepest, and arise from the dead, and Christ shall give thee light." Eph. 5: 14.

STATE OF THE SANCTIFIED.

1. *Perfect in Christ.* "Whom we preach, warning every man, and teaching every man in all wisdom; that we may present every man perfect in Christ Jesus." Col. 1: 28.

2 *Abundance of grace.* "Much more they which receive abundance of grace and of the gift of righteousness shall reign in life by one, Jesus Christ." Rom. 5: 17.

3. *Sanctified.* "For by one offering he hath perfected forever them that are sanctified. Whereof the Holy Ghost also is a witness to us." Heb. 10: 14, 15.

4. *Full of light.* "The light of the body is the eye: if therefore thine eye be single, thy whole body shall be full of light." Mat. 6: 22.

5. *Have peace.* "Therefore being justified by faith, we have peace with God through our Lord Jesus Christ." Rom. 5: 1.

6. *Have life.* "Verily, verily, I say unto you, He that heareth my word, and believeth on him that sent me, hath everlasting life, and shall not come into condemnation; but is passed from death unto life." John 5: 24.

7. *Have faith.* "For ye are all the children of God by faith in Christ Jesus." Gal. 3: 26.

8. *Love God.* "Peter was grieved because he said unto him the third time, Lovest thou me? And he said unto him, Lord, thou knowest all things; thou knowest that I love thee." John 21: 17.

9. *Babes in Christ.* "And I, brethren, could not speak unto you as unto spiritual, but as unto carnal, even as unto babes in Christ." 1 Cor. 3: 1.

5. *Have perfect peace.* "Thou wilt keep him in perfect peace, whose mind is stayed on thee: because he trusteth in thee." Isa. 26: 3.

6. *Have abundant life.* "The thief cometh not, but for to steal and to kill and to destroy: I am come that they might have life, and that they might have it more abundantly." John 10: 10.

7. *Full of faith.* "For he was a good man and full of the Holy Ghost and of faith: and much people was added unto the Lord." Acts 11: 24.

8. *Perfect in love.* "Herein is our love made perfect, that we may have boldness in the day of judgment: because as he is, so are we in this world." 1 John 4: 17.

9. *Men in Christ.* "Till we all come in the unity of the faith, and of the knowledge of the Son of God, unto a perfect man, unto the measure of the stature of the fulness of Christ." Eph. 4: 13.

GOD'S WILL.

TO THE SINNER.

Repentance. "The Lord is ...not willing that any should perish, but that all should come to repentance." 2 Pet. 3: 9.

Called to repentance. "I am not come to call the righteous, but sinners to repentance." Mat. 9: 13.

Commands repentance. "And the times of this ignorance God winked at; but now commandeth all men everywhere to repent." Acts 17: 30.

The reason for repentance. "I tell you, Nay: but, except ye repent, ye shall all likewise perish." Luke 13: 3.

TO THE JUSTIFIED.

Sanctification. "For this is the will of God, even your sanctification." 1 Thes. 4: 3.

Called to sanctification. "For God hath not called us unto uncleanness, but unto holiness." 1 Thes. 4: 7.

Commands sanctification. "Having therefore these promises, dearly beloved, let us cleanse ourselves from all filthiness of the flesh and spirit, perfecting holiness in the fear of God." 2 Cor. 7: 1.

The reason for sanctification. "Follow peace with all men, and holiness, without which no man shall see the Lord." Heb. 12: 14.

PROVISIONS MADE.

FOR THE JUSTIFICATION OF THE SINNER.

1. *The Word.* "For I am not ashamed of the gospel of Christ: for it is the power of God unto salvation to every one that believeth." Rom. 1: 16.

FOR THE SANCTIFICATION OF THE BELIEVER.

1. *The Word.* "Sanctify them through thy truth: thy word is truth." John 17: 17

2. *The Spirit.* "Jesus answered, Verily, verily, I say unto thee, Except a man be born of water and of the Spirit, he can not enter into the kingdom of God." John 3:5.

3. *The Blood.* "Unto him that loved us, and washed us from our sins in his own blood." Rev. 1:5.

4. *Jesus.* "And he is the propitiation for our sins: and not for ours only, but also for the sins of the whole world." 1 John 2:2.

5. *God.* "Which were born, not of blood, nor of the will of the flesh, nor of the will of man, but of God." John 1:13.

2. *The Spirit.* "That I should be the minister of Jesus Christ to the Gentiles, ministering the gospel of God, that the offering up of the Gentiles might be acceptable, being sanctified by the Holy Ghost." Rom. 15:16.

3. *The Blood.* "Wherefore Jesus also, that he might sanctify the people with his own blood, suffered without the gate." Heb. 13:12.

4. *Jesus.* "And inheritance among them which are sanctified by faith that is in me [Jesus]." Acts 26:18.

5. *God.* "And the very God of peace sanctify you wholly;...faithful is he that calleth you, who also will do it." 1 Thes. 5:23, 24.

The following diagram illustrates man's fall and redemption. To make our explanation clear and comprehensive we have numbered each line. No. 1 is a line used to represent the plane of God's holiness. "The Lord is righteous in all his ways, and holy in all his works." Psa. 145:17. No. 2 represents the plane of man's holiness in his creation. Gen. 1:26; Eccl. 7:29. No. 3 indicates the transgression or fall of man to the low plane of sin. Gen. 3:1-7; Rom. 5:12. Line No. 4 represents the plane of sin or transgression. No. 5, the plane of innocency or childhood state. Psa. 51:5; Eph. 2:3. No. 6, the falling of the child from innocency to the plane of sin after a wilful, known transgression. No. 7, the holiness of Jesus. Heb. 7:26. No. 8, spiritual resurrection or repentance and salvation. No. 9, innocency restored by being born again. John 3:3; Mat. 18:3. No. 10, consecration and elevation to the plane of holiness. No. 11, the plane of man's holiness in complete and full salvation. 1 John 3:3, 7; 1 John 4:17.

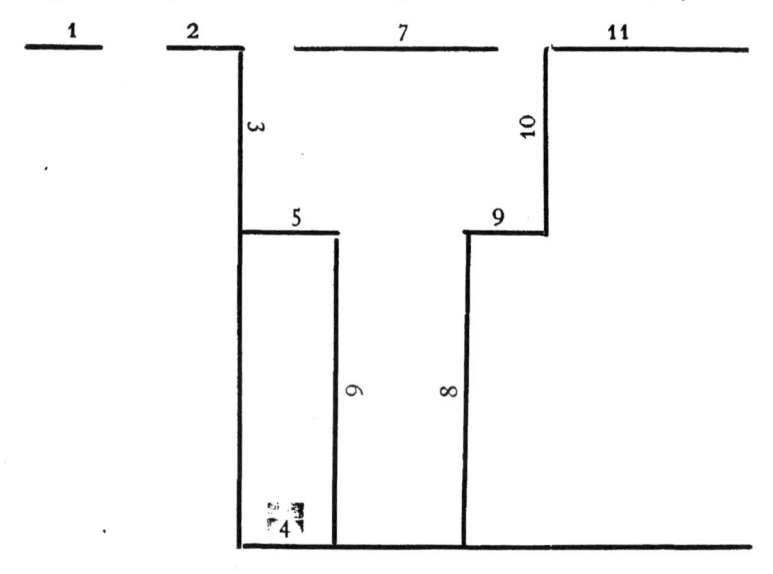

BEING LIKE JESUS.

Holiness is the image of God. A holy seer, in a vision, saw the Lord and his high throne. He saw the angels hovering over and heard one shouting, "Holy, holy, holy, is the Lord of hosts: the whole earth is full of his glory." Isa. 6:1-3. Nothing in earth or in heaven is so beautiful as holiness. The Scriptures are sublime in their description of the loveliness of the celestial world. Poets have sung of the exquisite delights of that better land. The crowning feature of attractiveness is holiness. Should the despiser of holiness be permitted to stroll through the fields of heaven he would find no object of beauty there. The rose of Sharon would be but a faded flower, "no beauty that we should desire him." Isa. 53: 2.

The one object and desire in the life of the sweet singer David, a holiness admirer, was to dwell in the house of the Lord all his days to "behold the beauty of the Lord." Psa. 27: 4. The beautiful holy image of God was seen upon man in his creation. He manifested the holy character of his Creator. He was in nature like God. The Almighty in looking over the works of creation saw that everything he had made, man included, was very good (Gen. 1: 31); therefore we can rightly conclude that as he looked upon man he looked upon a creature as pure and holy and faultless as an angel in heaven, else he would not have pronounced him very good. Such without controversy was the state of man by creation: as holy and as pure in his nature as his Maker. But a sorrowful change came to man. He transgressed the law of his God, and as a result the holy image of the Creator was supplanted by the hideous deformity of sin.

After the transgression, God again looked upon man and "saw that his wickedness was very great in the earth, and that every imagination of the thoughts of his heart was only evil continually." Gen. 6:5. This grieved him at his heart, and he repented of having made man. However he purposes that man shall yet enjoy the blessing of a holy state. Accordingly he sent his Son to this world to redeem him. This Son was in the image of the Father "in whom the god of this world hath blinded the minds of them which believe not, lest the light of the glorious gospel of Christ, who is the image of God, should shine unto them." 2 Cor. 4:4. "Who is the image of the invisible God, the first-born of every creature." Col. 1:15.

The Father has ordained that man in the Son should be made holy or in his original purity. "According as he hath chosen us in him before the foundation of the world, that we should be holy and without blame before him in love." Eph. 1:4. "In holiness and righteousness before him, all the days of our life." Luke 1:75.

In being restored to holiness man is conformed to the image of the Son. "For whom he did foreknow, he also did predestinate to be conformed to the image of his Son, that he might be the first-born among many brethren." Rom. 8:29. It is true God foreknew that some would not believe on his Son and be redeemed, and he foreknew that others would. Here we behold the wonderful mercy of God. He strives with the heart of the sinner and brings all influences possible to bear upon him to turn him from his sin, and all the time knowing he would never be saved; however he thus leaves him without excuse and makes him wholly responsible for his loss.

What is the image of the Son? He was holy, harmless, and undefiled. Heb. 7:26. He was equal with God. Phil. 2:6. He was in the glory and holiness of the Father. God after creation looked over the work of his hands and pronounced all very good. After the "transgression" he saw that all was very wicked. Now Jesus comes and presents to the Father one who has been redeemed by the all-atoning blood, and as God views him over he stands "holy and unblamable and unreprovable in his sight." Hallelujah! Read Col. 1:21, 22. The redemption obtained through the blood of Jesus is perfect and complete. It makes us "complete in him." Col. 2:10. Dear reader, this moment, with open heart before the all-seeing eye of God, does the Spirit witness clearly to your soul that you are "holy and without blame before him in love?" To be like Jesus includes only his holy nature. We are not to be like him in power to forgive sins, but in a holy life. We are to be thus like him in this present life; "because as he is, so are we in this world." 1 John 4:17. In this world we are to be like him in holiness. "But as he which hath called you is holy, so be ye holy in all manner of conversation; because it is written, "Be ye holy; for I am holy." 1 Pet. 1: 15, 16. God predestinated that we should be like him. He is holy, therefore he calls the believer unto holiness.

When we are restored to the holy nature of God it will be our nature to be as merciful as he is merciful. "Be ye therefore merciful, as your Father also is merciful." Luke 6:36. The mercy of God consists in showing favor unsolicited; in bestowing blessings upon the ungrateful. God in his mercy gave his Son to die for a wicked world. When we are made partakers of the divine nature, we go about showing favor and kindness to all; though men scorn us, revile us, and trample us down without mercy, we eagerly seize every opportunity to do them good.

With respect to the principles of Christianity we are, when fully redeemed, perfect as our Father in heaven. "Be ye therefore perfect, even as your Father which is in heaven is perfect." Mat. 5:48. By reading the contexts we find he is speaking of love. When fully saved there is naught in our heart but love, loving just as God loves. Such love enables us with joy to show kindness to our enemies, to feed them when they are hungry, and give them drink when they thirst. Rom. 12:20.

When we are fully saved we are like the Lord in purity: "And every man that hath this hope in him purifieth himself, even as he is pure." 1 John 3:3. Every crimson stain of sin is cleansed away and we are whiter than the snow. The evil nature incurred by Adam's sin is perfectly destroyed and we are made as pure as though there had never been a sin in this world.

We will be like our Creator and Redeemer in righteousness: "Little children, let no man deceive you: he that doeth righteousness is righteous, even as he is righteous." 1 John 3:7. Some do teach that we can not be righteous. The Word of God declares they are deceivers.

When we thus become of the pure, holy, righteous and merciful nature of Jesus it will of necessity separate us as far from this world and worldliness as he was separated. "I have given them thy word; and the world hath hated them, because they are not of the world, even as I am not of the world." John 17:14. There lies a great and wide gulf between the Christian and the world. Jesus is the bridge for the sinner to cross to the Christian's land. Sin and Satan is the bridge for the return of the Christian to the world.

When the children of God are fully redeemed they are one even as the Father and the Son are one. "And the glory which thou gavest me I have given them; that they may be one, even as we are one." John 17:22. This means a complete annihilation of every partisan spirit, a destruction of all strife and division. Should every professed Christian get salvation to the full Bible standard there would not be a sect left upon earth.

God predestinated you to be conformed to the image of his Son; holy as he is holy; merciful as he is merciful; perfect as he is perfect; pure as he is pure;

righteous as he is righteous; as far separated from the world as he is from the world, and one even as God and his Son are one. Such is the perfect redemption offered to man in this life through God's beloved Son. What can be more beautiful upon this earth than a soul redeemed from sin and a life reflecting the holy life of the Savior. "Christ before Pilate" is a rare and much admired work of art, but Christ in the soul and life is a work more grand and beautiful. For man to properly reflect the divine character necessitates a very close walk and deep communion with the Deity. There must be a constant feeding upon the divine life. There must be a careful watching and an effort to cultivate a deeper sense of the presence of God. Happy and blessed is the man whose heart is so filled with heavenly love and reverence to God as to cause him to give "all diligence" to develop into his own glorious image.

CHAPTER VII.
THE CHURCH OF GOD.

More than one hundred times the words church and churches are used in the New Testament. It is always translated from *ekklesia*. Most translators agree that a more correct translation of this Greek word would have been congregation. "The church of God" would then have read, "Congregation of God." "The church of the first-born" would have read, "The congregation of the first-born." The church that was at Antioch would have read, "The congregation that was at Antioch," etc.

WHAT IS THE CHURCH OR CONGREGATION?

The word church is a much misused word. It is commonly used at the present day when speaking of the edifices erected for the purpose of the assembling of the church to worship God. The quoting of a few texts will give us the Bible definition of this word.

"Likewise greet the church that is in their house." Rom. 16:5. This was the home of Priscilla and Aquila. This church was in their house. This house was not the church. The church was in their house. The command was to greet the church. This certainly begins to throw some light upon this subject. See 1 Cor. 16:19; Col. 4:15; Phile. 2. "And hath put all things under his feet, and gave him to be head over all things to the church, which is his body, the fulness of him that filleth all in all." Eph. 1:22, 23. "And he is the head of the body, the church." Col. 1:18. See also 24th verse.

These texts plainly teach the church to be the body of Christ. What is the body of Christ? Ans.—"Now ye [Christians] are the body of Christ, and members in particular." 1 Cor. 12:27. The body of Christ is the church. The church is Christians. This enables us to understand how the church could be in Priscilla and Aquila's house, and how we can greet the church. This is the Bible definition of church.

WHICH, ONE CHURCH OR MANY?

In the writings of the apostles the plural form of the word church is frequently used, but this argues nothing against the unity of God's church, nor in favor of the multiplicity of sects. If all the saved people in the world could be congregated in one place there would be no occasion for using the plural form of this word. Had it been so in the days of the writers of the epistles, the word would have been used only in the singular. But since there was a church or congregation of Christians at Antioch, also a church at Corinth, at Thessalonica, Ephesus, Smyrna, Pergamos, Thyatira, Sardis, Philadelphia, Laodicea, etc., to speak of the whole it would be proper to use the plural of church. "The churches of Asia." Please notice there is only one in each city, and the same writer addresses them all.

It does not take a town of so great a size to-day to find seven towering meeting-house steeples, where assemble as many different bodies of believers, termed sects. No one minister addresses them all. No one elder gives orders to all these different sects. 1 Cor. 16:1. No one minister ordains elders in all the separate bodies. 1 Cor. 7:17. The word churches was used to denote the different geographical location of the congregations of the Lord. The minister arguing in favor of the plurality of denominations from the plural term churches as found in the Bible is either ignorant or unfair. A plurality of sects is Babylon confusion.

The plural form is used in the Bible with reference to location and not to bodies having a different faith or belief. The church at Antioch had no contrary faith with the church at Corinth as we find existing between the denominations of to-day. They were separated by geographical distance, and not by difference of belief. Had these different churches come together in one place they could all have listened to Paul preach and said, Amen.

ONENESS OF GOD'S CHURCH.

"The multitude of them that believed were of one heart and of one soul." Acts 4:32. Can these same words be correctly used when speaking of the believers throughout the various denominations of to-day? "Now the God of patience and consolation grant you to be likeminded one toward another according to Christ Jesus: that ye may with one mind and one mouth glorify God, even the Father of our Lord Jesus Christ." Rom. 15:5, 6. "Now I beseech you, brethren, by the name of our Lord Jesus Christ, that ye all speak the same thing, and that there be no divisions among you; but that ye be perfectly joined together in the same mind and in the same judgment." 1 Cor. 1:10.

By these two texts we learn that the church of God has but one mind; it has but one mouth, and all speak the same thing. This is beautiful, this is heavenly. "Behold, how good and how pleasant it is for brethren to dwell together in unity." Psa. 133:1. It is only the church of the Bible that enjoys this pleasant unity, and we must never confound this church with the confusive sects. Babylon has as many mouths as there are sects, and they speak contrary things.

"For ye are all one in Christ Jesus." Gal. 3:28. "Only let your conversation be as it becometh the gospel of Christ: that whether I come and see you, or else be absent, I may hear of your affairs, that ye stand fast in one spirit, with one mind striving together for the faith of the gospel." Phil. 1:27. "Fulfil ye my joy, that ye be likeminded, having the same love, being of one accord, of one mind." Phil. 2:2. "For as we have many members in one body, and all the members have not the same office: so we, being many, are one body in Christ, and every one members one of another." Rom. 12:4, 5.

"Other sheep I have, which are not of this fold: them also I must bring, . . . and there shall be one fold and one shepherd." John 10:16. The Savior was here speaking of the Gentiles and the Jews. Before the coming of Christ there was a partition wall between these two nations, but Jesus came to break down the middle wall of partition, so there should be neither Jew nor Greek, bond nor free, male nor female: but all one in Christ Jesus. Gal. 3:28. "For as the body is one, and hath many members, and all the members of that one body, being many, are one body: so also is Christ. For by one Spirit are we all baptized into one body, whether we be Jews or Gentiles, whether we be bond or free; and have been all made to drink into one Spirit." 1 Cor. 12: 12, 13.

The "many members" here referred to are individual Christians, and not the ecclesiastical bodies now extant, as some do ignorantly teach. "But now are they many members, yet but one body." 1 Cor. 12: 20. In the fifteenth and sixteenth verses the apostle uses the physical body of man with its dependent members to illustrate the one body of Christ. These members work in blissful harmony and are dependent upon each other. A destruction of one member impairs the whole body. This is not illustrative of the different denominations; they are not dependent upon each other. Oftentimes they are opposed to each other, and thrive better when others are destroyed.

"And let the peace of God rule in your hearts, to the which also ye are called in one body; and be ye thankful." Col. 3: 15.

I am thankful that we are called as humble followers of the Lamb, into one body only, where the peace of God rules in évery heart. "Now therefore ye are no more strangers and foreigners, but fellow citizens with the saints, and of the household of God." Eph. 2: 19. God has a household of saints here upon the earth where peace rules. A contentious, quarrelsome, divided family is no part of God's united household. One family in heaven and earth. Eph. 3: 15. It is with great reluctancy that we pass by so many beautiful texts upon this subject, but we will only quote a few more lest this volume swell to too great proportions. "Holy Father, keep through thine own name those whom thou hast given me, that they may be one, as we are. While I was with them in the world, I kept them in thy name: ... neither pray I for these alone, but for them also which shall believe on me through their word; that they all may be one; as thou, Father, art in me, and I in thee, that they also may be one in us: that the world may believe that thou hast sent me. And the glory which thou gavest me I have given them; that they may be one, even as we are one: I in them and thou in me, that they may be made perfect in one; and that the world may know that thou hast sent me, and hast loved them as thou hast loved me." John 17: 11, 12, 20-23.

> Blessed oneness of God's own,
> Like the Father and the Son;
> One on earth like heav'n above,
> Bound with cords of perfect love.

> O holy Christian band, filled with Heaven's love,
> Living in sweet accord like angels above.

DIVISIONS CONDEMNED.

"Now I beseech you, brethren, mark them which cause divisions and offenses contrary to the doctrine which ye have learned; and avoid them; For they that are such serve not our Lord Jesus Christ, but their own belly; and by good words and fair speeches deceive the hearts of the simple." Rom. 16:17, 18. From the apostle they had learned the doctrine of oneness; he now warns them to avoid any contrary doctrine. "That there should be no schism in the body; but that the members should have the same care one for another." 1 Cor. 12:25. By consulting your dictionary you will find the word "schism" to be synonymous with the word "sect." "A man that is a heretic after the first and second admonition reject." Titus 3:10. Many translators have rendered heretic, sectarian.

"For first of all, when ye come together in the church, I hear that there be divisions among you; and I partly believe it. For there must be also heresies among you, that they which are approved may be made manifest among you. 1 Cor. 11:18, 19. Heresies and divisions are here spoken of as meaning about the same thing; or rather divisions are occasioned by heresies. If you will look in the margin of your reference Bible you will find this word translated "sect."

In Gal. 5:19, 20 is a number of deeds and dispositions classified and called the works of the flesh, and we are told that "they which do such things shall not inherit the kingdom of God." In this catalogue of evil works you will find the word "heresies." Upon examining other translations you will find it rendered sects. See Emphatic Diaglott.

"Now I beseech you, brethren, by the name of our

Lord Jesus Christ, that ye all speak the same thing, and that there be no divisions [schisms—margin] among you." 1 Cor. 1:10. "But there were false prophets also among the people, even as there shall be false teachers among you, who privily shall bring in damnable heresies, even denying the Lord that bought them, and bring upon themselves swift destruction." 2 Pet. 2:1. In the German version the words "damnable heresies" is rendered "destructive sects." Paul sternly reproves the Corinthians and declares them carnal because of a division that had been manifested among them. 1 Cor. 3:1-4; also 1 Cor. 1:10-13.

ORGANIZATION OF THE CHURCH OF GOD.

We will have to go to the dictionary to find a definition of the word "organize," since the word is not found in the Bible. "To arrange in parts; to form in due order; to furnish with organs," is the common definition. While the term "organize" is not contained in the Scriptures, yet the work of organizing God's church was performed, and his precious truth tells us how, and by whom it was done. "For to one [individual] is given by the Spirit the word of wisdom; to another the word of knowledge by the same Spirit; to another faith by the same Spirit; to another the gifts of healing by the same Spirit; to another the working of miracles; to another prophecy; to another discerning of spirits, to another divers kinds of tongues; to another the interpretation of tongues: but all these worketh that one and the selfsame Spirit, dividing to every man severally as he will." 1 Cor. 12: 8-11. Nothing need be plainer. It is the mission of the Holy Spirit to impart unto or bestow upon each member of God's church such qualifications as will make him a useful and effectual organ in this holy structure.

What is necessary for the building and furnishing of the church of God is not necessary in the formation and organization of a man-made ecclesiasticism. For man to build what he is pleased to call a church he does not have to furnish it with "a gift of faith," nor "a gift of healing," nor of "working of miracles," nor of "prophecy," nor of "discerning of spirits," nor of "diversities of tongues," nor of "interpretation of tongues." Neither does he require the "wisdom of God," nor the "knowledge of God." It is true he will require much knowledge and wisdom of the world, but of all the things necessary in furnishing the church of God, not one of them is necessary in the building of a sect.

"And he gave some, apostles; and some, prophets; and some, evangelists; and some, pastors and teachers; for the perfecting of the saints, for the work of the ministry, for the edifying of the body of Christ." Eph. 4: 10-12. "Take heed therefore unto yourselves, and to all the flock, over the which the Holy Ghost hath made you overseers, to feed the church of

God, which he hath purchased with his own blood." Acts 20:28. "Now ye are the body of Christ, and members in particular, and God hath set some in the church, first apostles, secondarily prophets, thirdly teachers, after that miracles, then gifts of healings, helps, governments, diversities of tongues." 1 Cor. 12:27, 28. "But now hath God set the members every one of them in the body, as it hath pleased him." 1 Cor. 12:18.

With this as with all other subjects of this work we must be brief.

WHO RECEIVES APPLICANTS INTO THIS CHURCH?

"Wherefore come out from among them, and be ye separate, saith the Lord, and touch not the unclean thing; and I will receive you, and will be a Father unto you, and ye shall be my sons and daughters, saith the Lord Almighty." 2 Cor. 6:17, 18. "But now hath God set the members every one of them in the body as it hath pleased him." 1 Cor. 12:18. "And the Lord added to the church daily such as should be saved." Acts 2:47. "For by one Spirit are we all baptized into one body, whether we be Jews or Gentiles, whether we be bond or free; and have been all made to drink into one Spirit." 1 Cor. 12:13.

By these texts we can plainly see that it is God by the Spirit that receives members into his church, therefore no sinner can enter there.

WHAT IS THE DOOR?

"I am the door: by me if any man enter in he shall be saved, and shall go in and out, and find pasture." John 10: 9. "I am the door of the sheep." ver. 7. "For through him [Jesus] we both have access by one Spirit unto the Father." Eph. 2: 18.

Jesus is the only entrance into the church of God. He that would climb up some other way is a thief and a robber. John 10: 1. We could get into a human organized body without coming in through Christ, but not into the divinely organized body.

"He that openeth, and no man shutteth; and shutteth, and no man openeth; ... behold, I have set before thee an open door, and no man can shut it." Rev. 3: 7, 8.

WHO IS THE BUILDER OF THE CHURCH?

Abraham "looked for a city, ... whose builder and maker is God." Heb. 11: 10. Like many other holy men who walked with God in those ancient days, Abraham looked by faith to the promise that was to come to bring deliverance to the captives. Christ says, "Upon this rock I will build my church, and the gates of hell shall not prevail against it." Mat. 16: 18. "Every house is builded by some man; but he that built all things is God." Heb. 3: 3, 4.

Jesus purchased the church with his own blood. Acts 20: 28. He gave his life for it. Eph. 5: 25. God, or Christ, who was God manifested in the flesh, **built** himself a glorious and pure church—holy, blameless, and spotless. It is all his own. He bestows upon it the fond title of Bride: "He that hath the bride is the bridegroom." John 3:29.

"For I am jealous over you with a godly jealousy: for I have espoused you to one husband, that I may present you as a chaste virgin to Christ." 2 Cor. 11:2. Paul addresses this letter to the church of God at Corinth. 2 Cor. 1:1. He presents this church as a chaste virgin to her one husband, even Christ.

John in conversation with an angel from heaven was bid to "come hither," and he would be shown the bride the Lamb's wife; and behold he was shown that great city, the holy Jerusalem, descending out of heaven from God, having the glory of God: and her light was like unto a stone most precious, even like a jasper stone, clear as crystal. Rev. 21:9-11. This is beautiful descriptive language. This holy city Jerusalem, clear as crystal, is

> The pure and holy virgin bride,
> The spotless church for which Christ died.

"I am my beloved's, and my beloved is mine: he feedeth among the lilies." S. of Sol. 6:3.

THE FOUNDATION OF THE CHURCH.

"For other foundation can no man lay than that is laid, which is Jesus Christ." 1 Cor. 3:11. "And are built upon the foundation of the apostles and prophets, Jesus Christ himself being the chief cornerstone." Eph. 2:20.

A quotation here from the Old Testament will only add strength and beauty to this subject: "Therefore thus saith the Lord God, Behold, I lay in Zion for a foundation a stone, a tried stone, a precious cornerstone, a sure foundation." Isa. 28:16.

God here gives promise of establishing Zion—the church—upon a sure foundation; namely, Christ in the great salvation day.

THE KINGDOM OF GOD.

Frequent reference is made throughout the New Testament to the "kingdom of God" and the "kingdom of heaven." When the "God which is in heaven" was "revealing the deep and secret things" unto Daniel concerning Nebuchadnezzar's dream, he also revealed unto him that in the days of those kings he would set up a kingdom which should never be destroyed, consequently would stand forever. Dan. 2:44.

When John, the swift herald of the gospel day, came preaching, he said: "Repent ye: for the kingdom of heaven is at hand." Mat. 3:2. The first words in the ministry of the Son of God were, "Repent: for the kingdom of heaven is at hand." Mat. 4:17. The kingdom which Daniel saw was to be set up. Great was the speculation throughout Jewry concerning the kingdom of God in John's days. They were expecting a kingdom to excel in temporal pomp and glory the grandeur of the kingdom of the Cæsars. The Savior in conversation with some Pharisees on one occasion astonished them by saying, "The kingdom of God cometh not with observation: neither shall they say, Lo here! or, lo there! for, behold, the kingdom of God is within you." Luke 17:20, 21.

Jesus one night explained to a ruler of the Jews how to enter this kingdom. He said, "Except a man be born of water and of the Spirit, he can not enter into the kingdom of God." John 3:5. Again he says, "Verily I say unto you, Except ye be converted, and become as little children, ye shall not enter into the kingdom of heaven." Mat. 18:3. The inspired apostle in Rom. 14:17 explains the nature of this kingdom: "For the kingdom of God is not meat and drink, but righteousness, and peace, and joy in the Holy Ghost." In the process of the mysterious birth of the Spirit the soul experiences a translation from a "power of darkness" into the kingdom of God's dear Son. Col. 1:13.

It certainly must have dawned upon your understanding ere this that the church of God and the kingdom of heaven are the same spiritual structure. In the twelfth chapter of Hebrews several terms are used to denote the church of God. In the twenty-second verse it is designated by "mount Zion," the "city of the living God," the "heavenly Jerusalem," and an "innumerable company of angels." In verse twenty-three it is denominated "general assembly," "the church of the first-born, etc. In the twenty-eighth verse it is called the "kingdom." By this we are made to understand that the church built by the Lord is identical with the "city of God," the "kingdom of God," the "heavenly Jerusalem," etc. With this understanding we will better comprehend the meaning of many other texts.

THE HEAD OF THE CHURCH.

"For the husband is the head of the wife, even as Christ is the head of the church: and he is the savior of the body." Eph. 5:23. "And he is the head of the body, the church." Col. 1:18. "But speaking the truth in love, may grow up into him in all things, which is the head, even Christ." Eph. 4:15. See also Eph. 1:22; Col. 2:18, 19.

Christ is the head of his church, and as such he is the sole governor, or legislator. "He that hath ears to hear, let him hear."

RECAPITULATION IN CONCLUSION.

The church is the body of Christ. Eph. 1:21, 22. There is but one body. Rom. 12:4, 5; 1 Cor. 10:17. Christians are this one body. 1 Cor. 12:27. They are of one heart and soul. Acts 4:32. There are no divisions. 1 Cor. 1:10. Christ is the head of this church. Col. 1:18. He is the door. John 10:7. He is the foundation. Eph. 2:21. He sets the members in the body (1 Cor. 12:18), and prays that they be kept in his name. John 17:11.

OFFICERS IN THE CHURCH OF GOD.

God sets the members in the body of Christ, which is the church, as seemeth best according to his unbounded wisdom. All are not an eye or ear or hand or foot. That the church of God may be complete as a body it has all the different members. Christ is the head, and the saved men and women are the other members of the body according to their calling, all governed by the head and consecrated to do his will. The ministry are the feet, the burden-bearers, the servants of all. They have the care or burden of the church. They carry the glad tidings of salvation. They are not to be carried about and served, but they are the servants. "How beautiful are the feet of them that preach the gospel of peace, and bring glad tidings of good things." Rom. 10:15.

The following officers are mentioned in the New Testament: apostles, prophets, evangelists, bishops, pastors, teachers, deacons, elders, and presbyters. Apostle is from the Greek "*apostolos,*" which is one sent forth to plant. Paul was an apostle. He was sent forth by the Holy Spirit. Acts 13:4. He was sent forth to plant. 1 Cor. 3:6. Prophet is from the Greek "*prophetes,*" which is one who is an expounder of prophecies and revelations and of future events. Agabus was a prophet, a teller of future events.

See Acts 21: 10, 11 and Acts 11: 28. Philip the evangelist had four daughters who did prophesy, or expound or explain the Scriptures. An evangelist is one who announces good tidings, while an apostle is one who plants churches or goes into new localities, and through whose preaching people are saved and a church thus planted. The mission of an evangelist is to visit those planted churches and water them. "I have planted, Apollos watered; but God gave the increase." 1 Cor. 3: 6.

Bishop is from the Greek *"episkopos,"* and means a superintendent or overseer. Pastor is from the Greek *"poimen,"* and means shepherd or feeder or overseer, the same as bishop; consequently bishop and pastor are the same, an overseer or shepherd. The word "overseer" occurs but once in the New Testament: "Take heed therefore unto yourselves, and to all the flock, over the which the Holy Ghost hath made you overseers, to feed the church of God." Acts 20: 28. Overseer in this text is translated from the Greek *"episkopos,"* from which same Greek word we have the word bishop. Paul was then addressing bishops, and tells them to feed the church of God. Now a pastor is a feeder; therefore bishop and pastor are two words used to denote the same office. To note the qualifications of a bishop or pastor as set forth in the New Testament will doubtless be edifying to the reader.

WHAT A BISHOP MUST BE.

A bishop must be blameless, the husband of one wife, vigilant, sober, of good behavior, given to hospitality, apt to teach; patient, ruling well his own house, a lover of good men, just, holy, temperate, etc. See 1 Tim. 3:2-4; Titus 1:7, 8.

Blameless. This word is synonymous with spotless, faultless, irreproachable. A person or thing is blameless when it is free from fault.

The husband of one wife. No one can meet the New Testament requirements for bishop or pastor who has two wives, though one be divorced.

Vigilant. He must be so watchful as to early discover danger of any kind and use the utmost precaution to avoid it.

Sober. This word is not applied only to freedom from intoxication by spirituous liquors, but is synonymous with calmness, quietness, grave, sedate, steady, serious, solemn, etc. The Greek *"sophron"* for sober in these texts means sound mindedness.

Of good behavior. Their conduct must be free from levity, folly, or anything that tends to degrade morals.

Given to hospitality. (Lover of hospitality. Titus 1:8.) He must love in his heart to receive and entertain strangers without remuneration, to be kind and pleasing in his manners.

Apt to teach. He must possess a talent or God-given ability to teach the Word to others in a simple manner.

Patient. He must be free from ill passion and irritableness. He must be calm, and possess a tranquility and evenness of life. His composure and holy tranquilness is such that commands and quiets all strife, contentions and heated discussions.

Ruling well his own house. Unless a man has sufficient wisdom, authority, love and firmness, to govern and control his own children he certainly can not be used of God to oversee the church of God.

Lover of good men. His very heart and soul must admire and appreciate and love the good he sees in men.

Just. In his admonitions, corrections and reprovings, he is always just and impartial.

Holy. His heart and life and affections must be pure and holy, free from sin.

Temperate. There are many things from which we are commanded by the Scriptures to abstain. In the use of all things God has given for use he must not be excessive. He must not be excessive in eating, drinking, sleeping, working, talking, sexual relation, etc.

WHAT A BISHOP OR ELDER MUST NOT BE.

A bishop must not be given to wine, no striker, not greedy of filthy lucre, not a brawler, not covetous, not a novice, not self-willed, not soon angry. See 1 Tim. 3:3-6; Titus 1:7.

Must not be given to wine. Not a wine drinker. He is to be an example and abstain from all appearance of evil.

No striker. A good translation from the Greek would render this *reviler*. He must not strike back with the tongue; in other words, not contentious.

Not greedy of filthy lucre. When man becomes greedy of filthy lucre—loves money—he can be influenced by it and thus be led to favor the rich.

Not a brawler. This is synonymous with wrangler or contender.

Not Covetous. Covetousness includes more than the love of money. Fame, honor, worldly pleasures, gratification of unholy appetites and passions, may be properly termed covetousness. To entertain for anything an affection that is not a pure and godly affection is idolatry, and idolatry is covetousness.

Not a novice. One newly converted.

Not self-willed. Not obstinate in contending for his views or desires in opposition to others.

Not soon angry. Soon is not found in the original. A more proper rendering would be, Not passionate.

DEACON.

Deacon is translated from *"diakonos,"* meaning minister. By reading the writings of those contemporary with the apostle and those immediately following we learn that a bishop or elder is the overseer or pastor of the flock, or the one upon whom the greatest responsibilities lie, while the deacons are helpers. This doubtless is what is meant by "helps" in 1 Cor. 12: 28. There was always at least one bishop in one congregation, but often more than one deacon. The qualifications for a deacon are very similar to those of a bishop. See 1 Tim. 3; Titus 1.

ELDERS OR PRESBYTERS.

Webster in defining presbyter, says, "An elder in the early Christian church." Young in his analytical concordance says of presbytery, "An assembly of elders." These two terms have the same Greek origin, "*presbuteros.*" An elder is one grounded in the faith with a sound matured judgment; one capable of giving good advice or counsel. An elder is not necessarily a preacher, but one calculated to advise and give counsel in his pastoral duties. They also are especially called of God to aniont and pray for the sick.

These church officers are all called of God. See Gal. 1: 15,16. They are commissioned by Christ. Mat. 28: 19. Sent by the Holy Spirit. Acts 13: 3, 4. They are qualified by God. 2 Cor. 3: 5, 6. They are ambassadors from the kingdom of heaven with a heavenly message to this lost world. God help them every one to faithfully declare it in the fear of him who has called them.

CHAPTER VIII.

THE ORDINANCES OF THE NEW TESTAMENT.

In the preceding chapter we considered the church of the New Testament. The Lord Jesus built his church and instituted some ordinances, which he commands the church to faithfully keep. The keeping of the commandments of God is proof that we love him: "For this is the love of God that we keep his commandments: and his commandments are not grievous." 1 John 5:3. "He that hath my commandments, and keepeth them, he it is that loveth me." John 14:21. "If a man love me he will keep my words." ver. 23. "He that loveth me not keepeth not my sayings." ver. 24.

We may profess great attainments in the divine life and wonderful devotion to God, but the proof is obedience to his commands. We have learned of people who have become so holy that they were raised above or passed beyond a great portion of the Bible and are not required to keep it. We have heard of but few things so ridiculously foolish. The better and more holy we become, certainly the more of the Word of God we will practise in our life; and who on earth can live a more perfect Christian life than he who lives in obedience to every word of the Bible? When one gets in possession of something that exempts him from obedience to the Scriptures he gets in possession of some very mysterious thing. The only way to heaven is by the commandments of the Bible. "Blessed are they that do his commandments, that they may have a right to the tree of life and enter in through the gates into the city."

We will consider some ordinances and ceremonies which belong to the church of God as recorded in the New Testament so plainly that a wayfaring man though a fool need not err therein.

BAPTISM.

"There was a man sent from God, whose name was John." John 1:6. In the thirty-third verse this same John declares that God sent him to baptize with water. Of the books written on this subject there is scarcely an end. The controversy is very great, and so often very ridiculous. Lexicographers have defined and analyzed the word baptize in its different forms. Liddell and Scott, Robertson, Parkhurst, Scapula, Stokins, Calvin, Luther, Campbell, Gill, Stuart, Vitringa, Brenner, Paulus, and many others of great erudition have defined the word, and to sum them all up we find the primary meaning is "to dip, to immerse, to plunge in water." Many of the English translators of the New Testament always render *baptizo*, immerse or dip, as "John the immerser," or "John the dipper."

This brief reference to the expositions of the learned must suffice for this work. It is with pleasure we resort to the plain and simple teachings of the Scriptures.

BAPTISM A NEW TESTAMENT ORDINANCE.

All Jerusalem, and Judea, and the region about Jordan, were baptized of John in Jordan. Mat. 3:5, 6. Jesus baptized by proxy. John 4:1, 2. He commissioned his ministry to preach baptism unto all the world. "Go ye therefore, and teach all nations, baptizing them in the name of the Father, and of the Son, and of the Holy Ghost." Mat. 28:19. "Go ye into all the world, and preach the gospel to every creature. He that believeth and is baptized shall be saved." Mark 16:15, 16. Those who have undertaken the dangerous and Christ uncommissioned task of freeing Christians from the obligations of this ordinance, hold high aloft the following texts: Eph. 2:15; Col. 2:14, 15; Col. 2:20. Since the Savior's commission to his disciples was forty days after his resurrection, such teachers are driven from this position, and to substantiate their doctrine they flee to a more fatally exposed one when saying that the baptism of this commission was the baptism of the Spirit. It is a pity that precious time must be taken for the correction of such erroneous teaching. How can men baptize with the Holy Spirit? God alone can do that.

It is evident that the apostles understood this baptism to be with water, since they taught it and practised it throughout their ministry. We shall take time and space to refer to but two or three instances of the administration of this ordinance recorded in the Acts of the Apostles. The first is that of a Christ commissioned preacher by the name of Philip, who was sent by an angel to preach the gospel to a Scripturally ignorant man of Ethiopia. Unlearned as he was, he readily understood from the preaching of Philip the importance of water baptism; therefore when they came to a certain water he said, "See here is water; what doth hinder me to be baptized?" Acts 8:36. By reading the following verses you will learn that this man was baptized in water and God witnessed to his approval by sending him rejoicing on his way. Obedience to the commands of God brings a joy to the Christian heart.

The second instance of baptism to which we wish to invite your attention is that of the devout Cornelius. He sent for Peter to learn more concerning the ways of the Lord. Peter came and told them of Jesus, of his resurrection and his power to save. As he spoke the Holy Ghost fell upon all them which heard his words. Then said Peter, Can any man forbid water that these should not be baptized which have received the Holy Ghost as well as we? And he commanded them to be baptized in the name of the Lord. How can an instance of water baptism be more plainly recorded? This occurred some eight years after the crucifixion of the Lord Jesus. To teach the abolition of this ordinance at the cross, in the face of these plainly stated instances of baptism, only proves to us the blinding and deceptive power of the spirit of error.

MODE OF BAPTISM.

Many of the professed teachers of the gospel have become very liberal. "We all have a right to our opinion," so many say; and "a thing becomes right unto us if we believe it to be right." Because of this teaching and the varied opinions, there have originated in the minds of the people several different modes of baptism. But this great liberality finds no warrant in the Word of God. The Scriptures teach that "there is one body." Eph. 4:4. If I should hold in opinion, as many do hold, that there are many bodies, would my opinion prove the Word of God to be in error? Let me say here, with emphasis, that there can be but one true, rightful body. If the Catholic body should be the right body, it is the only body upon the earth that is right. If the Presbyterian body is the right and true body, it is the only body. And so with any other denominational body. If we were a member of the Methodist body we would have to believe that that was the one true body and that all the others were wrong. If there be but one body, how can two bodies be that one body when those two bodies are different?

There is but one Holy Spirit, one true Lord, one gospel faith, and one true mode of baptism. God has not left us to follow our own peculiar fancies, but all must go the same way. Whatever is required of one individual, that same thing is required of every other individual. If sprinkling is a right mode of baptism it is the only right mode, and all others are wrong. If pouring is right it is the only mode that is right. If three dips, face forward is right it is the only mode that is right. If one single immersion is right it is the only mode that is right. The Lord did not set the example in all these different ways. He was baptized. He also baptized by proxy, and we believe that he thus baptized in the same manner he was baptized. This one mode was all they understood by baptism. The apostles perhaps had seen the Lord baptized, they administered baptism under his direction, and when he commissioned them with the authority to administer baptism after he had ascended to the Father, they did not question him as to which mode. The word baptism meant but one thing and the same thing unto them all. In the after years of their ministry they practised just what they had seen their Lord practise.

Now let us learn from the plain, easy language of the Scripture the mode as administered by John, the Lord and the apostles. In the third chapter of Matthew the inspired writer has given an account of John's baptism, which we kindly invite you to read. Now the way to correctly understand the Scripture is to take it in its easiest, plainest, most sensible way. Do not attempt to give it some complicated, mysterious meaning, but receive it as you would any easily understood historical fact of this present time. If you should read in your county paper of a man down by one of the rivers of your adjoining county who was administering baptism to the people, and the whole neighborhood round about went out to him and were baptized of him in the river, and when he had baptized a certain individual he went up straightway out of the water, what idea would you form as to the mode of the baptism? Would you think it was a little water sprinkled on the head somewhere in a meeting-house? There is nothing in the account to convey such an idea. How unreasonable it would be for you to study to change the meaning of the plain account and mystify it because it was not congenial to your desires.

Suppose you should read in your paper of two men traveling along the way. One of them had never heard of Jesus nor of the ordinance of baptism; the other talked to him of the Savior, of his death and his resurrection, and how he had authorized him to go into all the world and preach this gospel to every creature, and he that believed and was baptized, the same should be saved. And as they traveled on their way they came to a certain water, and the one said to the other, "See here is water, what doth hinder me to be baptized?" The other replied, "If thou believest with all thine heart thou mayest." He answered, "I believe that Jesus Christ is the Son of God." Then they stopped their carriage and they went down both into the water and there the one was baptized of the other, and when they came up out of the water the one went one way and the other another way, and they saw each other no more. What idea would you form as to the mode of baptism? This is all very plain to the candid heart.

The other instances of baptism recorded in the New Testament do not express so clearly the mode as the two we have given, yet they can not with propriety be made to express anything contrary to immersion. The apostle Paul in his letter to the Roman brethren speaks of baptism as a burial. Rom. 6:4. This only confirms in our mind (concerning the mode) the ideas suggested by the baptism of the Savior and of the man of Ethiopia. For yet greater clearness we will present a few thoughts suggested to us by the recent writings of a brother, which we consider very conclusive.

A word, perfectly synonymous with another word can be used in its stead with the same correctness of diction. As, for example, "The snow is slowly descending from the dark cloud." To use a word synonymous with "descending" in the above sentence it must express the same thought and present the same elegance of style. We find such a synonym in the word "falling." "The snow is slowly falling from the dark cloud." The idea expressed by these two sentences is precisely the same, and both are good grammar. Let us now read Rom. 6:4: "Therefore we are buried with him by baptism into death." To find a word synonymous with baptism it will not deprive the word "burial" of its proper meaning. Try the word "sprinkle." "Therefore we are buried with him by sprinkling into death." Please read Mat. 3:5, 6; Mark 1:9; John 3:2, 3, and use the word sprinkle or pour where the word baptize is used, and note the great absurdity. Why is so much time spent in discussion over declarations so simple, clear and plain? Because of the perversion of plain language by the spirit of error to a self-conceited mind.

TRINE IMMERSION.

There is a religious class of people that teach and practise three immersions; one in the name of the Father, one in the name of the Son, and one in the name of the Holy Ghost. Such teaching is based upon the construction of Mat. 28:19. Only a little unprejudiced consideration will enable you to see the fallacy of such an interpretation. These three are one. If they were separate and distinct so we could act in the name of the one to the exclusion of the others then we could better understand such an interpretation of the above text. The apostles well understood that to act in the name of one was to act in the name of the whole trinity; therefore Peter says, "Repent, and be baptized every one of you in the name of Jesus Christ." Acts 2:38. Why did not Peter use the formula of Mat. 28:19? Because to act in the name of one is to act in the name of all. "And he commanded them to be baptized in the name of the Lord." Acts 10:48. "They were baptized in the name of the Lord Jesus." Acts 8:16. "When they heard this, they were baptized in the name of the Lord Jesus." Acts 19:5.

Nowhere in the Acts of the Apostles is the triune name used in baptism. Pages could be written showing the absurdity of the teachings of trine immersionists, but we consider that what has been written is clear enough to convince candid, unbiased minds, and any amount of argument will not convince those who defiantly set themselves against any reasonings contrary to their established notions.

THE OBJECT OF BAPTISM.

There is a baptism taught in the Scriptures that is not water baptism. There is a baptism of the Spirit. See 1 Cor. 12:13; Mat. 3:11. Some not being able to rightly divide the Word of God have taken some texts that teach the baptism of the Spirit to be the baptism of water, and thus confused the true object of water baptism. We will frankly admit that there are some texts which if taken alone and interpreted literally do apparently teach that baptism is a saving ordinance. We will refer the reader to a few of these texts. Mark 16:16; Acts 2:38; Acts 22:16. These texts seem to plainly teach that water baptism does wash away or remit sins. I always prefer to give each text the simplest, plainest rendering when it does not conflict with some other text. Now to teach that baptism by water is a saving ordinance, and so interpret these texts, we place ourselves in direct opposition to other plain teaching. Some do teach that there is none righteous and base such teaching upon Rom. 3:10. We would ask such teachers to interpret Titus 2:12; 1 John 3:7, 10; 1 John 2:29; Luke 1:75. By such texts they are brought to confusion.

Elsewhere in this work we quote the scriptures teaching salvation from sin to be by the grace of God. Then to teach that water baptism saves us from sin makes the Word of God contradict itself. All is beauteous harmony in the Scriptures when all is correctly interpreted. Water baptism represents a burial. A burial must of course be preceded by death. We die or separate ourselves from a life of sin and accept Christ; he accepts us. The real death to, and destruction of sin and resurrection to life is performed by the power of God's grace, while baptism expresses in a figure the burial and resurrection to spiritual life. This is the true object of baptism.

PROPER APPLICANTS FOR BAPTISM.

Water baptism is the answer of a good conscience toward God. 1 Pet. 3:19-21. We must obtain a good or "undefiled conscience" before we are a Scriptural candidate for baptism. How can defilement be purged from the conscience? By the blood of Jesus. Heb. 9:14. We are taught in Mat. 3:8 that we must bear fruits of repentance to be worthy applicants for baptism. The man of Ethiopia was asked to profess faith in Christ before Philip considered him to be a proper subject for baptism.

Infants can not profess faith in Christ, therefore their baptism is unscriptural. We are aware that there are many who teach "infant baptism," and use a few texts of Scripture and by their misapplication make it look as plausible as possible. The commission of the Lord to his ministry is to "preach the gospel to every creature; he that believeth and is baptized shall be saved." Faith precedes baptism in the commission. Infants have not faith. Peter says, "Repent and be baptized." Acts 2:38. Repentance, therefore, precedes baptism. John understood it thus. Mat. 3:8. Infants need no repentance. There is not a case recorded in the New Testament of infant baptism. After one has reached the years of accountability and repents of his sins and is born of the Spirit he is then, and not until then, a proper candidate for baptism.

THE LORD'S SUPPER.

In the teachings of the holy inspired and unblamed apostle Paul, the expression, "The Lord's Supper" is to be found. In reproving the Corinthians for corrupting the sacred communion service, he says, "When ye come together therefore into one place, this is not to eat the Lord's supper." 1 Cor. 11:20. In the preceding chapter he uses the word communion when speaking of the same divinely originated ordinance. "The cup of blessing which we bless, is it not the communion of the blood of Christ? The bread which we break, is it not the communion of the body of Christ?" 1 Cor. 10:16.

The apostle in these texts is referring to an ordinance of the New Testament instituted by the blessed Savior just prior to his passion as recorded by the writers of the gospels and observed by the church when it was the light of the world. If this sacred and very impressive ordinance was abolished at the death of the Savior, as some erroneously teach, why does Paul more than a score of years after exhort Christians to its observance and warn them so faithfully against corrupting so sacred a rite, telling them that if they eat and drink unworthily they eat and drink damnation to themselves, and admonishing them to examine themselves and so let them eat? 1 Cor. 11. It must be clear to all unclouded, candid minds by the reading of this chapter that there was an ordinance solemnly observed by the Christians long after the Savior was "nailed to the cross." In very plain and positive language he tells us that the communion or Lord's Supper is a New Testament ordinance: "This cup is the New Testament in my blood." 1 Cor. 11:25. This is corroborative of Mat. 26:28: "For this is my blood of the new testament;" and of Mark 14:24: "And he said unto them, This is my blood of the new testament, which is shed for many." Also of Luke 22:20: "Likewise also the cup after supper, saying, This cup is the new testament in my blood, which is shed for you."

To one enjoying the full light of the precious gospel to teach the abolition of this solemn ordinance appears the very height of folly and ignorance. In the recording of the Acts of the apostles it is said that "upon the first day of the week, when the disciples came together to break bread, Paul preached unto them." Acts 20:7. The breaking of bread as here spoken of signifies nothing else but the observance of the Lord's Supper.

The few plain, comprehensive texts of apostolic teaching we have quoted upon this subject must make obvious to the mind of the reader that Christians of the morning time of this gospel day observed an ordinance termed the Lord's Supper or communion, done in remembrance of Jesus and showing his death till he come. We will learn in the noontime's awful darkness how the blinded minds and unregenerated hearts of teachers by misunderstanding and misapplying these plain texts caused their clear light to cease to shine.

THE HOLY KISS.

True love manifests itself in many ways. We embrace with the arms, we greet with a kiss, the object of our love. We speak of these love tokens ofttimes in a spiritual way: "Folded in the arms of Jesus;"

"Leaning on his breast;" "Sheltered beneath his wing." "The Psalmist says, "Kiss the Son, lest he be angry." Psa. 2:12. These were literally practised by the Savior and his beloved followers while he was here. After Jesus arose and went to the Father the apostles practised the holy kiss. "They all wept sore, and fell on Paul's neck, and kissed him." Acts 20:37. We behold the love they bore for him. It was not a cold kiss of formality, but of love. In the first verse we see the love Paul had for the disciples: "Paul called unto him the disciples and embraced them."

In the epistolary law of the New Testament the holy kiss is five times commanded. "Salute one another with a holy kiss." Rom. 16:16. Greet ye one another with a holy kiss." 1 Cor. 16:20. "Greet one another with a holy kiss." 2 Cor. 13:12. Greet all the brethren with a holy kiss." 1 Thes. 5:26. "Greet ye one another with a kiss of charity." 1 Pet. 5:14.

Satan ever ready to corrupt the pure precepts and practises of the sacred Word has led people into the disgraceful fanaticism of promiscuous kissing. Such is not a kiss of love, but a kiss of lust. Everything done in the order of the kingdom of heaven is done in the perfection of decency and respectability. How natural for the fond husband to embrace and kiss the beloved wife, and the devoted mother her child, the brother his sister, all because love exists consistent with natural relation. But the strongest tie of love that binds hearts together is the Christian love. Then how natural and becoming for the Christian to greet with a kiss his brother, and the Christian sister her sister in the Lord.

Christian love continued after the apostles' days were ended, and consequently the practise of greeting with a holy kiss. We will conclude this subject by referring the reader to history as quoted in "Ordinances of the New Testament": "The fraternal kiss used on admission to the church and at the Lord's Supper were not empty forms, but the expression of a true feeling, and of a real experience."—*Butler's Ecclesiastical History*, p. 132.

"After the prayers . . . we greet one another with the brotherly kiss."—*Justin Martyr*, p. 146.

"The communion was a regular part of the Sunday worship. In many places it was celebrated daily. It began after the dismissal of the catechumens, by the kiss of peace given by men to men and women to women."—p. 147.

It is natural for Christians filled with the love of God to greet each other with a kiss, but the cold distant forms of men have prevented Christians following the natural inclination of the heart.

LIFTING UP OF HOLY HANDS.

In the olden time when the chosen children of God were battling in the wilderness against their enemies, as long as the hands of Moses were kept uplifted Israel prevailed, and when his hands were let down the enemy triumphed. Ex. 17:8-12. See also Psa. 28:2; 63:4; 88:9; Lam. 3:41. This signal act of triumph is conveyed into the spirit of the New Testament. Paul says, "I will therefore that men pray everywhere, lifting up holy hands, without wrath and doubting." 1 Tim. 2:8. This is a single text of the New Testament teaching this ordinance. In connection with this text some have used Heb. 12:12; but to our mind it is only an exhortation to encourage the feeble and faint-hearted, and not an express command to the literally raising of the hands. However the one text quoted is sufficient for those who love the Lord, for those who love him keep his commandments.

This ceremony is suggestive of submissiveness and reliance upon God. It is natural for the Spirit-born child of God to imploringly lift his hands to God in petition or praise and thanksgiving. In the time when the spiritual battles wax hot we seek God in earnest imploring prayer, and the lifting up of our hands adds strength to our faith and draws God nearer. But, oh, let us make sure that our hands and hearts are holy. It is but mockery to spread forth your hands unto God when they are full of blood. From such the Lord hides his eyes, and closes his ears against their prayer. Isa. 1: 15.

FEET-WASHING.

To the proud heart the commandment to "wash one another's feet" is perhaps the most ridiculous ever given by the Son of God. In the semi-theatrical church entertainments men may pay a large sum for the privilege of kissing the most handsome lady, and for similar or more shameful indulgences, but to humbly wash a brother's feet would be shocking in the extreme. "If a man love me he will keep my words." John 14: 23. Where true love exists there is no disposition to spurn any of the Lord's commandments, however humiliating they may be.

The ordinance of feet-washing was instituted by the Savior, and is recorded in the thirteenth chapter of John. One objection that many bring against this sacred ordinance is that it is so seldom mentioned in the Bible. If a man does not love God deeply enough to obey him when he speaks but once, he would not obey him should he speak a dozen times. Jesus says, "If they hear not Moses and the prophets, neither will they be persuaded, though one rose from the dead." Luke 16: 31. It is never difficult to persuade a humble heart to believe the Word of God, though there be but one single commandment; but the proud in heart will not be persuaded by any number if they are not according to their inclinations. About the first objection offered against this humble ordinance is that it was a custom among the Jews to wash feet, and the feet-washing recorded by John was nothing more than the Jewish custom. There was more here than the mere custom of washing feet.

We will carefully weigh this objection. Bathing is a custom, naturally so, for cleanliness and health, and is observed by people of every civilized nation, and has been in every age of the world. Pharaoh's daughter went down to the river to bathe when she found the babe in the ark of bulrushes. Ex. 2:5. Bathing was not a custom of any particular nation, but a universal custom. God separated Israel from the world to be his own chosen people. He gave them certain laws, which stood as a partition wall between them and the Gentile world. Among the many ceremonies was that of bathing. By reading the fifteenth chapter of Leviticus you will learn of the bathings required of the Jews for certain sins and uncleannesses. These bathings were peculiar to this people alone and served to separate them from other nations. They observed the universal custom of bathing, but these bathings were additional and given by the Lord. When Jesus came he abolished the Jewish ordinances that distinguished them from the world and offers salvation to every nation. By his grace he separates his people from the world and institutes for them the ordinance of baptism. This is not the universal custom of bathing, neither is it the Jewish ceremony of bathings for cleansings, but a New Testament ordinance for saved people of this gospel day, representing their death to sin and consequent separation from the world. All continue in the custom of bathing, but the Christian is baptized.

All people in every age are accustomed, if we may call it a custom, to eating; but when God separated Israel from Egypt and gave them a law, he instituted a supper called the Passover. This they kept in commemoration of their deliverance from Egyptian bondage. The Passover supper was not the mere custom of eating supper, but was an ordinance peculiar to the Jewish nation, and served to distinguish them as God's own chosen people. In Heb. 9:10 we learn that these meats and drinks, and divers washings, and carnal ordinances, were imposed on them until the time of reformation. When Jesus came he instituted a new order of things. The Passover supper was with the rest of the Jewish ordinances blotted out and nailed to the cross. Col. 2:14. Jesus instituted a supper to be kept in remembrance of him by his peculiar, exclusive people. This consists of bread, which represents his body, and of wine, which represents his blood. This is not the custom of eating, neither is it the Jewish ordinance, but a newly instituted ordinance in this dispensation of grace. All continue the custom of eating, but Christians keep the communion.

When Abraham was in the plains of Mamre he was visited by three angels, unto whom he said: "Let a little water, I pray you, be fetched, and wash your feet, and rest yourselves under the tree." Gen. 18:4. Two angels came one evening to Sodom, and Lot rose up to meet them, and said: "Behold now, my lords, turn in, I pray you, into your servant's house, and tarry all night, and wash your feet." Gen. 19:1, 2. By these instances and others we understand that washing feet was a custom in that time. It was not a law of God, but people of all nations observed it as a law of health, comfort, and cleanliness.

In Ex. 30: 19-21 and 40:30-32 we learn that God instituted an ordinance or ceremony of washing feet. This was not the mere custom of washing feet, but was a Jewish rite and served among other rites and ceremonies to distinguish them as God's own peculiar people. When the Son of God set up the kingdom of grace, this priestly ceremony was blotted out and a new ordinance of feet-washing was instituted. See John 13. This was not the ancient universal custom of washing feet. That still continues the same as eating and bathing. It is not the Jewish ordinance, because they were all nailed to the cross; but it is a humble ordinance the Savior instituted for his people saved from sin in this blessed gospel day. The Lord's people love this precious ordinance. Jesus set the example and intends his own to do as he did. "If I then, your Lord and Master, have washed your feet; ye also ought to wash one another's feet. For I have given you an example, that ye should do as I have done to you." John 13:14, 15. Jesus set the example in baptism and intends for us to follow. Mat. 3:15, 16. He set the example in partaking of his newly instituted supper and intends for us to walk in his steps. 1 Cor. 11:25.

Since the word *ought* is used some appear to rejoice in the thought that it is not obligatory. I, for one, ever since the Lord made me a Christian, have always been willing and glad to do just what I *ought* to do. We scarcely think a man loves God when he refuses to do what he knows he ought to do. "Ye ought to support the weak." Acts 20:35. "Men ought always to pray." Luke 18:1. "We ought also to love one another." 1 John 4:11. "Ye also ought to wash one another's feet." John 13:14. Let us as professed followers of Jesus live and do what we *ought* to do. Happy are ye if you do, but what shall be the result if you refuse? "Therefore we *ought* to give the more earnest heed to the things which we have heard." Heb. 2:1. Will you do as you ought? Because the widow did what she ought she was recommended to the care of the church. 1 Tim. 5:9, 10.

CHAPTER IX.
DIVINE HEALING.

The thirty-fifth chapter of Isaiah is a prophecy beautifully extolling the glories and virtues of Christ's redemptive works. "The desert shall rejoice and blossom as the rose." "It shall blossom abundantly, and rejoice even with joy and singing: the glory of Lebanon shall be given unto it, the excellency of Carmel and Sharon, they shall see the glory of the Lord, and the excellency of our God. . . . Then the eyes of the blind shall be opened, and the ears of the deaf shall be unstopped. Then shall the lame man leap as an hart, and the tongue of the dumb sing."

In Isaiah sixty-one, is another prophecy of the Savior: "The Spirit of the Lord God is upon me; because the Lord hath anointed me to preach good tidings unto the meek; he hath sent me to bind up the broken-hearted, to proclaim liberty to the captives, and the opening of the prison to them that are bound; to proclaim the acceptable year of the Lord." Isa. 61: 1, 2. Where this text is quoted in the New Testament, there is added, "and recovering of sight to the blind." Luke 4: 18. This addition is found in the LXX.

Again the prophet speaking of Christ said, "But he was wounded for our transgressions, he was bruised for our iniquities: the chastisement of our peace was upon him; and with his stripes we are healed." Isa.

53: 5. The evangelist in speaking of the prophecy of Isa. 53: 4, 5, says, "When the even was come they brought unto him many that were possessed with devils: and he cast out the spirits with his word, and healed all that were sick; that it might be fulfilled which was spoken by Esaias the prophet, saying, Himself took our infirmities, and bare our sicknesses." Mat. 8: 16, 17. In verse thirteen is recorded the healing of the centurion's servant: "Go thy way, and as thou hast believed, so be it done unto thee. And his servant was healed in the selfsame hour." When Jesus saw the mother of Peter's wife lying sick of a fever, he touched her hand and the fever left her, and she arose and ministered unto them. ver. 14, 15.

In the ninth chapter of Matthew is recorded the instance of the healing of the man sick of the palsy, and of a woman who had been diseased for twelve years, and of the raising to life of the daughter of a certain ruler; also the restoring of the sight of two blind men. Jesus saith unto them, "Believe ye that I am able to do this? They said unto him, Yea, Lord. Then touched he their eyes, saying, According to your faith be it unto you. And their eyes were opened." "And Jesus went about all the cities and villages, teaching in their synagogues, and preaching the gospel of the kingdom, and healing every sickness and every disease among the people." ver. 35.

John, when in prison, hearing of the works of Jesus, sent two of his disciples who asked the Savior, "Art thou he that should come, or do we look for another?" Now John was acquainted with the prophecy of Isaiah concerning the Christ, so Jesus said to the disciples, "Go and show John again those things which ye do hear and see: the blind receive their sight and the lame walk, the lepers are cleansed, and the deaf hear, the dead are raised up, and the poor have the gospel preached unto them." Jesus told them that he was doing just what was prophesied that Christ should do when he came, then this must certainly be he and we need not look for another. Throughout his ministry the Savior continued to cast out devils and to heal the sick. He gave his twelve disciples power "against unclean spirits, to cast them out, and to heal all manner of sickness and all manner of disease." Mat. 10:1. Not only did he give the twelve such power over Satan and sickness, but in sending out the seventy he said: "And into whatsoever city ye enter, and they receive you, eat such things as are set before you: and heal the sick that are therein, and say unto them, The kingdom of God is come nigh unto you." Luke 10:8, 9.

Before Jesus ascended to the Father he commissioned his disciples to preach the gospel, saying, "Go ye into all the world, and preach the gospel to every creature. He that believeth and is baptized shall be saved; but he that believeth not shall be damned. And these signs shall follow them that believe: In my name shall they cast out devils; they shall speak with new tongues; they shall take up serpents; and if they drink any deadly thing, it shall not hurt them; they shall lay hands on the sick, and they shall recover." Mark 16:15-18. Jesus was the "light of the world," because he had power over sin and disease. The church becomes a light in the world in proportion to her power and purity, and when she reaches the zenith of her power the same power is exercised by her as by the Lord himself. After commissioning the disciples to preach, Jesus was "received up into heaven, and sat on the right hand of God. And they went forth, and preached everywhere, the Lord working with them, and confirming the word with signs following." Mark 16:19, 20. Although Jesus had ascended to heaven, yet it is said that he was working with them as they preached the word. Here was the secret of their power, "workers together with God."

Again Jesus said, "Go ye therefore, and teach all nations, baptizing them in the name of the Father, and of the Son, and of the Holy Ghost: teaching them to observe all things whatsoever I have commanded you: and, lo, I am with you alway, even unto the end of the world." Mat. 28:19, 20. The Lord here gives promise to be with them unto the end. Although he ascended, yet he says, "I will not leave you comfortless: I will come to you." John 14:18. The Holy Spirit on the day of Pentecost came and dwelt in the midst of God's church in the same authoritative power over sin and demons that Christ exercised before his passion. He now comes in the power of the Holy Spirit, performing great deeds of wonder through his church. The church only was visible, therefore became the light of the world. After Pentecost the disciples did as Jesus commanded. They began to preach the gospel, and Jesus working with them, many souls were saved. Peter and John on one occasion "went up together into the temple at the hour of prayer, being the ninth hour. And a certain man lame from his mother's womb was carried, whom they laid daily at the gate of the temple which is called Beautiful, to ask alms of them that entered into the temple; who seeing Peter and John about to go into the temple asked an alms. And Peter, fastening his eyes on him with John, said, Look on us. And he gave heed unto them, expecting to receive something of them. Then Peter said, Silver and gold have I none; but such as I have give I thee: in the name of Jesus Christ of Nazareth rise up and walk. And he took him by the right hand, and lifted him up; and immediately his feet and ankle bones received strength. And he leaping up stood, and walked, and entered with them into the temple, walking, and leaping, and praising God. And all the people saw him walking and praising God." Acts 3:1-9. This miracle of divine healing was done by faith in the name of Jesus. ver. 16. The Lord was with his disciples confirming the preaching with signs following.

In the ninth chapter of Acts is recorded an instance

of the dead being raised to life. Dorcas, who was a good woman, was taken sick and died. Two men were sent for Peter, who when he was come was brought into the upper chamber: "and all the widows stood by him weeping, and showing the coats and garments which Dorcas made while she was with them. But Peter put them all forth, and kneeled down and prayed; and turning him to the body said, Tabitha, arise. And she opened her eyes: and when she saw Peter she sat up. And he gave her his hand, and lifted her up: and when he had called the saints and the widows, presented her alive. And it was known throughout all Joppa; and many believed in the Lord." This was when the church was the light of the world; when the whole pure gospel was preached for the gospel's sake, and men lived humbly before God, and were workers together with him.

Paul escaping the waves was cast upon the island of Melita. He says, "The barbarous people showed us no little kindness; for they kindled a fire, and received us every one, because of the present rain, and because of the cold." And when he had gathered a bundle of sticks, and laid them on the fire, there came a viper out of the heat, and fastened on his hand. And when the barbarians saw the venomous beast hang on his hand, they said among themselves, No doubt this man is a murderer, whom, though he hath escaped the sea, yet vengeance suffereth not to live. Acts 28:1-4. Now was the promise given in the commission to prove true? Jesus said, "They shall take up serpents." Here Paul had taken one up. Should he trust in the promise of the Savior, or resort to some antidote? It is said, He shook off the beast into the fire and felt no harm. The natives were astonished and God was glorified. Had Paul sought and obtained relief by medical means, whatever brought the relief would have been worthy the praise. He was living solely for the glory of God, and by trusting in God and God protecting him it was thus that God was glorified.

The "gifts of healing" were placed in the church. See 1 Cor. 12:28. As late as the year 60 A. D., twenty-seven years after the Lord had ascended, James tells us what to do when sick. He says, "Is any among you afflicted? let him pray. Is any merry? let him sing psalms. Is any sick among you? let him call for the elders of the church; and let them pray over him, anointing him with oil in the name of the Lord: and the prayer of faith shall save the sick, and the Lord shall raise him up; and if he have committed sins, they shall be forgiven him." Jas. 5:13-15.

Thus the Lord worked in the midst of his people in the morning of the gospel day. He gave them grace and power to live the same holy, humble life he lived. He gave them power to cast out devils and to heal the sick. By performing the works and living the life of Jesus the church was a city set upon a hill, which could not be hid—a light in the world.

CHAPTER X.
THE SOUL.

Man as we behold him is not all there is of man. He is a wonderful being. He stands in the highest order of God's creation.

HE IS A COMPOUND.

Man was created a physical and spiritual organism. He possesses an animal and a spiritual life. Thus he is connected with two worlds. The physical creation is termed the "outward man," and the spiritual, the "inward man." "For which cause we faint not; but though our outward man perish, yet the inward man is renewed day by day." 2 Cor. 4:16. "For we know that if our earthly house of this tabernacle were dissolved, we have a building of God, a house not made with hands, eternal in the heavens." 2 Cor. 5:1. "Yea, I think it meet, as long as I am in this tabernacle, to stir you up by putting you in remembrance." 2 Pet. 1:13.

In the quotation from second Corinthians the pronoun "we" is applied to the inward man, and the "earthly house of this tabernacle" is spoken in reference to the outward man. In the quotation from second Peter the pronoun "I" has for its antecedent the "inward man," and tabernacle refers again to the outward man.

THE OUTWARD MAN IS DENOMINATED "BODY."

In the fifth chapter of Mark's gospel there is recorded an instance of a woman who was diseased and suffered many things of many physicians in the outward man. She came to Jesus and touched his garment and she felt in her body she was healed of the plague.

THE INWARD MAN IS DENOMINATED "SOUL."

By the one text given above it is plainly to be seen that the outer man is the body. Many additional texts could be given but we consider it unnecessary, because all at once believe it.

But why not as readily believe one text which calls the inner man the "soul"? Some will not. This is the inconsistency of man. We will quote more than one. "When my soul fainted within me I remembered the Lord." Jonah 2:7. "But his flesh upon him shall have pain, and his soul within him shall mourn." Job 14:22. "And the man of God said, Let her alone; for her soul is vexed within her." 2 Kings 4:27.

THE INNER MAN IS THE RESPONSIBLE MAN.

"Will the Lord be pleased with thousands of rams, or with ten thousands of rivers of oil? shall I give my first-born for my transgression, the fruit of my body for the sin of my soul?" Micah 6:7. Since it is the soul that sins, of necessity the soul becomes the responsible man.

SIN PRODUCES DEATH TO THE SOUL.

"The soul that sinneth, it shall die." Ezek. 18:4.

THE VALUE OF THE SOUL.

"For what is a man profited, if he shall gain the whole world, and lose his own soul? Or what shall a man give in exchange for his soul?" Mat. 16:26. Here the "soul," the "inner man," is considered of greater worth than this world. He who secures the eternal safety of his soul has accomplished more than he who should gain this whole world.

THE SOUL DOES NOT LOSE CONSCIOUSNESS WHEN THE BODY DIES.

"For to me to live is Christ, and to die is gain. But if I live in the flesh, this is the fruit of my labor: yet what I shall choose I wot not. For I am in a strait betwixt two, having a desire to depart and to be with Christ; which is far better: nevertheless to abide in the flesh is more needful for you." Phil. 1:21-24.

If there is no conscious existence after death until the final resurrection from the grave, how could it be "far better" for Paul to depart? For him to depart this life is to be with Christ. "We are confident, I say, and willing rather to be absent from the body, and to be present with the Lord." 2 Cor. 5:8. How can language be plainer than this? To be absent from the body is to be present with the Lord.

THE PLACE OF THE SOUL WHILE THE BODY LIES IN THE GRAVE.

The Son of God in his beautiful narrative of the rich man and Lazarus certainly teaches a conscious existence of the departed souls of both the wicked and the righteous. The soul of the rich man was in torment in the flames of hell. The angels carried the poor beggar to rest and bliss in Abraham's bosom.

"There was a certain rich man, which was clothed in purple and fine linen, and fared sumptuously every day: and there was a certain beggar named Lazarus, which was laid at his gate, full of sores, and desiring to be fed with the crumbs which fell from the rich man's table: moreover the dogs came and licked his sores. And it came to pass, that the beggar died, and was carried by the angels into Abraham's bosom: the rich man also died, and was buried; and in hell he lifted up his eyes, being in torments, and seeth Abraham afar off, and Lazarus in his bosom. And he cried and said, Father Abraham, have mercy on me, and send Lazarus, that he may dip the tip of his finger in water, and cool my tongue; for I am tormented in this flame. But Abraham said, Son, remember that thou in thy lifetime receivedst thy good things, and likewise Lazarus evil things: but now he is comforted, and thou art tormented. And beside all this, between us and you there is a great gulf fixed: so that they which would pass from hence to you can not; neither can they pass to us, that would come from thence. Then he said, I pray thee therefore, father, that thou wouldest send him to my father's house: for I have five brethren; that he may testify unto them, lest they also come into this place of torment. Abraham saith unto him, They have Moses and the prophets; let them hear them. And he said, Nay, father Abraham: but if one went unto them from the dead, they will repent. And he said unto him, If they hear not Moses and the prophets, neither will they be persuaded, though one rose from the dead.'' Luke 16:19-31.

SOUL-REST.

The immortal soul of man is a conscious entity, whether in sin or in righteousness. If in righteousness, there is a blessed consciousness of peace, rest, and contentment. This internal sense of happiness man enjoyed in his primeval state. By disobedience an awful change came over him, by which the peaceful rest and full satisfaction of the soul was destroyed, and the terrible miseries of sin were experienced. In sin the soul still retains its consciousness. There is in fallen man an internal knowledge of incompleteness. There is a missing link, an awful vacancy, and a kind of intuitive knowledge that he must give answer for certain moral responsibilities unto a great Creator. There are deep longings, restless fears, dark uncertainties, and desperate strugglings for a satisfactory hope.

By the entrance of sin into the world there was implanted in the nature of man a "lust of the flesh," which seeks the pleasures of the world. This never brings contentment to the soul. It reaches to something far beyond for rest. Jesus came to this world as the soul's Rest-giver. "Come unto me, all ye that labor and are heavy-laden, and I will give you rest. Take my yoke upon you, and learn of me; for I am meek and lowly in heart: and ye shall find rest unto your souls." Mat. 11: 28, 29. The name of Jesus is sweet to the soul whose cry is not stifled by the "lusts of the flesh." It is the disposition of the "carnal mind" to hush the pleadings of the hungry, thirsting spirit by bidding it wait until some future time when its demands will be given attention. The "flesh" gains its pleasures at the cost of the soul's rest, and when the soul gains rest it must be at the cost of the lust of the flesh, and thus the war goes on between the flesh and the spirit. How often in the days of one's youth the soul struggles hard for freedom and pleads for rest; the "flesh" quiets its fears by promising to yield to its desires in maturer years. Old age comes on, and the flesh, unwilling yet to make a sacrifice of the world, bids the restless soul to hope for joy in heaven.

This delusive scheme often proves a success, allowing the flesh to go on reaping its carnal lusts with the soul endeavoring to satisfy itself with the hope of rest above. It is true there are wondrous joys in heaven, but it is not all who shall get to enjoy them. It is very dangerous and delusive to encourage the heart to hope for a home in heaven when the flesh still loves this world. Bright hopes of endless glory in the world above cheer us on amid the storms of life to that precious goal, but we would not desire you to pass through this world heavy-laden, with a hope of unloading your cargo of sorrow and pain somewhere in the beyond and being happy there. As we cross the ocean of life, there is to be found a blessed port where you can discharge your load of sin and sorrow and take on joys to your vessel's full capacity. Beyond life's sail there remains no port of exchange. The soul fitted for the delights of heaven, enjoys heavenly delights in this world. In the divine economy there is a sufficiency of grace to enable the soul to be blessedly at rest amid the most trying circumstances of life. When our happy spirits, no longer holden by the house of clay, shall soar away to heavenly rest, scenes and experiences will arise of such a nature as to greatly enhance the felicity of our hearts, but the revelation of heaven upon a pardoned soul, and

"The enjoyment of heavenly bliss
E'en in a world like this,"

to the humble Christian heart can never be told. Do not therefore, dear reader, permit the thoughts of great happiness in the paradise above, nor of some fancied coming age of universal peace and joy on earth, to hide from your soul the precious realization of heavenly enjoyments, sweet walks with God, and tastes of love in this present life and time. We repeat, there is wondrous peace and happiness in heaven; all is joy there, and upon the soul yielded to God's control the sweets of heaven's graces are distilled like the gentle siftings of the evening dew upon the flower, transporting the soul to wondrous joys all along the way of life. "Oh, this blessed holy rest" is to be found only "on Jesus' loving breast." Trials may come, storm-clouds gather, and billows threaten, yet "in Jesus all is bright." Make him your haven of rest.

ETERNAL HAPPINESS.

Happiness forever—these words sound sweet and dear to almost every heart. There is nothing repulsive in their tone, but, oh, what strength they give to the weary, waiting soul. The hope of never-ending happiness in a bright celestial world enables us to patiently endure the tortures and afflictions of this sin-cursed, terrestrial sphere. It is not difficult to persuade most people that somewhere in the great beyond there is a place of peace and bliss, prepared for the children of God to inhabit forever. But few men have disposition of spirit to wrest the clear declarations of inspiration on this delightful theme. Perhaps no other subject in the Bible is so universally received. Eternal rest to the Christian is the voice of the Word forever settled in heaven. Oh, how our hearts glow with rapture and our bosoms heave with waves of love and praise to God as we by faith look into an eternity of perfect bliss prepared for us. "Come, ye blessed of my Father, inherit the kingdom prepared for you from the foundation of the world." Mat. 25:34. "Well done, thou good and faithful servant, enter thou into the joy of thy Lord." "In thy presence is fulness of joy; at thy right hand there are pleasures forevermore." Psa. 16:11. "The righteous shall go away into eternal life." Mat. 25:46. "Then we which are alive and remain shall be caught up together with them in the clouds, to meet the Lord in the air; and so shall we ever be with the Lord." 1 Thes. 4:17.

These few texts are sufficient to convince the reader that there is a heaven of eternal joys, but before leaving this subject we will give one text of caution. "Not every one that saith unto me, Lord, Lord, shall enter into the kingdom of heaven; but he that doeth the will of my Father which is in heaven." Mat. 7:21.

ETERNAL PUNISHMENT.

Misery, wretchedness and woe forever—these words have an unpleasant sound. They form no enjoyable theme for meditation. People usually reject all thoughts of eternal unhappiness. Because of its unpleasantness many have sought to explain the doctrine away. However it is as positively declared in the sacred volume as the doctrine of eternal happiness. "And these shall go away into everlasting punishment: but the righteous into life eternal." Mat. 25: 46. The punishment of the wicked in duration is equal with the life of the righteous, but some, who no doubt have not been rescued from the fears of hell, have endeavored to make the words everlasting and eternal as used in the above texts differ in meaning with respect to time.

Upon this subject we will quote from the treatise entitled, "What Is the Soul?" by D. S. Warner: "The words 'eternal life,' as the great gift of God to men, occur in the New Testament just twenty-nine times, and in every instance the word eternal is derived from the Greek word *aionios;* the same word which tells how long the punishment of the wicked shall last in Mat. 25: 46, and elsewhere. The words 'everlasting life' and 'life everlasting' occur in the New Testament fourteen times, and by reference to the Greek Testament you will find the word everlasting is, without a single exception, translated from the same Greek word—*aionios.* Here then we learn the wisdom of Heaven finds and uses no stronger term in all the forty-three promises and statements of eternal and everlasting life to the righteous in the New Testament than the word *aionion*, the very same word which he uses to declare the eternal and everlasting punishment of the wicked. . . . The Lord Jesus Christ and the Holy Spirit have described the duration of their own existence, attributes and glory by the use of the same word which we have seen fixes the eternal punishment of the wicked.

"In Heb. 5:9 we read that Christ became the author of 'eternal [*aionion*] salvation unto all them that obey him.' If therefore this word does not mean eternal, our salvation will finally fail and drop us back into the hands of the devil. In Heb. 9:12 we read that Christ has obtained eternal (*aionion*) redemption. If then the word only means a long period of time our eternal redemption is not yet secured. In Heb. 9:15 we are told that by means of Christ's death for our redemption, we have 'received the promise of eternal [*aionion*] inheritance.' Will the inheritance that Christ has purchased by his death come to an end?"

In speaking of hell-fire in the ninth chapter of the gospel by Mark the eternal—*aionion*—immortal Son of God five times says it is a fire "which is not" and "never shall be quenched." If it never shall be quenched, can we possibly err in supposing that it will burn forever? "Then shall he say also unto them on the left hand, Depart from me, ye cursed, into everlasting fire, prepared for the devil and his angels." Mat. 25:41. "And shall be tormented day and night forever and ever." Rev. 20:10. "And the smoke of their torment ascendeth up forever and ever." Rev. 14:11.

There are yet many other scriptures which positively teach everlasting punishment in an endless hell. Whatever fears this doctrine may bring to deluded souls, and however zealously they may labor for its refutation, it stands unshaken. If you fear eternal punishment do not endeavor to calm your fears by seeking to believe there is no endless torment, but seek the Savior, who will save you from your sins and fears, and give you hope, blessed hope, of everlasting peace and rest.

CHAPTER XI.
SPIRITUAL CULTURE.

"And this is the record, that God hath given to us eternal life, and this life is in his Son." 1 John 5:11. There is eternal life in Jesus, but for man to come into possession of this life he must comply with the requirements made by the Bible. After getting into possession of this life there are certain duties which man must faithfully perform to retain and develop it. After entering the wide fields of grace development is necessary. "But grow in grace, and in the knowledge of our Lord and Savior Jesus Christ." 2 Pet. 3:18. Nutrition necessary for the development of spiritual life is contained in the Word of God. "Man shall not live by bread alone, but by every word that proceedeth out of the mouth of God." Mat. 4:4.

"As new-born babes, desire the sincere milk of the word, that ye may grow thereby." 1 Pet. 2:2.

By proper culture—attending to Christian duties—the Christ-life in the soul will be strengthened, and daily we will become stronger in faith, richer in virtue, deeper in knowledge, more strictly temperate, exercise a greater degree of brotherly kindness and godliness, and enjoy more of heaven's pure love in our hearts. Neglect the proper Scriptural culture of the spiritual life and the Christian will degenerate into a few irksome duties of cold formality. By the writers of the New Testament we are urgently exhorted, yea, commanded, to attend to certain duties necessary to keep us in the love of God. Of these especially important are reading the Scripture, prayer, fasting, examination, meditation, etc.

READING THE SCRIPTURE.

"Thy word is very pure: therefore thy servant loveth it." "I love thy commandments above gold; yea, above fine gold." "The law of thy mouth is better unto me than thousands of gold and silver." Psa. 119: 140, 127, 72. The Bible, to the Christian, is a richer treasure than gold. No other book is read with such deep, amazing interest. The soul ravishingly feasts upon the pure, simple truth. It is manna. It is life. "How sweet are thy words unto my taste! yea, sweeter than honey to my mouth." Psa. 119: 103. When the soul gets to taste of the honeyed sweetness of God's Word it endears it to God and the Bible so as to make death preferable to separation. "O how love I thy law! it is my meditation all the day." Psa. 119:97. Exile to Patmos would not be so lonely to the Christian did he but have his Bible.

"All scripture is given by inspiration of God, and is profitable for doctrine, for reproof, for correction, for instruction in righteousness: that the man of God may be perfect, thoroughly furnished unto all good works." 2 Tim. 3:16,17. The Word of God contains sufficient instructions and corrections to properly develop the Christ-life in the soul, if it is heeded. By looking into this perfect law of God and continuing in its teaching one will imbibe its spirit, its life, its power, until his own life will reveal the truly high and ennobling principles of the precious volume from heaven. The true sentiment of the Bible will be so interwoven into his very existence that his decorum will be so influenced by the power of divine truth that all who read his life will but read God's Holy Book.

The Bible tells us of heaven, the eternal, happy home of the righteous. It tells us of sin and how it deprives the soul the privilege of entering that bright mansion of everlasting rest. It tells of a Savior who saves from sin, and fits and prepares man to receive from God's hands great eternal rewards. It unfolds to us the beautiful character of God and encourages our souls to imitate his perfect example. It speaks of our Heavenly Father's loving providence, how that he is ever watching over us, and guiding us with his eye; how that no harm shall ever befall us, and when we pass through the rivers they shall not overflow us; when we walk through the fire we shall not be burned; how that he will withhold no good thing from us, but will cause all things to work for our good: how that he bears our burdens and shelters us beneath his wing. The Bible is the Christian's guide to a haven of rest; to make sure he is traveling in the right course, he must study it well. He must run the way of its commandments. To be a fruitful Christian he must search it and be a doer of its precepts, ever gaining knowledge and practising what he knows. Ah, my Bible! it is a lamp unto my feet and a light unto my pathway.

> Precious volume, ever lie
> Very near my heart and eye;
> All the precepts of thy page
> Ever shall my soul engage.

PRAYER.

Prayer has brought a comfort to many a sorrowing heart. It has wiped away many a tear. Prayer is the Christian's stronghold. There can be no real progress in the divine life without earnest prayer. A decline in spiritual life usually begins at the secret closet. Satan knows what a powerful weapon prayer is in the hands of a saint. As Cowper has said,

> Satan trembles when he sees
> The weakest saint upon his knees.

The Bible says, "The effectual fervent prayer of a righteous man availeth much." Jas. 5:16.

Prayer to be effectual must be offered in faith. The prayer of faith has accomplished wonders in every age of the world. It has stopped the mouths of lions. It has subdued kingdoms, obtained promises, quenched the violence of fire, and escaped the edge of the sword. By the prayer of faith the weak have become strong and turned to flight the armies of the aliens. The weak child of God by prayer develops into strong manhood. When engaged in a severe contest with the enemy of your soul the prayer of faith draws upon the strength of heaven and thus you become stronger in God. In a time of heavy and sore trials by looking upward unto God in confidence we conquer. For this reason the trial of our faith is more precious than gold. "What things soever ye desire, when ye pray, believe that ye receive them, and ye shall have them." Mark 11:24. "If ye abide in me, and my words abide in you, ye shall ask what ye will and it shall be done unto you." John 15:7. "And whatsoever ye shall ask in my name, that will I do, that the Father may be glorified in the Son. If ye shall ask anything in my name, I will do it." John 14:13, 14. "Hitherto have ye asked nothing in my name: ask, and ye shall receive, that your joy may be full." "And whatsoever we ask, we receive of him, because we keep his commandments, and do those things that are pleasing in his sight." 1 John 3:22.

With these promises before us we certainly ought to be encouraged to strive earnestly for the faith once delivered to the saints. It is the prayer of faith that moves God upon his throne. Words offered in mere form are powerless. "He that cometh to God must believe that he is, and that he is a rewarder of them that diligently seek him," for "without faith it is impossible to please him." Heb. 11:6. Man that asks of God and wavers in his faith is compared to the restless waves of the sea. "But let him ask in faith, nothing wavering. For he that wavereth is like a wave of the sea driven of the wind and tossed. For let not that man think that he shall receive anything of the Lord." Jas. 1:6, 7.

There is a difference between simple faith and presumption. Some people take things for granted because God has promised similar things, without considering well if their prayer is according to the will of God. The Lord has promised bodily healing to his children. He says, "The prayer of faith shall save the sick, and the Lord shall raise him up; and if he have committed sins, they shall be forgiven him." Jas. 5:15. This is conditional, the conditions being recorded in the following verse: "Confess your faults one to another, and pray one for another, that ye may be healed." The glorious Bible doctrine of divine healing has many times been disgraced by mere presumption. Many when they are anointed presume they are healed because God has promised it in his Word when they have failed to sit in the valley of humiliation to learn of God their faults that need correction. They find in a short time that their presumption does not prove effectual and witnesses are made to scorn the idea of divine healing. We hear of no relapsing in a few days of those who were healed by the Lord and his church in the morning light. If any had such severe trials of faith as to be as sick or worse than ever apparently, it was thought wisdom to exclude such testimony from the Bible, and if wise to exclude it from the Bible, we are persuaded it is wise to exclude it from public testimony at any time.

The same may be said of prayers for spiritual and temporal blessings. Never mistake presumption for faith. An individual might ask God for some temporal blessing and because God has promised to supply "all our needs," and if "we ask anything he will do it," take it for granted he is soon going to receive it, and when it fails to appear is disappointed and discouraged. By close examination it will be found that there was not a humble resignation of all things into the hands of God. The prayer was tinctured with selfish desire and more presuming than heart-felt faith. For a perfect operation of faith that will draw blessings and life and power from

God to the soul there must be a humble yielding, a perfect surrender of all to the Father's loving control. When all is resigned, and we sit in holy submission at his feet, faith will spring up, and if it is for some temporal blessing we are asking, God will answer to the soul and we will know and feel within us that we have the object desired. Though we have it not as yet in our possession it will never fail to appear at God's own appointed time, which is never too late. We believe that many presume that they are sanctified, but afterwards discover that they have not a perfect and pure heart. In all probability there was a lack in the consecration, which hindered a perfect operation of faith, and presumption was mistaken for belief. Such has doubtless been the result also in seeking justification. Positive faith affects God on his throne and brings a clear understanding consciousness to the soul.

Some one may wonder in what way the prayer of faith offered when we are sick, or prayers for temporal needs can advantage us in the development of spiritual life. God has so arranged that the prayer of faith that brings healing virtue to the afflicted body also brings a blessing and an increase to the soul. Prayer that reaches God in a time of temporal need not only moves him to grant the petition, but also adds new strength and energy to the inner being. Thus God may permit us to be afflicted or to be in great need of food or raiment to awaken our souls to earnest imploring prayer for our spiritual advantage. When all is dark before and behind us, when storm-clouds hang heavy over us and temptations grow manifold, we are made keenly conscious that our whole and only dependence is upon God. Then on wings of faith the trembling soul comes into God's majestic presence to implore his aid, his help, in time of need. In his fatherly care he extends his hand and lifts us above the storm-clouds of affliction and temptation into beautiful light. It will be found that our soul is wonderfully increased in God. Thus prayer offered in these times of greatest need always prove a blessing to the spiritual life. Our own dear children could save themselves from much chastisement by obedience. Thus the children of God would doubtless be spared many an affliction if they were more strictly obedient to him.

How often should we pray? David says,"Evening, and morning, and at noon, will I pray, and cry aloud: and he shall hear my voice." Psa. 55:17. Again he says, "Seven times a day do I praise thee because of thy righteous judgments." Psa. 119:164. The apostle Paul exhorts us to "pray without ceasing." 1 Thes. 5:17. We do not understand by this last text that the Christian is to be constantly in an attitude of prayer. No one can reasonably demand such a strict interpretation. For constant spiritual growth we should follow the example of the holy prophets and apostles and have regular daily visits to our altar of prayer. Beside this if you desire the beautiful character of Christ to unfold in your soul and life you should be careful to constantly maintain a prayerful frame of spirit. How often one should go within their closet, circumstances must decide. Where circumstances afford much time for **prayer we** assure you to be no loser by living much behind your closed door.

The spiritual man may be compared to the physical man in a sense, or to a certain extent. The physical man demands food for its sustenance. It feasts at the breakfast table, then goes, using the strength derived in performing the vocations of life. In a few hours there will be a demand for more, as the force of the former meal is spent. "But man shall not live by bread alone." The soul feasts upon the life of God in prayer and is strengthened, you then engage in the duties of life. In a short time you will feel the pangs of hunger in your soul. There is a longing for a deep communion with God. This is your best guide as to how often you should pray if your soul is in a good healthy state. It may not be convenient for you to go into your closet every time you feel your soul "panting after God," but you can lift up your heart to him in the best manner you can under the circumstances, and then go and feast at your private altar at your very earliest convenience.

The physical and spiritual man differ with respect to overeating. Too much food is injurious to the animal man, but the danger of surfeiting was not spoken of the soul. The inner man may feast and banquet and drink of spiritual stores and streams and the soul will grow and develop accordingly. There is but little danger of lingering too long at the feast. There is much danger of famine while the Christian as a citizen of this world has certain secular duties to perform, yet amid these he communes and walks with God. While he may be intellectually engaged in the problems of life, the higher affections of his soul live upon heavenly things. He thus drinks of the refreshing dews of glory until the beauteous graces of Christ are imbibed and infused throughout his very existence and the holy image of God is seen upon him.

The effect of a prayer of faith is almost without limit. By it Daniel shut the mouths of lions. The Hebrews walked unhurt amid the flames. Elijah shut up the heavens until it did not rain for more than three years. The waters of the sea have been divided, the walls of cities thrown down, armies turned to flight, kingdoms subdued, the prison-doors opened, the barren womb has become fruitful, the lame have been made to walk, the deaf to hear, the blind to see, the dead raised to life and the soul redeemed. Oh, the wonders of prayer!

Satan, knowing how disastrous to his kingdom is the Christian's prayer of faith, will do all he can to hinder. He will heap upon you duties of life; tell you that you have no time for prayer. When you do pray he will try to make your prayers hurried and insincere. He will try to divert your attention when at the altar of prayer. He will be constantly presenting thoughts of secular duties. He will strive to make your devotions formal and irksome. He will cast over you a feeling of awful indifference and then advise you not to pray until you feel more like it. He will make the heavens appear as brass above you, and tell you God does not hear you. Christian, you know by the Word of God what is your duty. It is to pray. Then pray you must. It is the language of the Bible. Disregarding your feelings, pray. Disregarding the suggestions of Satan, pray. As you value your soul, pray, and "pray without ceasing."

FASTINGS.

That the apostle Paul considered fasting an excellent means for spiritual development is evident from his writings. He says that the ministers of God should approve themselves by "much patience, in afflictions, in necessities, in distresses, in stripes, in imprisonments, in tumults, in labors, in watchings, in fastings." 2 Cor. 6:4, 5. In speaking of himself, he says he was "in weariness and painfulness, in watchings often, in hunger and thirst, in fastings often." 2 Cor. 11:27. In Acts 27:33, we learn that on the occasion of the shipwreck fourteen days were spent in fasting. This is not the doing of penance that the priests of mystic Babylon bind upon their subjects, but the cheerful service of a humble, devoted heart. God has not left this at the direction of man, but it is alone at the dictation of the Holy Spirit.

There is a secret power in fasting. It separates us farther from self and deepens us in humility, spirituality and reliance upon God. On occasions where great faith was required, fastings were recommended by the Savior. In speaking to his disciples concerning the devils which possessed a child, he said, "This kind goeth not out but by prayer and fasting." Mat. 17: 21. When Paul and Barnabas were separated by the Holy Spirit unto the work of the Lord, after fasting and prayer hands were laid upon them and they were sent away. When fasting, the mind is clearer and the faith more active. It is a self-denial, which has a tendency to develop the graces of the Spirit.

It is said of a certain prophetess that dwelt in Jerusalem in the days of our Savior's nativity, that she departed not from the temple, but served God with fastings and prayers night and day. Luke 2: 36, 37.

The most spiritual Christians are ready to acknowledge that fasting is an excellent means of drawing us into a deeper and more intimate communion with God. We scarcely think that any one will attain to any great spiritual depth without fasting. When the Christian's soul is burdened for this lost world it is natural for him to unburden his soul to God in fasting and prayer. How beautifully has the Lord arranged all things in the kingdom of heaven! He by his Spirit lays a burden upon our heart for the souls of lost mankind. This burden causes us to seek God in fasting and prayer for these lost ones, and our prayers move him to send forth his Spirit to convict this world of sin. Thus it is arranged in the economy of grace, and thus we can all be "workers together with him."

It is sad that comparatively so few know the value of the sincere prayer of faith. Fasting and prayer affect this whole world, and heaven and hell. Christian, do not be sparing in them. Christians are few, but there are enough of them upon the earth, that if all were earnest in fasting and prayer this world would be disturbed in her slumber and sinners be made to fear before the wrath of God. To be unwilling to fast when we feel the movings of God's Spirit upon us to that end, is to soon become so dull and stupid spiritually that we will have but little burden or concern for perishing souls. If we want to walk with God and have a deep concern for his cause and love for lost mankind we must be self-denying and "in fastings often."

TRIALS AND TEMPTATIONS.

You may wonder why we have arranged the subject of "Trials and Temptations" in the chapter of "Spiritual Culture." It is because they are an excellent means of our growth in divine things. "**All things work together for good to them that love God.**" Trials prove to be for our good in the spiritual life if we will boldly and bravely meet them in Jesus' name. We are encouraged by the apostle James to count all temptations a joy. It is evident that the apostle would not exhort us to count temptations a joy if they were not for our good. The Bible tells us there is a tempter. 1 Thes. 3:5. We also learn from the sacred page that God does not tempt any man. Jas. 1:13. Matthew tells us that the devil is the tempter. Mat. 4:1. God permits Satan to try and tempt us as we learn from Job's experience. Satan can not tempt us beyond what God permits, and God will not permit him to tempt us beyond what we are able to bear. He does not permit one to be tempted more than another, but we all have temptations such as are common to man. 1 Cor. 10:13.

Jesus was tempted in every manner that man is tempted, yet without sin. Heb. 4:15. Jesus was not overcome by temptation, but he faithfully endured. Because he was thus tempted and overcame, he knows how to deliver the godly out of temptation. 2 Pet. 2:9. Not only does he know how to deliver us out of temptation, but he is fully able to do so. Heb. 2:18.

Temptations and trials are necessary in the Christian life. But few people realize the **value of temptation.** But few people, or perhaps none but what would backslide if they did not have any trials. God has so arranged it in the nature of Christianity or spiritual life that in order for the soul to grow and develop it must be tested and tried. Leaning upon God in time of strong temptation only increases our strength in God. Man would become independent of God, however much he may think to the contrary, if he had no trials and temptations. No true-hearted Christian has trials only such as he needs. Peter says, "Wherein ye greatly rejoice, though now for a season, if need be, ye are in heaviness through manifold temptations." 1 Pet. 1:6. Christian, do you not value your spiritual prosperity above all else? Then never complain nor become discouraged because of the heavy and manifold temptations. God knows how to deal with you. You may sometimes think you know best, but in this you are mistaken. Father knoweth best. He loves you and will not suffer you to be tempted beyond what your needs are, and what he will enable you to bear, if you will but trust in him.

When your way grows very dark and temptation's billows roll high, when the flames of fiery trials seem to almost consume your soul, will you not remember that just as you are being tempted, Jesus was also tempted, yet he was not overcome? Also remember that he knows how to deliver you, and is able to do it. God sees that you need this and he is permitting it to mold you and fashion you into his own holy image. These are the refining flames that serve to consume the dross and make you perfectly pure. Our heavenly Father chasteneth us for our profit, that we might be partakers of his holiness. Heb. 12:10. God has given us a promise, which, if you will remember in faith, will enable you to endure. "Blessed is the man that endureth temptation: for when he is tried he shall receive a crown of life, which the Lord has promised to them that love him." Jas. 1:12.

> When in trial's heated furnace,
> In temptation's deep, wide sea,
> Like with sainted Hebrew children,
> Jesus walketh there with me.

MEDITATION.

That meditation does affect one's spirituality is an unquestionable fact. Vagrant thought is well calculated to dull the finer sensibilities of the soul, thereby rendering it less capable of impression by the Spirit of God. "Keeping in touch with God," is a very familiar expression among holiness people at this present time, but what does it imply? We are all at sea when not in touch with him. To be so kept is to have everything in us fully alive to God. Every Christian grace must be in a state of perfect health and vigorous growth. If there be any dwarfed condition of the spiritual being in any part it will be less sensible to God's touch.

The blind have been known to cultivate the sense of touch in the physical being to the amazing acuteness of being able to distinguish color. The sense of touch in the soul by careful, earnest husbandry can be refined to such a degree as to make it susceptible to the slightest impression of the Holy Spirit.

In the creation, the moral being was given the capability of being influenced and controlled by the Spirit of the Lord. By sin this electric current from God's presence to man's soul, like the separation of the Atlantic cable, was divided. Man becoming thus disconnected from God's power and impressive guidance was left to be operated by the influences of a wicked world. Through the redemptive power of Jesus' blood man is again brought into union with God. The divided cable is taken up and united, and man's soul wondrously animated by God's presence.

So cultured may become the sensibilities of the inner being, and so thoroughly impregnated by God's enlivening power, that one empty thought, causing the slightest ebbing of life's current flow is keenly felt. To keep in perfect touch with God is to live where there is a soul consciousness that he is pleased with every act of life; where there is a witnessing "sweet and clear" of the Spirit to the inmost soul that the words of your mouth and the meditations of your heart are acceptable unto him.

Pure and holy meditations are an excellent means for the culture and refinement of man's moral being. Useless thought makes the soul coarse, and difficult of impression by good influences. By associating with God through prayer and meditation man's spiritual entity will develop into his own glorious image. By communion with the Lord his pure character is assimilated into our own until our lives become but the fruit of a vine which has its origin in the rich soil around Heaven's throne. If you can indulge a train of careless, vagabond thought, and not be severely smitten in conscience, you are far from being in touch with God. The spiritual depression and awful benumbing stupidity, the disrelish for prayer and reading the Bible, is often the result of entertaining empty, fruitless meditations. The Scriptures tell us what are wholesome subjects for thought, and what are not. "The thought of foolishness is sin." Prov. 24:9. "I hate vain thoughts." Psa. 119:113.

Vain and foolish thoughts are very destructive to spirituality, and should be hated and carefully guarded against by every lover of God's law. Many people find it difficult to stay their mind upon the Lord. While reading the Bible and in secret prayer their thoughts are disposed to wander. The wonderful works of God scarcely awaken any admiration within them. They can not elevate their soul into a profound awe before his awful presence, and there is but little conscious depth of inner reverence and devotion to his dear name. There is a blessed remedy for this serious trouble. Carefully watch your meditations. Call the oftener upon God in some silent secret place. Select some secluded, hallowed place for meditation. It is said of Isaac that he went into the field at eventide to meditate. Gen. 24:63. This is a time well suited to draw the soul out into deep, intimate communion with God. Learn to admire the wondrous works of the Creator. Meditate upon them. The setting of the sun, the starry heavens, the fleecy floating clouds, the silent hills, all will serve to fill your soul with reverential fear before God's majestic presence, and all within you be awed to solemn stillness at his footfall. Then you can say with the Psalmist, "O how love I thy law! it is my meditation all the day." Psa. 119:97. "I will remember the works of the Lord: surely I will remember thy wonders of old. I will meditate also of all thy work, and talk of thy doings." Psa. 77:11, 12. "My soul shall be satisfied as with marrow and fatness; and my mouth shall praise thee with joyful lips: when I remember thee upon my bed, and meditate on thee in the night watches." Psa. 63:5, 6.

Idle, careless thoughts generate a stupidity that will rob you of joy and soul satisfaction. It will deaden the sensibilities of your inner nature and prevent your hearing God's footstep, and deprive you of many a blessing. Communion with the Lord and meditating upon his Word will elevate the soul to a plane all radiant with Heaven's light and love, and put a humility in your heart and a sweetness in every expression that will distinguish you from the coarse ways of the world. "I will sing unto the Lord as long as I live: I will sing praise to my God while I have my being. My meditation of him shall be sweet: I will be glad in the Lord." Psa. 104: 33, 34.

EXAMINATION.

Close and impartial examination of our moral character is indispensable to spiritual prosperity. He who does not watch the inclinations of his heart, nor note the course of its affections, and direct them in the channels of heavenly grace, will soon have naught but a "name to live." As you read the infallible Word of God, ask him to let its light find entrance to the remotest chambers of your soul. Too many read the Scriptures in a careless way. The severity of God's judgments are turned aside by the enemy of their soul. We fear that too many people are to-day building hopes of heaven upon an experience of years ago. They will talk of the time when they found the Savior and enjoyed his love. But now they have become formal and do not sit in impartial judgment upon their actions. The holy apostle said, "Examine yourselves, whether ye be in the faith; prove your own selves." 2 Cor. 13: 5.

Closely examine your actions, your life, your nature, and prove your spiritual condition by the Word of God. Thousands to-day are deceived and on the broad way to eternal night and woe because they never stop to reason and to carefully examine their lives and spiritual condition in what light and knowledge they have of the Scriptures. How many will read, "Love not the world, neither the things that are in the world; if any man love the world the love of the Father is not in him," and pass on with a heart filled with the love of the world, consoling themselves that they are on their way to heaven. If they were but serious enough to examine their hearts they would feel the condemnation of God's Spirit as they read such texts, but ofttimes when they are brought to any consideration they will search for evidence to neutralize their guilt. They will again read, "Man shall give an account of every idle word," and go on talking foolishly and jesting, seeking to believe they are God's own children. And thus goes the world.

If you value your soul and hope of heaven, see to it that your life is in strict accordance with every requirement of the Scriptures. People are having idle talk, impure thoughts, evil surmising, feelings of pride, envy and hatred. They are speaking evil of their neighbors, laying up their treasures upon earth, loving the world and self, rendering evil for evil, backbiting, reveling, and professing to be traveling the narrow way that leads to eternal rest the same as if there was no Bible. Such have no examination of their lives, and should they have they use some satanic sophistry to gloss their sin. "Who is a wise man and endued with knowledge?" It is he that shows out of a godly life that he is a Christian. It is he that carefully examines every act and thought and word and by Heaven's grace tolerates nothing in his life in opposition to the Word of God. Careful examination is an important factor in our spiritual prosperity. By carefully watching our life we can detect its defects and then by earnest prayer these defects can be removed and we grow up into the image of God. If you hold but little or no examination of your conduct there may be many imperfections in your ways of life displeasing to God, and yet unknown to you. You will find it beneficial to frequently seclude yourself from the busy whirl of life, and enter into profound meditation and careful examination.

We will suggest a few general questions, which may help you in your retrospection. Have my meditations been pure and acceptable to God through this day? Have I not spoken one idle word? Am I as thankful to God for blessings as I should be? Has there been any feeling of pride in my heart? Has there been any feeling of impatience within me? Have I felt and manifested any selfishness? Have I had a due regard for the welfare and happiness of others? Have my devotions been spiritual and full of reverence? Do I love God? Am I dead to sin? Do I love secret prayer and the reading of the Bible? Do I feel as deeply as I should the sins of this lost world? Have I spent my money for self and withheld from God? All told, what have I done for Jesus? These and many other questions the Christian may ask himself to see if he is in the faith.

BACKSLIDINGS.

In the chapter of "Spiritual Culture" we have included the subject of Backsliding, not that backsliding is in any sense advantageous to spiritual development, but it is our certain destiny if we do not assiduously employ the means necessary to our growth in grace. By *backsliding* is meant the gradual turning back or away from God; to apostatize. The Savior gives us warning to "watch and pray," that we "enter not into temptation." The tempter will lay in your pathway all things possible to induce you to turn away from God. He will suggest that it is not necessary to pray so much, and we do not have to keep such a strict vigil over our lives and govern and rule the whole by the Word of God. He may tell you that now since you are saved you are safe. God is able to keep you, and you have nothing now to do but to silently fold your arms and sail to heaven on "flowery beds of ease." There never was a soul created of God or recreated by his Spirit, not excepting the Savior himself, since the day Adam was made of the dust, to this present time, but what Satan has endeavored, by lies and machinations to turn him away from God. Thousands of millions have gone down the rapids of negligence and carelessness, and been lost in the whirlpool of a cold, formal religion.

Some teach that the soul once born of God can

never apostatize. "Once in grace always in grace," is the manner in which they state it. We are fully persuaded that the individual who teaches such a doctrine is wholly ignorant of grace and devoid of God's enlightening Spirit. What would be the need of Christians being warned to "watch and pray, lest they enter into temptation," if there be no possibility of being overcome by it? If there is never a return to sin after regeneration, why does John say to his little children, "If any man sin, we have an advocate with the Father, Jesus Christ the righteous"? 1 John 2:1.

The reader will not understand us to favor the teaching that Christians must of necessity occasionally commit sin and that none live a sinless life. It is impossible for man to be committing sin and at the same time be a Christian. A sinning Christian is a phenomenon never known in the kingdom of grace. The Scriptures plainly teach that when once we enter a state of grace, we should always, by living a pure, holy life, continue in the same. But the teaching that when we once enter a state of grace we always remain in that state, no matter what we do, is certainly very foreign to the Holy Scriptures and soul deluding. God spoke by the mouth of an Old Testament prophet nearly six hundred years before the coming of "grace and truth" by the Savior, saying, "When a righteous man doth turn from his righteousness, and commit iniquity, and I lay a stumbling-block before him, he shall die: because thou hast not given him warning, he shall die in his sin, and his righteousness which he hath done shall not be remembered." Ezek. 3:20. What need be, and what can be, plainer than this text? Here iniquity and sin are used interchangeably and are perfectly synonymous. If a righteous man (one in possession of grace) commits sin his righteousness is no longer remembered. This is as much as to say he is no longer in grace, but is fallen. In the next verse this holy seer receives words from the mouth of the Almighty and gives the righteous man warning that he sin not. If he does not sin he shall live. It is sin that brings death to the soul. Ezek. 18:4. It is sin that separates us from God. Isa. 59:2. It is sin that causes our names to be blotted out of the book of life. Ex. 32:33. It is sin that withholds good things from us. Jer. 5:25. It is sin that destroys grace. Rom. 6:1, 2.

What is sin? Sin is the transgression of God's law. 1 John 3:4. Who in all the earth has become so boldly defiant that he can in the face of clear and plain Scriptural statements testify that he is in a state of grace when he is living in known violation of some of God's commandments? His boldness will forsake him and he wither like the frail flower beneath the hoary frost when he comes into the awful majestic presence of a righteous Creator in that great avenging day.

One of the inspired writers of the New Testament exhorts Christians to give all diligence that we add virtue to our faith, and knowledge to our virtue, and temperance to our knowledge, and to temperance patience, and to patience godliness, and to godliness brotherly kindness, and to brotherly kindness charity. 2 Pet. 1:5-7. In the following verses he tells us if these things abound in us we shall be neither barren nor unfruitful in the knowledge of our Lord, and if we do these things we shall never fall. Does not this obviously imply that if we do not do them that we shall fall? Dear reader, if you are now a Christian and feel the glowing of God's pure love in your heart, if you neglect to employ the means for growth in grace that the Bible commands, that certain you will backslide, or fall from grace. You may retain a form of worship, but you will be devoid of spirituality and your worship be unacceptable. We are commanded to "grow in grace." 2 Pet. 3:18. In the verse above we are warned against being led away by the error of the wicked and falling from our own steadfastness.

Now it is a well established fact in the very nature of things that it would be impossible to grow if there was no possibility of a decline. If there be no retrogression, there can be no progression. The beloved John from the lonely isle writes unto the church of Ephesus and tells them that God had somewhat against them because they had left their first love.

He tells them to remember from whence they are fallen and repent. They once enjoyed the love of God—they were spiritual. His redeeming grace had removed the guilt of sin, but now they are fallen. He that hath an ear, let him hear.

How often the apostle Paul warns the Christian against backsliding. His motto was, "I press toward the mark for the prize of the high calling of God in Christ Jesus." Phil. 3:14. In writing to the Colossians he says, "Luke, the beloved physician, and Demas," greet you. A greeting was sent from Demas by Paul to the Colossians in the year 64, A. D. In writing his letter to Philemon, A. D. 64, Paul says, "There salute thee Epaphras, my fellow prisoner in Christ Jesus; Marcus, Aristarchus, Demas, Lucas, my fellow laborers." ver. 23, 24. Demas was one of Paul's coworkers, and undoubtedly enjoyed the experience of salvation by grace. In writing to Timothy two years later Paul says, "For Demas hath forsaken me, having loved this present world." 2 Tim. 4:10.

As on the other subjects of this volume many more texts and strong points of reasoning could be given to fixedly establish the New Testament teaching of the possibilities of spiritual degeneration and death, but we conclude that we have made all plain to the understanding of every candid mind. It has not been our purpose to exhaust any subject. It has not been our expectation to convince many gainsayers, but to bring light to the hearts which the Lord has prepared.

One text of Scripture used by propagators of the doctrine, "We can never fall from grace," is found in 1 John 3:9, and reads thus: "Whosoever is born of God doth not commit sin; for his seed remaineth in him: and he can not sin, because he is born of God." We believe it is safe to always give the Scriptures the plainest, simplest meaning when it does not conflict with the Word of God elsewhere. We should never mystify a text, but accept it as it reads. In 1 John 2:1, the author of this epistle says, "My little children, these things write I unto you, that ye sin not. And if any man sin, we have an advocate with the Father, Jesus Christ the righteous." Certainly every reader understands John to here teach that it is possible for man to sin, or in other words, no man in this life passes beyond the possibilities of sin. Now to understand him to say in the ninth verse of the third chapter that when we are once born of God we can not possibly sin, makes him to teach contradictory doctrines. Such we know he does not do, and since 1 John 2:1 is too plain to be misunderstood, we must look about to harmonize with it, in the most simple way, 1 John 3:9. We will quote Rotherham on this text: "No one that hath been begotten of God doeth sin, because his seed in him abideth, and he can not be sinning, because of God has he been begotten." To be begotten of God is to be pardoned or saved from sin.

The seed (the Christ-life) abides in the soul in the regenerated state. The seeds of life are supplanted by the seeds of death when we commit sin. No one is born of God when spiritual life has been destroyed by sin. No man can be "sinning" and be a child of God. One who has been saved may be overcome and commit sin, but when he does so he is not God's child. This text does not teach the impossibility of committing sin after we are born of God, but only the impossibility of committing sin and being a Christian.

CHAPTER XII.
THE COURSE OF THE WORLD.

Unmistakably there exists a wide gulf of separation between the children of God and the children of the world. Christ is the only avenue of escape from the world. The wide, open door of salvation is the exit. He who would return from the blissful shores of Christianity to the beggarly elements of the world can do so only on the transporting barges of Satan. As a tree is known by its fruits, so is a true follower of Christ. The fruit borne by a Christian is directly opposite in its nature to the fruit borne by the worldling. It is not the profession merely that produces the separation, but it is the manner of life. The Son of God is the great exemplar of Christianity. Just what true Christian principles did in him will in the very nature of things do for all who possess like principles. We are forced to the conclusion that the professed follower of Christ is destitute of Christian principles when he delights himself in worldliness. Jesus said of himself, "I am not of this world." John 8:23. He says of his followers, "If ye were of the world, the world would love his own: but because ye are not of the world, but I have chosen you out of the world, therefore the world hateth you." John 15:19.

Paul bears testimony to his separation from the world by the grace of God. In Eph. 2:2, 3 he speaks of the time when he lived among those who were worldly. He says, "Wherein [in sin] in time past ye walked according to the course of this world, according to the prince of the power of the air, the spirit that now worketh in the children of disobedience: among whom also we all had our conversation in times past in the lusts of our flesh, fulfilling the desires of the flesh and of the mind; and were by nature the children of wrath, even as others." In the next two verses he testifies to the effects of saving grace: "But God, who is rich in mercy, for his great love wherewith he loved us, even when we were dead in sins, hath quickened us together with Christ; by grace ye are saved." It must be made obvious to all by these texts that salvation from sin by grace saves from walking according to the course of the world.

Again the apostle gives testimony: "But God forbid that I should glory, save in the cross of our

Lord Jesus Christ, by whom the world is crucified unto me, and I unto the world." Gal. 6:14. How true! When man accepts Christ he is by him separated from the world. Jesus was not of the world. He was the light of the world. The world was in darkness. Light is the opposite of darkness. Had he been of the world and like the world he would not have been a light. Christians are said to be "the light of the world," and are to shine as lights in the world. They are lights in the world because of the righteous principles they possess and manifest. They are like Jesus and in as direct contrast to the world as he. The Savior says, "I have given them thy word; and the world hath hated them, because they are not of the world, even as I am not of the world. I pray not that thou shouldest take them out of the world, but that thou shouldest keep them from the evil. They are not of the world even as I am not of the world." John 17:14-16.

It is impossible for the heart's affections to be centered upon opposing natures. For instance, it is impossible for man to admire honesty and dishonesty; to love temperance and intemperance; to enjoy peace and strife. It is equally impossible for man to both love and possess sin and righteousness. "No man can serve two masters: for either he will hate the one, and love the other; or else he will hold to the one, and despise the other. Ye can not serve God and mammon." Mat. 6:24. It is impossible to love

God and the world: "Love not the world, neither the things that are in the world. If any man love the world, the love of the Father is not in him. For all that is in the world, the lust of the flesh, and the lust of the eyes, and the pride of life, is not of the Father, but is of the world. And the world passeth away, and the lust thereof: but he that doeth the will of God abideth forever." 1 John 2: 15-17. "For do I now persuade men, or God? or do I seek to please men? for if I yet pleased men, I should not be the servant of Christ." Gal. 1: 10. Ye adulterers and adulteresses, know ye not that the friendship of the world is enmity with God? whosoever therefore will be a friend of the world is the enemy of God." Jas. 4: 4.

These are plain declarative texts. It is not meant by them that Christians do not love sinners and can not be friends to them. Christ loved and died for sinners. He visited them in their homes while here on earth, but never did he approve of their sinful ways. He never participated with them in anything that was worldly. He was not influenced by the world into any spirit of worldly merriment. He loved the souls of men, but he did not love the world. He was holy, harmless, undefiled, and separate from sinners." Heb. 7: 26. Christians, like Christ, love mankind, and are friendly and treat with respect and kindness the sinner, but never participate with him, nor become influenced in sinful, worldly ways. The affections of the Christian are set on things above. Col. 3: 1.

PERSECUTIONS.

In the early ministry of the Savior there is an intimation that the righteous shall be persecuted. It is found in these words: "Blessed are they which are persecuted for righteousness' sake: for theirs is the kingdom of heaven. Blessed are ye, when men shall revile you, and persecute you, and shall say all manner of evil against you falsely, for my sake." Mat. 5: 10, 11. From whence may the righteous expect these persecutions? We learned in the preceding subject that Christians were not of the world. We learn also by the Scriptures that they are hated by the world. Jesus was hated by the world because of the light of Christian virtue and righteousness that shone through him. Those that glorify God by reflecting the righteousness of Christ to the world will be regarded with the same feeling. "If the world hate you, ye know that it hated me before it hated you." John 15:18. In every age of the world, from the days of Cain and Abel to the present, true Christians have been hated and persecuted by the wicked, and especially by false worshipers.

We will farther quote the language of the Savior: "If ye were of the world, the world would love his own: but because ye are not of the world, but I have chosen you out of the world, therefore the world hateth you. Remember the word I said unto you, The servant is not greater than his Lord. If they have persecuted me, they will also persecute you; if they have kept my saying, they will keep yours also. But all these things will they do unto you for my name's sake, because they know not him that sent me." John 15: 19-21. When pretended worshipers of God are free from persecutions for Christ's sake it is because they are worshipers in form only, but in spirit they are worldly. In truth these people are usually foremost in persecuting the true children of God. Jesus was persecuted and hated by the very pretentious Pharisees and Sadducees. "He came unto his own, and his own received him not." John 1: 11. Those who professed to be children of Abraham sought to take the Savior's life. John 8: 39, 40. Because Jesus by a pure, holy life rebuked sin, because he in burning words of Heaven's glorious truth exposed the hypocrisy of the proud Jews, because he told them of their sins, they gnashed upon him with their teeth; they told him he had a devil; they spit upon him; they smote him; they mocked him; they placed a crown of thorns upon his brow, and were the instigators of his death.

Jesus says to his own beloved followers: "If they have persecuted me, they will also persecute you." John 15: 20. "If they have called the master of the house Beelzebub, how much more shall they call them of his household?" Mat. 10: 25. "And ye shall be hated of all men for my name's sake." Luke 21: 17. Those who live like Jesus, those who will boldly declare the truth of the gospel, and rebuke sin and hypocrisy, they shall receive persecutions from wicked men, and cold, proud-hearted professors, as did the Savior. "Yea, and all that will live godly in Christ Jesus shall suffer persecution." 2 Tim. 3:12.

Christians must suffer the taunts of a sinful world, but they "rejoice, inasmuch as ye are partakers of Christ's sufferings; that, when his glory shall be revealed, ye may be glad also with exceeding joy. If ye be reproached for the name of Christ, happy are ye; for the Spirit of glory and of God resteth upon you." 1 Pet. 4:13, 14. "Blessed are ye when men shall hate you, and when they shall separate you from their company, and shall reproach you, and cast out your name as evil, for the Son of man's sake. Rejoice ye in that day, and leap for joy: for, behold, your reward is great in heaven: for in the like manner did their fathers unto the prophets." Luke 6:22, 23.

One evening, shortly after God by his saving grace had separated us from the world and bestowed his righteousness upon us, we for Christ's sake received insults and abuse from the wicked. We turned away from our persecutors and entered the privacy of our home, when a rich glory rested in such a heavenly sweetness upon our souls that we cried out, "O God, why am I so wonderfully blessed?" The answer came: "If ye be reproached for the name of Christ, happy are ye; for the Spirit of glory and of God resteth upon you." "Rejoice ye in that day and leap for joy." The grace and glory that was poured out upon our soul on this occasion would have made the coals and flames of martyrdom a bed of sweet repose.

Stephen as he faced death at the hands of cruel persecutors, saw the glory of God and the heavens opened and saw the Son of man for whose sake he was now stoned. Paul and Silas with their feet made fast in the stocks at midnight prayed and sang praises to God. Is it not an occasion of wonder and astonishment how the bigoted zeal of deceived and blinded, high-minded professors leads them to become the most vile persecutors of the righteous? Paul persecuted the church of God and wasted it. He thought he was doing God's service. The children of God in every age have received their persecutions from religious bigots, and so will it ever be. We rejoice to be counted worthy to suffer for Jesus' sake. We glory in the midst of tribulations. The Spirit of God and of glory rests upon the devoted Christian in affliction's furnace, and a bright, blessed hope of great eternal reward ever cheers and nerves his faltering soul. He, who, in this dark world will suffer with the Savior shall share a blissful eternity with him.

.

AMUSEMENTS.

The affections of a Christian's heart are set on things above, and not on things on the earth. Col. 3:2. The entertainments, such as suppers, festivals, parties, concerts, regardless of what may be the ultimate object, are engaged in and enjoyed only by the worldly minded and graceless hearted. "She that liveth in pleasure is dead while she liveth." 1 Tim. 5:6. Those who find enjoyment in the amusements afforded by the world are without spiritual life. "Go to now, ye rich men, weep and howl for your miseries that shall come upon you. . . . Ye have lived in pleasure on the earth, and been wanton." Jas. 5:1, 5. A life of pleasure here on the earth in wantonness is directly opposed to a life with Christ. "No man can serve two masters." People who participate in and enjoy the socials, the suppers, the fairs, and picnics, the Christmas festivities and church entertainments of the present time have but little or no comprehension of true Christianity. They are ignorant of God's true character and the power and beauty of his holiness. Children of God are to live "soberly, righteously, and godly in this present world." Titus 2:12.

Revelry is one of the fruits of the flesh, which if borne in our life, or, in other words, if we engage in, Paul tells us we shall never inherit the kingdom of God. Gal. 5:21. Peter tells us that the time of his life when he walked in sin, when he indulged in the lusts of the flesh was sufficient to have wrought the will of the Gentiles, to walk in lusts and engage in revelings and banquetings. Salvation saved him from such a life, and his former worldly associates think it strange that he will not engage with them in the worldly riotousness and pleasures any longer, and because he is saved from such a course they speak evil of him. This is the substance of 1 Pet. 4:1-4. The gay scenes of a worldly life with their pleasures and mirth have no delight for the heart filled with Christian love. He who loves God has no love for worldly sports. The pleasurable society of Jesus destroys all taste for the society of the world. The Christian's walk is alone with God.

CONVERSATION.

An individual saved by grace will experience a marked change in his language. The apostle says that in the time of his life when he walked according to the world he had his conversation in the lusts of the flesh. Eph. 2:2, 3. It is true the word "conversation" in this text, and many others, is by many translators rendered "conduct," which is a more correct translation. But this is made to include the words of speech. "Out of the abundance of the heart the mouth speaketh." Mat. 12:34. Where worldliness and foolishness is lodged in the heart it will be manifest in the conversation. Gay, frivolous, foolish talk, mirthful stories, and language in jest, indicate a graceless heart. Listen at the world in conversation. Note the idle bywords, the slang phrases, the jestings, the gay, giddy, foolish expressions, the low and impure speech, which is all foreign to the kingdom of grace. Man is not to be known by his profession, but by his fruits: "Wherefore by their fruits ye shall know them." Mat. 7: 20. Thus we know regardless of profession, when man's conversation is as the above, that he is destitute of God's pure love and grace.

"Be ye holy in all manner of conversation," is the command of God's holy Word as recorded in 1 Pet. 1: 15. From a pure heart can only flow a pure and holy speech. "Let no corrupt communication proceed out of your mouth, but that which is good to the use of edifying, that it may minister grace unto the hearers." Eph. 4: 29. Our words are to be in such gravity and sincerity, in such depth of wisdom, and so flavored with the seasoning qualities of grace as to be elevating or inspiring to a higher degree of piety the listener. "Let your speech be alway with grace, seasoned with salt, that ye may know how ye ought to answer every man." Col. 4: 6. God's saving grace effects a change in the heart, and as a natural result a change in the conversation. Paul no longer walked according to the course of this world in conversation when saved by the grace of God.

Where there are amusing stories told, idle expressions, unmeaning remarks, jestings and jokings, regardless of the assumed sanctity in the hour of public worship, it is a life after the manner of the world, and betrays a heart devoid of God's sober, solemn, holy presence, and the sanctimonious appearance on sacred occasions is but an effort of the human will, and not the deep piety and spontaneous reverence of the heart. Jesus said that for every idle word that men shall speak they shall give an account thereof in the day of judgment: "For by thy words thou shalt be justified, and by thy words thou shalt be condemned." Mat. 12: 36, 37. "Young men likewise exhort to be sober-minded. In all things, showing thyself a pattern of good works: in doctrine showing uncorruptness, gravity, sincerity, sound speech, that can not be condemned." Titus 2: 6-8. "But fornication, and all uncleanness, or covetousness, let it not be once named among you, as becometh saints; neither filthiness, nor foolish talking, nor jesting, which are not convenient." Eph. 5: 3, 4. Slang phrases, gay, frivolous, foolish talking, and unholy conversation is degrading to society, disgraceful to Christianity, and a shame and a reproach to any people.

DRESS.

When the new birth is experienced a marked change is made in the life. The individual is made a new creature, old things are passed away and all things become new. The heart that loved this world is gone, and a heart filled with the love of God and heaven takes its place. The radical change effected within the heart will affect the exterior man. "Make clean the inside of the cup and platter and the outside will be clean also." "Out of the heart are the issues of life." "Out of the abundance of the heart the mouth speaketh." It is impossible for a proud heart to receive the grace of God. "God resisteth the proud, and giveth grace to the humble." 1 Pet. 5:5. The wonderful salvation of God which changes the heart will also change the manner of dress, if the dress formerly was worldly, which is very natural. The dear Lord has been so very careful to distinguish his loved children from the world and make them a shining light that he has given them plain directions how to dress. What a privilege the Christian has in obeying God in what is considered the "little things" of his Word, which however small are of such importance as to cause the eternal loss of the soul if wilfully disobeyed.

Respecting the manner of Christian dress we will quote from 1 Tim. 2:9, 10: "In like manner also, that women adorn themselves in modest apparel, with shamefacedness and sobriety; not with broided hair, or gold, or pearls, or costly array; but (which becometh women professing godliness) with good works." This is a much abused and wrested scripture. The proud-hearted, who have endeavored to persuade themselves to believe they are Christians, have surmised and planned to enforce upon themselves the conclusion that

God did not here mean what he has said. In earlier days when the human systems of religion were more consistent with the Word of God such texts were incorporated in their creeds, but so deep has been their plunge into the whirlpool of worldliness that they are rejected from both Bible and creed. Many tell us that this was for the women in the primitive days of Christianity when it was the custom to plait the hair with gold and silver strands. This is only a ready sophistry to allure the soul. We will admit it was for women in the early days of Christianity, but we deny it is any less for women and men also in any other day. With respect to Christianity some people are shamefully dishonest. All the duties and sacrifices not congenial to a proud heart they are glad to impose upon the Christians of some past or future time, but all the blessings God has promised the saint they would gladly receive in this present time.

The Christian is commanded to dress in "modest apparel" "with shamefacedness." It frequently happens that people become so boldly proud that they can dress in the height of fashion and profess to be Christians without a shame upon their face. One who is really and truly saved will dress in modest apparel, while humility, meekness, and modesty are depicted in loveliness upon their countenance. Those who adorn themselves in pearls and gold and costly array usually bear a proud, disdainful look. When redeemed by grace the fashionable dress and proud look give place to a sweet Christian modesty. A humble heart and a fashionable dress are incompatible. Shamefacedness is derived from *aidos* in the Greek, and has "modesty" and "bashfulness" for its primary meaning.

How beautifully the teachings of the apostles harmonize. Peter tells us that the Christian's adorning should be the hidden man of the heart adorned by a meek and quiet spirit. This man in the heart, hidden as he is, does however reveal himself. "Out of the heart are the issues of life." When the heart is meek and humble, lowliness, gentleness, and modesty will be seen in the countenance. A meek, modest, Christlike countenance under a fashionably decorated hat is the greatest incongruity. With shamefacedness the Christian is to be adorned with sobriety.

Fashionable dress is directly the opposite of sobriety. This word is translated from the Greek word *sophron*, which is properly defined, soundness of mind. The weary toil and labor that many undergo to earn money and then make the unnecessary expenditure in buying costly, fashionable dress does certainly betray a lack of wisdom, which might in reality be termed an unsoundness of mind. Gold and pearls and costly array is intemperance in dress. Instead of dressing in sobriety many are crazed or drunken on the spirit of worldliness in dress. There is a beautiful consistency in Christianity, but how inconsistent with divine things is the expenditure of money for the adornment of the physical being. No one can spend money for gold rings and chains and charms, for pearls and beads, for plumed hats, and such like, with the number around that are destitute, penniless, and starving, without incurring the displeasure of a merciful God. Man shall have to give an account in the day of awful judgment how he has expended the money the Lord has entrusted to his care. In the purchasing of any unnecessary article of dress there will be a reproving of the Spirit unless the heart is so intoxicated with the love of self that it is unconscious of the things and voice of God.

Ah, how shamefully inconsistent with the tenderheartedness and sympathizing spirit of Christianity in this lavishing of charms and adornments upon self! Our dress should be only such as is necessary for protection and health. Going about in the world doing good in all humility of heart, modest and unassuming in our manners and dress, making ourselves as little conspicuous as possible, but lifting up Jesus everywhere, is the true Christian life.

SECRET ORDERS.

The present-day institutions known as "Secret Orders," are of an earthly, worldly origin. They are one of the things of this world which man can not love and continue in the love of God. Within those secret organizations are bundled together by strong oaths the professed Christian, the infidel, the lawyer, the doctor, the saloon-keeper, the gambler, and almost every character upon the earth. By the bonds of this secret union the preacher is made a brother with an infidel. The apostle Paul tells us, "Be ye not unequally yoked together with unbelievers: for what fellowship hath righteousness with unrighteousness? and what communion hath light with darkness? and what concord hath Christ with Belial? or what part hath he that believeth with an infidel?" 2 Cor. 6: 14, 15.

The preacher who professes to believe in God is here having a part with an infidel contrary to the Word of God. You who are professing to be a light in the world, how can you in the fear of God take the oaths necessary to make you a member of a secret order? How can you join in the worldly hurrah and laughter, and foolish, ungodly pranks as played upon the candidate within the secret walls? What do you think of a preacher, or layman, becoming the laughing-stock of infidels, lawyers, saloon-keepers, drunkards, and gamblers, as he trembles beneath the blindfold? What kind of light are they letting shine? I appeal to your reason and common sense. Is it Christlike? Do you think Jesus would engage in such dark works? Some have charged the Savior with being a freemason. Such is a libelous statement. In Isa. 45: 19, the Lord says, "I have not spoken in secret, in a dark place of the earth: . . . I the Lord speak righteousness, I declare things that are right." Christ only speaks the things that are right and never the dark, ungodly oaths and sayings of the secret lodge. Again, the Savior said, "I spake openly to the world; I ever taught in the synagogue, and in the temple, whither the Jews always resort; and in secret have I said nothing." John 18:20. Jesus spake nothing in secret, and to charge him with having connection with the dark, secret mysteries of masonry is as slanderous as the charge made by the people who said, "Thou hast a devil." John 7:20. The Savior not only knew that men would, in order to defend their unrighteous systems, charge him with having a devil, but he also knew that for the same purpose men would charge him with having connections with such systems; therefore he said, to uncloak the falsity of such charges, "Wherefore if they shall say unto you, Behold, he is in the desert; go not forth: behold, he is in the secret chambers; believe it not." Mat. 24:26. Jesus gives commandment to preach upon the housetop what ye hear in the ear. Mat. 10:27. "For God shall bring every work into judgment, with every secret thing, whether it be good, or whether it be evil." Eccl. 12:14.

It is not the mission of this work to reveal the awful oaths and secret works of these various orders. Other men by many volumes have done this. We only hope to help you to see that secrecy is contrary to the Bible and the Spirit of Christ and Christianity. It is a thing of the world and conducted on a worldly basis. Connected with many of these orders are life insurances—a thing of the world. The Christian is separated from the world and Christ becomes his all in all. To make prominent the good qualities of their secret systems men tell us of their obligations to help their brother and his family. How these orders provide help for a man in time of need, and how true each member is to his obligation, etc. Such might do if there were no God nor Christianity. Secrecy provides only for its own members. Salvation provides for all. A member of a secret order is under no obligation from his order to visit a poor sick man by the way who is not a member of his order, but is under obligation to visit and care for a sick fellow member, though he be rich. We see no Christianity in this. We see no humanity. It is having respect of persons, forbidden by Scripture. Humanity, and much more Christianity, will not only send man to do good to the rich, but to the poor also, be they of any class or nation. A man that is a Christian will visit the sick and afflicted, no matter what may be their station in life.

If a man thinks he is a light in the world because he is true to the obligations of his secret order in visiting and administering to the needs of his sick brother, he is very much deceived. Such is a false light. When a man has to place himself under such solemn oaths to do good, it proves that he has but little or no humanity. "Do good to all men," is the spirit of Christianity. A man need not take the obligations of a secret order to be furnished with the qualifications for doing good. The Word of God is all that is needed for reproof, correction, and instruction, that a man may be thoroughly furnished unto all good works. 2 Tim. 3:16, 17. A man need not seek membership in some secret organization in order to be provided for in his old days, or his family in case of his death. The Psalmist says, "I have been young, and now am old; yet have I not seen the righteous forsaken, nor his seed begging bread." Paul says, "But my God shall supply all your need." Phil. 4:19. "Wherefore come out from among them, and be ye separate, saith the Lord, and touch not the unclean thing; and I will receive you, and will be a Father unto you, and ye shall be my sons and daughters, saith the Lord Almighty." 2 Cor. 6:17, 18. "They are not of the world, even as I am not of the world." John 17:16.

CHAPTER XI.
THE DOMESTIC RELATION.

When we speak of home life with its relations and duties we are not digressing from the subject of gospel light. Nowhere does the light of Christianity shine so peaceful and beautiful as in the home. Nowhere is the power of its influence so felt as in the home circle. The public worship of Christians is an inspiring scene, but nothing apparently is so heavenly as the sacred family altar. A father and mother whose hearts are filled with holy love together with happy, obedient children bowing together at the shrine of devotion is the most imposing scene the eye and heart can witness.

MARRIAGE.

The union of man and woman in marriage is the work of the Creator. God saw after he had created man that it was not good for him to be alone. Such was his constitution. So he made a helpmeet for him. God from the rib of man made woman and brought her unto him, who said, "This is now bone of my bones, and flesh of my flesh: she shall be called Woman, because she was taken out of Man. Therefore shall a man leave his father and his mother, and shall cleave unto his wife: and they shall be one flesh." Gen. 2: 22-24.

In conjunction with the divine institution of marriage there is also a legal institution. While the civil contract is acceptable unto God by way of preventing promiscuous sexual intercourse, it is powerless to make both one flesh and bone. It is only the power of God that can make two hearts to beat as one. By the power of his grace he makes Christians of "one heart and one soul," and of man and woman he makes "one flesh and bone." The apostle to illustrate the blessed union of Christ and the church makes use of the union of man and wife. "They two shall be one flesh." Eph. 5:31. "Man shall leave his father and mother and shall be joined unto his wife." The union between husband and wife is stronger than between parent and child. The all-wise God has a design in all his works. He reveals to man in his Word his purpose in the union of man and wife. One object in the marriage union, as we have before said, is to prevent promiscuous sexual commerce. "Nevertheless, to avoid fornication, let every man have his own wife, and let every woman have her own husband." 1 Cor. 7:2. The union of man and woman is a holy and sacred institution, however the union of Christ and the church is still a higher and more important work of God. Therefore Paul advises all who can live a pure life in an unmarried state they can be more useful to God, for he careth for the things that belong to the Lord, how he may please the Lord. But he that is married careth for the things that are of the world, how he may please his wife.

Another object in the divine mind for uniting male and female is for the purpose of procreation. "And God blessed them, and God said unto them, Be fruitful, and multiply and replenish the earth." Gen. 1:28. Alas! how few properly reverence and esteem the divine purpose. Marriages are too often contracted for the comforts of a home, or for affluence, or for elevation in society, or, worst of all, for the gratification of lustful desires. Of such too many murderously resort to the devices of art to thwart the designs of the Creator. Procreation was the highest purpose in the divine mind for the union of man and wife. For this purpose he implanted in their natures a sexual desire. They who avoid to act this part in life come short of the purpose of their creation.

DIVORCE.

Because the contracting parties at the marriage shrine do not feel and have not properly considered the obligations and responsibilities of a married life, but enter in from selfish desires, then finding it attended with cares and responsibilities they do not care to bear, they seek opportunities for release. The legal union is often severed by the same authority as was given. But as the civil power can not create two hearts into one, nor make of twain "one flesh and bone," neither can such authorities create two of what has been made one. The law of Heaven is, What God hath joined together, let not man put asunder. Mat. 19:6.

The Word of God fixes death as the limit to the bond of union. "For the woman which hath a husband is bound by the law to her husband so long as he liveth; but if the husband be dead, she is loosed from the law of her husband. So then if while her husband liveth, she be married to another man, she shall be called an adulteress: but if her husband be dead, she is free from that law; so that she is no adulteress, though she be married to another man." Rom. 7: 2, 3. "The wife is bound by the law as long as her husband liveth; but if her husband be dead, she is at liberty to be married to whom she will; only in the Lord." 1 Cor. 7: 39. "And he [Jesus] saith unto them, Whosoever shall put away his wife, and marry another, committeth adultery against her. And if a woman shall put away her husband, and be married to another, she committeth adultery." Mark 10: 11, 12. In Mat. 19: 9, we read, "And I say unto you, whosoever shall put away his wife, except it be for fornication, and shall marry another, committeth adultery: and whoso marrieth her which is put away doth commit adultery."

Some have thought there was a lack of harmony in the teaching of Jesus as recorded by Mark and Matthew. Mark makes the plain statement that whosoever puts away his wife and marries another commits adultery. He makes no exceptions. Matthew says, "Except it be for fornication." There is no disagreement here. It is the prominent thought each has that makes the difference in the statements. The truth that Mark wishes to teach is that there is no just cause for a man marrying who has a divorced wife. The plain statement is if a man puts away his wife and marries another he commits adultery. There is no exception. There is no just cause for his marrying, and if he does it is adultery, no matter what may be the cause of divorcement. The truth that Matthew teaches is that there is one just cause for putting away the wife. This is a just cause for putting her away, but not for marrying again. Every one that divorces his wife, even though it be for fornication, and marries another violates Mark 10:11 and Luke 16:18. A man may put away his wife for fornication, and not transgress a single text in the Bible. Fornication is the only just cause for man to put away his wife, or the wife the husband.

Some have fallen into the dangerous error of putting away the wife because the Scriptures say, "Be ye not unequally yoked together with unbelievers." 2 Cor. 6:14. This is a wrong application of this text. No doubt but it does forbid the unmarried Christian yoking up with an unbeliever, as in 1 Cor. 7:39 the woman whose husband is dead is at liberty to marry whom she will; only in the Lord. However, it does not teach the breaking of the marriage yoke. Matthew gives the only cause. Paul says, "If any brother hath a wife that believeth not, and she be pleased to dwell with him, let him not put her away. And the woman which hath a husband that believeth not, and if he be pleased to dwell with her, let her not leave him." 1 Cor. 7:12, 13.

A man once told us that God showed him to leave his wife. (She was a true wife.) He was decidedly mistaken and should have tried the spirit. "What therefore God hath joined together, let not man put asunder." The word joined is from the Greek *suzeugnuo*, and means "yoked together." This yoke man can not break. When God by his saving grace unites a soul with Christ, no man can break the bond of union. Sin, and sin only, will sever the tie that binds them together. When God unites husband and wife into one flesh and bone, no civil court can break the bond. When woman has become so untrue to her husband and false to her marriage vow as to have sexual connection with another man, God allows such an unchaste sin, and such a sin only, to dissolve the union. Why is fornication the only just cause for disuniting husband and wife? Why is sin the only cause of separation between Christ and the Christian? It is because the design of God in sending his Son to the world was to destroy and prevent sin. Then of necessity when his purpose fails there can be no union. The design of the Almighty in instituting marriage was to secure a legitimate population of the world, or to prevent the lewd, indiscriminate sexual intercourse. When this purpose fails the object of marriage fails, and there can be no union.

> Brooklets joining form the river,
> Rivers joining form the sea;
> Love uniting hearts together
> Beat as one eternally.

God by law of his creation
   Creates in one the happy twain;
Hand and heart they are united
   As they pass adown life's stream.

See the flowers greet each other,
   And the sunlight kiss the sea;
See the waves clasp one another,
   Why not hearts united be?

Birds in springtime mate each other,
   'Tis a law decreed above;
For the sake of procreation
   God creates connubial love.

DUTIES OF THE HUSBAND TO THE WIFE.

Great are the responsibilities resting upon the husband. The wife is termed the "weaker vessel," unto whom the husband is to give honor and to dwell with according to knowledge. 1 Pet. 3:7. The Word of God gives instruction how the husband should dwell with the wife. It is his duty to glean knowledge from the same and dwell with her accordingly. He is her example. She looks unto him as her instructor, both in precept and example. She is to be honored by receiving the benefits, by way of counsel, support and protection, of his superior strength. He in his strong, courageous construction, and she in her feminine frailty, are both heirs together of the grace of life. When each understand their true position and dwell together according to knowledge their prayers rise unhindered to the throne of grace.

The Scriptures grant man authority over the wife: "But I would have you know, that the head of every man is Christ; and the head of the woman is the man; and the head of Christ is God." 1 Cor. 11:3. "For the husband is the head of the wife, even as Christ is the head of the church." Eph. 5:23. You understand the protection and care Christ has for his bride—the church; in like manner man is responsible for the protection and care of the wife. He takes the position of head of the wife as Christ takes the position of head of the church—in love. "Husbands, love your wives, even as Christ also loved the church, and gave himself for it." Eph. 5:25. "Husbands, love your wives, and be not bitter against them." Col. 3:19. The love of the husband must be as deep and true for the wife as the love of Christ for the church. He gave himself for it. Man considers not his life for the care and protection of his wife when he loves her. Where there is bitterness there is wanting true love. Bitterness drives love and heaven away from the home. "Let all bitterness, and wrath, and anger, and clamor, and evil speaking, be put away from you, with all malice: and be ye kind one to another, tender-hearted." Eph. 4:31, 32.

Man should take the wife into his confidence and entrust her with the secrets of his private life. He should respect and regard her counsel. Jacob has given us an example. Gen. 31. Elkanah has set us an example of comforting the wife. 1 Sam. 1:8. It is a comparatively easy thing, unless you are abounding in the love of God, to become neglectful of the comfort, welfare and happiness of the wife. She in her tender, sympathetic nature seeks for attention and delights in being loved. Do not therefore be sparing in your attention toward her. The fond, affectionate wife will meet the duties, trials, afflictions and responsibilities of life without a murmur does she but know that she is loved. Enter into her joys and sorrows with a regard. "Let thy fountain be blessed: and rejoice with the wife of thy youth.... Be thou ravished always with her love." Prov. 5: 18, 19. Malachi exhorts the husband to faithfulness. "Yet ye say, Wherefore? Because the Lord hath been witness between thee and the wife of thy youth, against whom thou hast dealt treacherously: yet is she thy companion, and the wife of thy covenant." chap. 2:14. Such are some of the duties of a husband, and he who has cast aside regard for such duties, is a stranger to the covenant of grace.

DUTIES OF THE WIFE TO THE HUSBAND.

It is a just cause of lament that so comparatively few wives have a perfect knowledge of their rightful position in the domestic circle. We will briefly give a few texts from the Holy Book showing the wife her true place in the family and her duty toward her husband, trusting God to give her a desire to be all that a wife should be. The fundamental principle is love. Without sincere, conjugal love she can scarcely fill the mission of wife. When woman becomes a wife she takes a position fraught with the greatest responsibilities. Oh, how many idle dreamers take such positions with little feeling, thought or comprehension of its responsibilities, and pass through life away below the true mission of a wife. The instruction of the inspired apostle is that the young women be sober, love their husbands, love their children, be discreet, chaste, keepers at home, good, obedient to their own husbands, that the word of God be not blasphemed. Titus 2:4, 5.

Such are the demands of the young wife made by the Word of God. The demand made of the aged wives is that they set a proper example in all these things. When they do not fill these demands the Word of God is blasphemed. When wives professing to be Christians and a light in the world are neglectful of home, of husband and children, they bring Christianity into disrepute. Wives are commanded to be sober. Instead of sobriety how often we see them gay, silly, foolish and worldly-minded. Their thoughts are trashy, and their conversation the same; talking about one another, busybodies, no depth of thought or feeling of their mission in life, but are concerned more about the fashions and society than the duties of home. Such characters disgrace the cause of Christ. True love will manifest itself, and where the wife loves the husband, home is her dearest place. Her great life work is to make home happy and attractive. She has a deep regard for the comforts of her lord, and love lightens all her labor for him. The true wife loves her children, which will also find its manifestation.

Among the coarse and vulgar we have heard mothers in provocation speak thus to their children: "Haven't you any sense?" "You are the foolishest thing I ever saw." "I'll box your head off." "I'll beat you to death." "I wish you were dead," and other like expressions. Such is awful language, but it has escaped the lips of many a mother. Before the public they like to appear gentle, mild and sweet tempered, while in the privacy of their homes they are snarly, snappish and cross. When it pleases God to remove one of their little ones to a more peaceful home above they mourn most bitterly; more because of remorse of conscience than from a fountain of pure love. There is, however, many a mother who longs to be tender and kind to her loved ones, but because of her bondage to the tyrannical power of an ill, impatient temper, she utters, under provocation, unfeeling, inhuman speech toward her little ones. In her calmer hours she weeps because of bondage. To all such we would say, There is help for you in God. Jesus can set you free. Yield yourself to him. He will pardon your sins and sweeten your life by his grace. To be discreet, wise, prudent, selecting the best means to accomplish a noble purpose is the wife's mission in her home.

The wife is a type of the church. "Let us be glad and rejoice, and give honor to him: for the marriage of the Lamb is come, and his wife hath made herself ready." Rev. 19:7. "Come hither, and I will show thee the bride, the Lamb's wife. And he carried me away in the spirit to a great and high mountain, and showed me that great city, the holy Jerusalem, descending out of heaven from God." Rev. 21:9, 10. The husband is to love the wife as Christ loved the church; and as the church reverences and obeys, is faithful and subject to Christ, the wife is to reverence, obey and be faithful and subject to her husband. "Nevertheless let every one of you in particular so love his wife even as himself, and the wife see that she reverence her husband." "Wives, submit yourselves unto your own husbands, as unto the Lord. Therefore as the church is subject unto Christ, so let the wives be to their own husbands in every thing." Eph. 5:22, 24. "Wives, submit yourselves unto your own husbands, as it is fit in the Lord." Col. 3:18. "Likewise, ye wives, be in subjection to your own husbands; that, if any obey not the word, they also may without the word be won by the conversation [conduct] of the wives." 1 Pet. 3:1.

Such is the true position of the wife, giving the husband reverence. This means to fear. Not the slavish fear, but a fear in love, like as one would fear God whom he loved with all his heart. Fear to purposely displease him. Fear to wilfully neglect him. Fear to obstinately disobey him. To be in subjection with reverence. Such words are full of solid thought, and we would ask every wife to wisely consider them, especially if she places any value upon Christianity. The husband is to command in love. She is to obey in fear. He is to govern without giving vexation, and she is to be in subjection without feeling herself a slave. He is to watch over her conduct and guard her from every act that would be damaging to her character or her soul. She is to trust in him, and obey.

> Let the wife be in subjection,
> Let the husband give protection;
> He to honor, love, defend,
> She to trust him to the end.

The humble apostle, after exhorting the wives to be in subjection to their husbands, commands them to not adorn themselves by plaiting the hair or wearing gold or apparel. 1 Pet. 3:3. "But let it be the hidden man of the heart, in that which is not corruptible, even the ornament of a meek and quiet spirit, which is in the sight of God of great price." ver. 4. Can the wife in the fear of God, profess to sincerely love her husband, and to be a true wife, when she is spending his hard earnings for gold and pearls, and costly apparel for adornment? he to struggle against poverty, and she to embarrass him to satisfy a proud, selfish heart? Such is not true love to husband nor to God. The wife who adorns herself with modesty and sobriety (1 Tim. 2:9), with a meek and quiet spirit (1 Pet. 3:4, 5), with good works (1 Tim. 2:10) is a blessing to her husband. "A virtuous woman is a crown to her husband." Prov. 12:4. "Who can find a virtuous woman? for her price is far above rubies. The heart of her husband doth safely trust in her, so that he shall have no need of spoil. She will do him good and not evil all the days of her life." Prov. 31:10-12. "A prudent wife is from the Lord." Prov. 19:14.

DUTY OF PARENTS TO CHILDREN.

Great are the responsibilities of the husband. Great are the responsibilities of the wife, but greater are the responsibilities of parents. Father and mother, God lays a responsibility upon you as you receive your new-born child. A precious little immortal soul, whose eternal destiny depends largely upon you. The proper training of children is attended with many difficulties, and every parent certainly needs instruction from God. Your child is given you from God, and you in return should give him trustingly to God, like a mother of olden time: "For this child I prayed; and the Lord hath given me my petition which I asked of him: therefore also I have lent [see margin] him to the Lord; as long as he liveth he shall be lent to the Lord." 1 Sam. 1:27, 28. This is the consecration of children to God, which is the first duty of parents.

The successful training of a child, especially in the first years of its life, is due more to example than to commandment. The influence of example upon youthful minds is rarely comprehended. We are commanded to be an example in faith, purity, conversation, charity, spirit, and to be a pattern of good works. It is the parents' duty to love their children. Titus 2:4. Perhaps every parent thinks and is ready to say, "I love my child." True love as required by the Bible comprehends more than you may have been aware. They who indulge their children in a worldly life do not love them as the Bible commands. Because the priest Eli did not restrain his children from the ways of sin, God sent an awful judgment upon him. 1 Sam. 3. If parents love their children as they should they will do the very best thing for them. Now the instructions given in the Bible are the safest and best to follow.

As you looked into the face of this thine own child did you remember the little treasure was a heritage from the Lord? "Lo, children are a heritage of the Lord: and the fruit of the womb is his reward." Psa. 127:3. It may be that you were unmindful of this "fruit of the womb" being a gracious heritage from God; but such it was. In the creation of man and woman they were formed to bear offspring. When Esau and Jacob met after their long separation and enmity, Esau inquired, "Who are those with thee?" Jacob replied, "The children which God hath graciously given thy servant." Gen. 33:5. Blessed and happy is the man that can look into the face of the newly-born and feel in his heart that this is a child graciously given me of God.

Because children are a heritage from the Lord is the real secret of the joy experienced in the parents' hearts when a child is born. An angel from God's presence anoints the spirit of man with the "oil of joy" when he obeys Heaven's ordained laws of procreation. Alas! how many husbands and wives, who fear to meet the responsibilities involved thus upon them, seek to avert God's laws. And when a child is conceived they, instead of rejoicing as did Rachel, the mother of Joseph, and Mary, the mother of Jesus, sorrow in heart, thus allowing the enemy of human happiness to deprive them of the blessing God designed for them.

God, in his own mysterious way, from the mother's life and blood is creating a new life. But did you know that at the same time he was creating an immortal soul? That new-born life contains an immortal part, and very much depends upon you as to where shall be its eternal existence. We want you to feel this deep in your hearts. God has given into your charge a life and a soul. When you come to appear before him in the day of judgment then you will have to render an account of how you have dealt with your child. Oh, what awful responsibilities! What a charge! God help us! With such a sacred trust, what shall we do? Like she of olden time, who petitioned the God of heaven for a child, carry him back to the Lord and there implore grace and wisdom and guidance from above to train these little feet in the way that leads to endless joys.

Parents, as you look into the face of your slumbering child, and then along down through his life, what do you want him to become? Do you want him to grow up to manhood a poor, delicate, frail body with but little energy or vitality with which to meet the sterner duties of life? Do you want him to be indolent, shiftless, unmanly and addicted to such as will bring him to shame, ruin and death? What! would you picture such a life for my innocent boy? Such a thought is instantly banished from you. With all your heart you desire him to become a true and noble man. You want him to be strong, full of energy and vitality, of great mental and physical worth, of manly ways, of pure habits, and in every way a worthy son. Yes, that is the life you fondly picture for your son. Well, here he lies an infant in thine arms. He is at thy mercy. You can make of him about what you will. You can lead him in the paths of virtue and to a generous Christian manhood, or you can neglect him and allow him to go to shame and ruin. Let me say again that the life and destiny of your child depends largely upon you. You can make it what you will. God help and bless you.

PHYSICAL CARE.

When your child is born then comes the care of the little body. It must have food. It must have air. It must have clothing. The supplying of temporal needs is a duty that falls to the father. May he do his duty with a will and see that his child's health is not impaired by an insufficient amount of clothing or of food. "But if any provide not for his own, and especially for those of his own house, he hath denied the faith, and is worse than an infidel." 1 Tim. 5:8. The parent that will not industriously make use of every legitimate means to secure temporal comforts, does not love his child. It has been known that the awful curse of tobacco, opium and rum, have robbed the father and mother of parental love. Some may have become so in love or so in bondage to tobacco that they would rather see their child go hungry or naked than to deprive themselves of the accursed thing.

Parents should acquaint themselves with hygienic laws and teach them to their children. Show them the danger of overeating, and of too frequent eating. Parents are destroying the health of their children by irregular feeding, and by nuts and candies. Teach the little ones to avoid sitting in a cool place when heated and of retaining wet clothing. Above all, avoid giving your child tea, coffee and "soothing syrup." Paregorics and laudanums pave the way to the formation of other bad habits. They have an effect which may answer your purpose at the time, but you gain your purpose at the cost of your child's vitality. If your attention has ever been called to the evil effects of such, you can not dope your children with them without bringing condemnation to your soul.

Good health is a great blessing, and our heavenly Father wills us to observe natural health laws. Parents by carelessness can in a very short time ruin the health of their child forever. Oh, the misery and distress originating from ill health entailed upon the human family through the ignorance and carelessness of parents is appalling. Had the writer's parents compelled their child to observe health laws in his youth he would enjoy better health to-day. By proper care and help from God he has largely overcome difficulties, but does not possess the strong constitution he otherwise would.

We kindly make an earnest appeal to all parents to look well to the health of your children. If you value their happiness, and a pleasant, happy home, acquaint yourself with the laws of health, and follow them as strictly as circumstances will allow. Many parents care more for their children's appearance in public than they do for their health. Mothers following the pride of their heart instead of the laws of health expose the bodies of their children to disease. In public gatherings, in order to make a show of their rich clothing, they will not wrap them sufficiently to protect them from cold; they will deform the feet of their little ones and bring them pain in after life, because of the pride of their heart. By lacing they will mold and shape the bodies of their daughters after the fashion of the world, entailing upon them disorder and disease, weakness and woe. In all love, but without hesitancy, we declare that such shameful treatment of children is a sin and is sufficient of itself to destroy the soul.

GOVERNMENT.

Great wisdom is required in the government of children. For parents to properly govern their children they need that wisdom and direction which comes from above. There are so many different natures which must be controlled in as many different ways, making it impossible to fix certain rules for all. However all these different dispositions among our children must be met. "If any man lack wisdom, let him ask of God."

Many parents ask, "At what age shall we begin to train and govern our child?" Wisdom makes answer, "From the beginning." You can train your babe to nurse regularly, say every two hours, or to stifle his cries, you can nurse him irregularly, and make him a cross, fretful babe by over and irregular feeding. Your babe will sleep sweetly and soundly upon its little bed, but you can very early accustom it to be rocked to sleep so it will not go to sleep unless it is rocked. Nature never designed that we be tossed to and fro in order to go to sleep. What is man's experience on board a ship in a rough sea? He becomes dizzy, nervous and sick, and when he steps upon the land he walks like a drunken man. The infant's first rock in the cradle has a similar effect. Its little muscles are strained to prevent falling. Its brain is dashed about until it becomes dizzy, but which it soon learns to enjoy because of the peculiar sensation.

Your little babe sees some bright object and reaches out its little hands to take it. You know it ought not to have it. It may injure itself with it, so you say, "No, baby can not have this." Then baby begins to cry. You try to quiet him. You try to turn his mind and attention somewhere else, but, no, he keeps his eye on the forbidden object and cries the harder. At last to quiet him you give it to him, even if you have to hold to one end to keep him from hurting himself. Baby has now learned a very valuable lesson, which he is not going to forget. He has learned that if he cries long enough and hard enough he can obtain what he desires.

As he grows older he becomes more determined to have his way. When company comes you want your boy to give the rocker to the lady, but no, the little man prefers the rocker for himself. You endeavor to remove him by force, but he kicks and bites and holds tight and cries very loud, and you call him a naughty boy, and give up the struggle. Then you begin to tell the ladies about your boy, how he will have his way and you can not do anything with him; that you sometimes whip him, but it does not do him any good. You are educating your child out of your control.

If you desire your child to obey you, be kind, loving and firm. Scolding is never in order, but does great harm. Unhappy and unholy is the home where children obey only through fear. So deal with your little ones that obedience is gained through love. So rarely is such obedience obtained that many have concluded it can not be accomplished. It is natural for children to love their parents, and if parents deal with their little ones in love and kindness they can make home the most desirable place on earth to them.

To rule by physical force is not government. It is a most pitiful sight to see a child fear and tremble before a parent's stern looks and cross words. There is a way, though but few have found it, of mingling tenderness with firmness that demands obedience in respect and love. It brings a joy to the parents' hearts to behold their child obeying willingly. By the help of God such obedience can be obtained. Some one may ask, "Would you never punish a child?" Yes; it is sometimes necessary, but not so often as many have supposed. Training, and not arbitrary government is what is the more successful.

GIVE ATTENTION TO YOUR CHILD.

It takes but little to wound the tender feelings of a child. It is not the angry look and cross word only that sends the little one away in tears; but oftentimes it is neglect. What may seem to us as a very little thing, or small achievement, may be a very great thing to the child, and a notice and an encouraging word has a good and lasting effect. Your little boy has done a piece of work, and done it poorly enough to be sure, but to him it is done in the most artistic style. Do not depress his spirit by showing your disapproval, but encourage him by telling him that it does very well for a child; then kindly help him to see how he can make it still better.

You should not become so absorbed in your occupation that you can not stop to notice the newly drawn picture. If the child's interruptions are too frequent, in kindness teach him that papa is not to be interrupted now. By all means show a deep interest in your children. Help them to see that you delight to make things pleasant for them. Do not make them feel that they are servants. Have pleasant conversations with them. Read some good story to them, or better still, tell them one; not a "fairytale," but something real. We have seen parents who scarcely ever spoke to their children only when reproving. Take them with you to the meeting. Take them with you if at all convenient when you go on your charitable errand. Take them for a drive. Take them to the woods and the fields, and there tell them of God.

Many opportunities will be afforded for you to show an interest and an appreciation in your child. Give him your attention and you will win his love and obedience and make him feel that there is freedom at home. Neglect him, treat him with indifference, and you will make his little heart cold and make him feel he is your slave.

BE PATIENT WITH YOUR CHILD.

For the sake of your child, your own happiness, and the happiness of your home, be patient. In dealing with your little "olive plants," "let patience have her perfect work," and of a truth you shall "be perfect and entire wanting nothing." Much of redeeming grace is needed to enable the parent to be calm and kind under the many trying circumstances connected with the pruning and training of the "fruit of the womb." It is a source of great joy, however, to know that God's grace is sufficient for me.

Dear parents, the only remedy we have to offer you for this qualification is the sweet controlling influence of saving grace. When you have gained control of your own spirit you are far on the way to conquer the rebellious spirit of your child. How sad it is that a mother who loves her child will find sometimes a feeling of hatred in her heart against it. We have heard mothers in a time of provocation use such words as these, "You foolish thing;" You naughty little imp;" "You mean thing, I have a mind to put you out where the dogs will get you;" "You do that again and I'll give you to the bad man;" "I'll slap your head off;" "I wish you were dead," etc. How awful! Mothers, who, if their little one was sick, would gladly sit night after night and watch by its bedside—no slumber for those eyelids now, for baby is very sick—when the dear one is restored to health and provokes the mother, she uses some of the above expressions, or similar ones.

As you stand some night by the casket that contains that lifeless little body, oh, what anguish at heart as you remember the hasty words you have spoken to that dear one. How those ugly expressions ring in your ears. They will follow you for days in thought and dream. How sad that the human heart is of such disposition, but what joy to know that the precious blood of Jesus will remove all such dispositions and fill the heart with love and sweetness that will enable you to deal with your child in loving patience, even in the hour of deepest trial, and should you be called to its death bedside you can look into the pale face and then up to God without a sting of conscience. Parents, be firm, but be patient with your child. Let love shine out of every reproval and you will find it is not so difficult to train him and govern him as you supposed.

NEVER SCOLD OR THREATEN.

How heart-rending to see almost a constant contention between parents and children, parents scolding their children for almost every little thing, and threatening to "give them to the Gypsies," or to "cut off their ears," or "put a split stick on their tongues," and many other foolish and hurtful threatenings, father and mother make when they are provoked. Be always calm in your own feelings and never be hasty to speak or act. When the child really needs reproval, take him quietly and show him the evil of such things, how it will lead to other bad things, and these to others, and should he continue in that way he would grow up to be a bad man. Tell him how you love him, and how you want to see him become a good and noble man, a blessing to his parents, to the community, and to the world. Tell him you hope he will not do those bad things any more, and should he do them you would be under obligations to punish him.

If the child is reasoned with rightly the corporal punishment will not be of frequent necessity. It is a shame and a sin to act so hastily and punish your little ones in some way without patiently and coolly explaining matters.

GIVE YOUR CHILD SOME PRIVILEGE.

Do not answer, "No," to every request of your child. Allow them some privilege, let them engage in certain plays. Do not be so fastidious in your home that the little ones can not have a little play indoors. Certainly they should be taught to be clean, to remove dirt from their shoes before coming into the house, and not to tumble things all up in the room, yet they should not be expected to sit perfectly still.

When the child makes a request of you that your wisdom decides best not to grant do not answer by a decided "no," but tell the little one that you think it not best to do so, and be firm. When you tell him you do not think it best do not be persuaded out of it, and he will soon learn that your mild "I do not think it best to give you that," means just as much as a sharp "no," but his feelings will not be disturbed like they are by that hasty "no."

ALWAYS BE CALM WHEN YOU PUNISH.

When it becomes necessary to use the rod upon your child be sure you possess a calmness in your soul. It requires much grace for true parents to whip their children. Before you punish them you should show them what great wrong they have done and how God is displeased, and that you do not punish them for your own pleasure, but because you love them.

To the dear parents who read this we wish to exhort you to give great diligence in cultivating the affectionate side of your nature. Do not be careless and unmindful of the dear little ones' happiness. Do not be cold and indifferent toward them. Enter into their joys and sorrows with a warm heart. Parents oftentimes remark when their child gets hurt in some way, "Well it is good enough for you; may be it will teach you something." Oh, may that heart be softened to tender sympathy, so you will make the dear child feel how sorry you are because he has been hurt, then teach him how he must not engage in such things, and then he will avoid being injured. Your kind words of sympathy will relieve the pain by their influence upon the heart. Your cold indifferent words make deeper wounds in the heart than were made in the flesh.

Seek God in much earnest prayer to tender your affections, to refine your nature, to make you very sensitive to the feelings of your child, and to help you to love the tender "olive plants" round about thy fireside. Some day there may be a vacant chair, and there can be no sweeter joy on earth to your sorrowing heart than to know you did what you could to make the little one happy and train its feet for the glory world.

> Kind words are flowers of beauty rare;
> Keep them blooming throughout the year.

MENTAL TRAINING.

The mental, moral and spiritual training of children go hand in hand. We shall speak of them under separate chapters, but the one has a great influence upon the other. It is true, the intellectual faculties may be cultivated to a high degree while the moral powers are unimproved, but the individual is out of harmony with true manhood. The spiritual and moral being may be in a fair state of health and the mental powers very much dwarfed, but still he is not in perfect harmony with manhood as designed by the creative mind. Without a blending of the intellectual, moral and spiritual forces there can be no perfect character in the fullest sense. We do not mean by this that man must be a philosopher or a scientist to be a moral or spiritual man; but we mean for man to be a perfect character in every respect and to glorify God in the whole realm of his being, he must cultivate every talent God has given him. The created mental powers must be improved by right study. In order to know and understand God we must have a sound mind. A sound mind is helpful to the enjoyment of grace, and grace is helpful to the enjoyment of a sound mind; so to enjoy existence necessitates a soundness in every part.

It is through the mental powers that we acquaint our children with God: "Faith cometh by hearing." Parents can not be too careful about the impressions made in the mentality of their children; it may affect their morality and spirituality in the whole of after life. Select such books for them as will develop the mental faculties, something that contains food for the brain. There are certain articles of diet that do not contain sufficient nutrition for the development of the physical body. Children fed upon such diet would become weakly. There is also a certain kind of literature that contains no brain nutriment. Reading such degenerates the mental powers. Stimulants or excitants are hurtful to the physical system. All fictitious, exciting tales are hurtful to the mental system. We are persuaded it were better if the unreal, fairy stories were excluded from our common school readers and supplanted by something real. Select such literature as is pure. Reading that produces pure thought in the child's mind not only improves his moral state, but furnishes the best mental food.

Educate your children as well as you possibly can. It is a duty you owe to them and to God. Keep before them the ultimate object—a developed mind for the glory of God. Encourage your children to an education. Do not think the buying of a good book an unnecessary expenditure. Better make a physical sacrifice than a mental one. Keep your children away from the physical, mental, moral and spiritual destructive party and dance by interesting them in sound and pure literature and providing it for them. If your children show a disposition to love and desire to spend the evening at the "parties" or the "balls," get up a "reading circle" or "composition exercise" at home. God will bless you and reward you in all your efforts in this direction. Much more of importance could be said upon this subject, but with these few suggestions we will leave the interested and inventive mind to enlarge.

MORAL TRAINING.

Man is an intellectual and a moral being. By his intellectual powers he gains a knowledge of facts. By his moral faculties he experiences a sense of responsibility and a feeling of certain relations existing between him and some higher power. Your child possesses an intuitive knowledge and upon this is where your moral training begins. The little brother knows it is wrong to injure his little sister. He does not have to acquire that knowledge, he knows it intuitively. This is the foundation for your moral training, and, of course, spiritual training naturally hinges upon this; but we shall speak of that in a separate chapter.

The wisest man that ever lived said, "Train up a child in the way he should go: and when he is old, he will not depart from it." Prov. 22:6. So many having failed, some have been almost persuaded to doubt this man's wisdom. The saying is true; the failures arise from the lack of understanding of how to train properly. All the moral principles sustain a close relation to each other; thus one moral principle influences another, therefore the violation of one principle makes it easier to violate a second, and the child is carried on until he can do wrong without any reproval of conscience.

Training should begin very early in the life of a child. Never allow this intuitive knowledge or the voice of conscience to be hushed by repeated wrong doing. The child who does wrong should be told why it is he feels a sense of guilt—God is displeased. Show him how one evil leads to another, and what will be the awful end. Call to his mind the differences in his feelings arising from wrong doing and right doing. With the one God is displeased, with the other he is pleased. The way then to be happy in life is to always do right.

You must be indefatigable in your efforts at training. Constant daily training is needed. As one wrong act makes it easier to do a second wrong act, so one right act makes it easier to do a second right act. It is comparatively easy for the child to fall into bad habits. Training, constant daily training is needed to keep the little one from evil ways. Lead him into right action. By repeating a right action it becomes easy to perform it. You must never think of becoming discouraged, although it appears so natural for your child to do wrong and so difficult to get him to do right. You must go on training, trusting in the promise, teaching, reproving, correcting, punishing, ever looking upward for grace and wisdom.

Be careful of your example. It exerts a powerful influence. At one time in his life, the writer was quick in his actions and his words. He never received such a reproving as when one day his little boy under a provocation acted and spoke in the exact manner and tone of his papa. It cut to the heart.

It may seem at times that the voice of conscience is almost stifled, but you must hope on and labor zealously as in the command: "And thou shalt teach them diligently unto thy children, and shalt talk of them when thou sittest in thine house, and when thou walkest by the way, and when thou liest down, and when thou risest up." Deut. 6: 7.

Many parents seeing their young child doing or saying something wrong often think it of not much consequence, because the child is young and the wrong is very slight. You do not know the power of habit, and how one wrong, howsoever slight, leads to a greater one. Habit has been likened to a spider's web, which at first can be easily broken, but after continued indulgence binds its victim as with a strong cable, making reformation almost impossible. The same is true of good and right conduct. At first it may require an effort to perform a certain right act, but after repetition it is accomplished naturally and without thought. Therefore be vigilant in training your child to right action, and carefully avoid everything that would lead to evil acts or feelings. To tease a child is to develop an angry disposition. Some fathers think it quite laughable to hear the little two-year-old say to its mamma, "I won't do it," but he shall afterward pay dearly for his sport.

Parents think it "cute" to see their little one shake its little fist at papa and mamma. Through such education the day will probably come when he will shake his fist at you so that it will strike like a hammer on your heart. We have heard many parents laughing at their little children saying "smart things," little conscious of what these things are leading to.

"Train up a child in the way he should go," comprehends much more than many have understood. Just recently we heard a little child being taught to say, "Peter, Peter, pumpkin eater," etc. Such teaching is horrifying to Christian hearts. It is better to train your child to make reply in the polite, "Yes, sir" and "No, sir," or, "Yes, ma'am," and "No, ma'am," instead of that coarse, impolite "umgh," "humgh," which is no language. Remember the first step to child training is to set the example before them in your own life. Frequently we find parents endeavoring to teach their children to say, "Please" and "Yes, sir," when they in their own speech neglect such politeness. Your efforts will prove fruitless.

Parents have been known to tease their little daughter and the daughter of other parents about some little boy companion, and their little son about some girl companion. Such is very shameful and harmful. It fills the minds of their children with impure thought. Keep your own language very modest and pure and the language of your children the same. Keep their thought pure. Impure language and impure thought leads to impure and injurious habits.

Be familiar with your child and talk to him about his secret life. Teach him of the awful evils in the secret lives of many children and how impure words and thoughts lead to such injurious vice. Parents, see to it that there is a loving confidence between you and your child. Be familiar in telling them how wonderfully they are made and what was the design of God in thus creating them. Teach them what a noble and sacred thing it is to use every member and organ of our body to the glory of the Creator. Teach them of the awful crime to misuse any part. Mothers, acquaint your young daughters of the event that must soon come into their life, and thus prevent their doing an injury to their health.

By precept upon precept and by example, train your child to grow up into a beautiful moral life. In love restrain every immoral tendency in your child. Also be very zealous in teaching your children good manners. Civility and refinement are beautiful in the life of any one, and is very closely associated with the morals. Teach your little ones to respect each other, to have a regard for each other's happiness, to practise self-denial for the benefit of others. By precept and example instil gentleness and kindness into their actions. Dear parents, never grow weary in training the little feet of thy tender "olive plants" in the paths of virtue,

SPIRITUAL TRAINING.

The moral life is beautiful, but there is a higher and more beautiful life. In the true, deep spiritual life is found the highest degree of morality. However we may train our children into a high standard of moral life, and yet not attain to the spiritual. It is reported that the homes of certain infidels are most exemplary in moral conduct. Ancient heathen philosophers through restraint, self-sacrifice, and force of will attained to beautiful moral lives. But the spiritual life, which includes the moral, is the perfection of beauty. The life out of which the Christ-life and character shines is the grandest and noblest upon the earth.

Parents, bring your children to Jesus, for of such is the kingdom of heaven. Bring up your children in the nurture and admonition of the Lord, is commanded in the Holy Scriptures. Your child possesses an immortal soul. This soul will exist either in happiness or wretchedness eternally. It is so ordained in the plan of redemption that the soul can be brought into possession of spiritual life, which, if retained, insures its eternal bliss. He who has attained to a high degree of morality through the force of human will holds communion only with the better qualities of manhood, all of which must perish. He who has attained to spirituality holds communion with God and heavenly things. He does not trust to human powers, but in the power of the divine life.

Moral life will not admit us into the paradise above. We must possess spiritual life—the life of Christ. It is well to train our children in the way of good morals with a view to leading them into the spiritual life. Then it is necessary to lead them into the spiritual life to aid in the moral training. Comparatively few parents have accomplished any great results in the moral training of their children without divine assistance. In the moral derangement of our children the inward tendency to immorality makes it impossible to educate them to a true and perfect standard of morality without God's aid. Have we and our children no other source of strength to do battle with the evil passions but the force of the human will? Who has succeeded in subduing or controlling an angry disposition in themselves or their children to the extent that there is no impatient speech or abrupt action, by their own will power? We admit that some men—as the ancient heathen philosophers—have succeeded in educating themselves to a high standard of morality by using all the power of the human will as a vigilant police force and carefully avoiding occasions of temptation. It is said of one of these philosophers that in order to absent himself from the races and games and bullfights and other worldly gatherings he would only shave one-half of his face, thereby making himself too ridiculous in appearance to assemble among men. Such is the struggle to attain any moral excellence without divine assistance.

Children should be taught what sin is, and of God's judgments against it, and as early in life as possible be led by instruction and seeking the aid of the Holy Spirit into a Christian experience. Some seem to think that children have no correct ideas of God, and never feel the influence of his Spirit. In this they may be mistaken. The tender heart of a child very often receives a deep and sacred impression by the Holy Spirit. Were we watchful and took advantage of these seasons to tell them of God and heaven we would be workers together with him, and he would reward us by faithful children. The communication of the Spirit with the hearts of children is more wonderful and frequent than we may sometimes understand. A lady recently told us that her parents never taught her to pray, but very early in life she was inclined by the Holy Spirit to kneel at her bedside and pray when unobserved.

Who is the reader that can not remember instances in his early life when he felt the influence of some good spirit and had thoughts of God? Had he in those tender childhood days been rightly instructed he could have been led into the beautiful walks of a Christian life. We remember a child of less than ten years of age, who, hearing his father using bad language, fell upon his knees and clasping his arms around his father told him of his sin and besought him to pray for forgiveness.

A lady writer in one of her excellent works

("Mothers' Counsel to Their Sons"), records the instance of a little girl of four and a half years who felt the guilt of sin, and by her Christian mother was led to Jesus, and there she was blessed by him, even to the witnessing of his Spirit that her sins were gone and she was his child. The child was at one time moved to plead with an unsaved relative to come to Jesus. She lived triumphant in the sweetness of redeeming grace until the age of fifteen, when her mission on earth was ended and she went to her home in heaven. Oh, how glorious! What if that mother, when this child came expressing her sense of guilt, had not instructed her in the ways of salvation? In all probability it would have resulted in a lost soul.

When our children are brought into a Christian experience the victory is only partly won; life lies before them with its temptations. Many are the allurements to turn those young feet into worldly paths. We have witnessed the bright, happy conversion of many children. We have seen their countenances beaming with the light and joy of Christian love and heard their voices ring with spiritual praise, only to soon yield to the influence of the world and lose that sincere devotion to God. This is not the inevitable course, thank God, but it is the course of many. To teach our children the fear of God and enable them to retain in their hearts a deep reverence and devotion to him has been a subject of much prayer with us. We find the Christian life is a warfare. There are temptations to be resisted, there are watchings and prayings, there must be a constant looking upward to God for his aid and direction.

One trouble with many parents has been that as soon as their children were converted they seemed to think the battle was over and the victory was won, when really the battle was only begun. •The first thing necessary in keeping our budding "olive plants" in deep spirituality is to keep very spiritual ourselves. Now whatever means are necessary to promote a growth of spirituality in our hearts, the same means are necessary to develop and deepen the spiritual life of our children. A habitual effort to cultivate a deeper sense of the divine presence is necessary and one of the most beautiful employments of the sanctified heart. Those reverential feelings toward God must daily become stronger. Those inmost affections of the soul must reach out with greater yearnings and deeper longings toward the Holy One. A benevolent regard in our hearts for our fellow men must become stronger and more true. O beloved, if you would have your child to grow up into a beautiful Christian character you must teach him to suppress every selfish feeling, to banish every idle, careless thought, and to resist all temptations to envy or impatience. The purest of meditations must be entertained. We and they must be strictly disciplined by the sacred Scriptures, "Watch and pray." Spiritual prayer unfolds the life into the beautiful life of God as the bud unfolds into the blooming rose.

A CHRISTIAN HOME.

Nowhere is Christianity more effectual and more beautiful than in the home life. Nowhere is the power of divine love so truly manifested as in a sincere Christian home. We will set a picture before you. A father and mother with their children are grouped together for the evening worship. The father out of the deep affections of his soul, in spiritual tones, speaks of God and his holy commandment. A tear of gratitude and joy is glistening in the mother's affectionate eye. The children's faces are beaming with admiration as they hear extolled the character of Christ. They kneel in prayer; a holy awe and sacredness rests upon the scene; their prayers arise as sweet incense into the nostrils of God and delight his great heart.

Such a scene as we have pictured only fitly represents a true Christian home. The father is all tenderness and love to his wife and children. He is kind and sympathetic. He regards his wife as the weaker vessel and is mindful of her happiness. The wife deeply reverences her husband. Affection and appreciation sparkle in her eye. To attend to the husband's wishes is her delight. They love their children and in gentleness are bringing them up in the nurture and admonition of the Lord. The children love each other and are kind and self-denying. They obey their parents through love. Alas! such a family is rarely found upon this sin-cursed earth. But such is taught and commanded in the Bible, and it is possible.

If a father and mother and children lived toward each other just as the Bible says they should live, we would have a scene that would fitly represent heaven. It is our privilege to have just such a home. "Ask, and it shall be given you." A happy home life is the most blessed life on earth. "Thy wife shall be as a fruitful vine by the sides of thine house: thy children like olive plants round about thy table." Psa. 128:3.

DUTY OF CHILDREN TO PARENTS.

It was the original design of God that children should be a blessing to their parents. "My son, be wise, and make my heart glad." Prov. 27:11. "The father of the righteous shall greatly rejoice: and he that begetteth a wise child shall have joy of him. Thy father and thy mother shall be glad, and she that bare thee shall rejoice." Prov. 23:24, 25. "A wise son maketh a glad father." Prov. 15:20.

You will observe, children, in each of the above texts that it is wisdom in a child that makes parents rejoice. Then you should "seek wisdom, seek understanding." "Wisdom is the principal thing; therefore get wisdom." Prov. 4:7. What is wisdom? "The fear of God is the beginning of wisdom." The highest honor a child can pay to a true parent is to honor and obey God: "And shalt return unto the Lord thy God, and shalt obey his voice according to all I command thee this day, thou and thy children, with all thine heart and with all thy soul." Deut. 30:2.

"Remember now thy Creator in the days of thy youth, while the evil days come not." Eccl. 12:1.

The duty of children is to fear their parents: "Ye shall fear every man his mother, and his father." Lev. 19:3. To honor them: "Honor thy father and thy mother: that thy days may be long upon the land which the Lord thy God giveth thee." Ex. 20:12. This, it is true, is an old-time commandment, but the spirit or principle of it is carried into the dispensation of the gospel. "Honor thy father and mother." Eph. 6:2.

Children should attend to the faithful instruction of their parents: "My son, hear the instruction of thy father, and forsake not the law of thy mother; for they shall be an ornament of grace unto thy heart, and chains about thy neck." Prov. 1:8, 9. "Hear, ye children, the instruction of a father." Prov. 4:1. "My son, keep thy father's commandment, and forsake not the law of thy mother." Prov. 6:20. "Children, obey your parents in the Lord; for this is right." If it is right to obey, it is wrong to disobey. Many children do not have a due regard for the instruction of the father and mother. They oftentimes think they know more than their parents and so follow their own ways without natural affection.

Children should imitate the example of righteous parents, but are commanded not to walk in the footsteps of the unholy: "But I said unto their children in the wilderness, Walk ye not in the statutes of your fathers, neither observe their judgments, nor defile yourselves with their idols." Ezek. 20:18.

One important duty of children is to care for the parents. If the parents become old and feeble, or the mother a widow, the Word of God places children under the obligation of caring for them. "But if any widow have children or nephews, let them learn first to show piety at home, and to requite their parents: for that is good and acceptable before God."

DUTIES OF MASTERS TO SERVANTS.

Masters are commanded to forbear threatening their servants: "And, ye masters, do the same things unto them, [servants], forbearing threatening: knowing that your Master also is in heaven, neither is there respect of persons with him." Eph. 6:9.

In our land the days of slavery are no more, but men and women have their hired man and maid servant. Their duty toward such servants is to treat them with kindness, not to threaten them, or treat them in an overbearing, authoritative manner because they are servants. Be as kind and mild and respectful to them as to the children of the rich, for God is no respecter of persons.

Masters should give unto their servants that which is just and right for their labor done. If a man's labor is well worth two dollars per day, but because he is needy (or for any cause) and must work at any price, you take advantage of him and give him but one dollar, you are a dim light in the world. In truth your light has gone out, and your deeds have become darkness. "Masters, give unto your servants that which is just and equal: knowing that ye also have a Master in heaven." These words, "Knowing that ye also have a Master in heaven," are contained also in Eph. 6:9, where masters are commanded to forbear threatening. They are intended to impress the master with his obligation of dealing with his servants in the fear of God, before whom he must some day appear and give an account for the deeds done in the body, or in this life.

The rich man's fraudulent deeds toward his servants is taken account of in heaven: "Behold, the hire of the laborers who have reaped down your fields, which is of you kept back by fraud, crieth: and the cries of them which have reaped are entered into the ears of the Lord of Sabaoth." Jas. 5:4.

DUTY OF SERVANTS TO THEIR MASTERS.

Servants should honor and respect their masters: "Let as many servants as are under the yoke count their own masters worthy of all honor, that the name of God and his doctrine be not blasphemed." 1 Tim. 6:1. Especially are they to reverence them if they are believers: "And they that have believing masters, let them not despise them, because they are brethren; but rather do them service, because they are faithful and beloved, partakers of the benefit." 1 Tim. 6:2.

Servants are under obligation to obey their masters: "Servants, be obedient to them that are your masters according to the flesh, with fear and trembling, in singleness of your heart as unto Christ." Eph. 6:5. The servant's service to his master should not be wholly for the hire. He should not fear to do him ill service because of not receiving his wages, but his service should be in singleness of heart—an honest, upright purpose—as unto Christ.

They should seek to please their masters: "Exhort servants to be obedient unto their own masters, and to please them well in all things." Titus 2:9. They are to be subject to them: "Servants, be subject to your masters with all fear; not only to the good and gentle, but also to the froward." 1 Pet. 2:18. Servants are to do good service and not defraud their masters, and thus adorn the doctrine of God. "Not purloining, but showing all good fidelity; that they may adorn the doctrine of God our Savior in all things." Titus 2:10. The word "purloin" is from the Greek word "*nosphizomai,*" and means "to hide or to secrete, to steal. In this text it would include the idling away of time that belonged to the master.

We believe we have done justice to the subject of "Domestic Relationship." In conclusion we would be pleased to set before you a picture, not to be excelled in sublimity, sacredness, elevation of character, or soul inspiration by anything on earth. "For thou shalt eat the labor of thine hands: happy shalt thou be, and it shall be well with thee. Thy wife shall be as a fruitful vine by the sides of thine house: thy children like olive plants round about thy table." Psa. 128: 2, 3. This picture is set in a beautiful frame, found in the preceding verse and the one following. "Blessed is every one that feareth the Lord; that walketh in his ways." ver. 1. "Behold, that thus shall the man be blessed that feareth the Lord." ver. 4. The picture of a happy Christian man, a loving wife, devoted children, embossed with the blessings and glory of God, is one of greatest admiration.

CHAPTER XIV.

EVIL HABITS AND INJURIOUS INDULGENCES.

The Word of the Lord may not denominate in plain terms every particular sin and evil practise man may engage in; however there are general terms and principles of righteousness that prohibit and condemn every possible sinful act man may perform. The words card-parties, picnics, fairs, shows and theaters are not found in the writings of the apostles; however indulgence in these is "revelry," "living in pleasure," "rioting" and worldliness, of which the Scriptures say the participants do not love God and can never enter heaven. Also the terms "whisky," "alcohol," "opium," "morphine," "tobacco," "tea and "coffee," "secret vice," etc., are not made use of by the New Testament writers. They are included, however, in the general term "lust of the flesh." To make mention of all the things that may be done as a lust of the flesh would make a lengthy catalogue indeed. Anything, no matter what it may be, if done to satisfy the lust of the flesh is very damaging to spiritual life.

"Dearly beloved, I beseech you as strangers and pilgrims, abstain from fleshly lusts, which war against the soul." 1 Pet. 2:11. "This I say then, walk in the Spirit, and ye shall not fulfil the lust of the flesh. For the flesh lusteth against the Spirit, and the Spirit against the flesh: and these are contrary the one to the other: so that ye can not do the things that ye would." Gal. 5:16, 17. "For if ye live after the flesh ye shall die: but if ye through the Spirit do mortify the deeds of the body, ye shall live." Rom. 8:13.

By these texts we plainly understand the "flesh" to be antagonistical to the Spirit. God has created us with a fleshly nature, or made us a fleshly being. He has also created things for the sustenance of this fleshly life. He has created food and drink for man's use. A proper use of these is not a lust of the flesh. An improper use may be considered lust. Our eating and drinking should be to the glory of

God. The primary object in our eating should be to sustain life and promote health and strength, that we may be able to labor for and glorify God.

If we have a pure and undefiled conscience and are conscientious before God, and fully comprehend that we are not our own, but that we are God's property and that we should glorify him in our body and our spirit, we then most certainly would eat and drink such things to the extent of our knowledge as are most conducive to development of physical energy, and mental activity. It is not a lust of the flesh if we eat and drink to the glory of God. Temperance in natural God-given food and drink is the law of Heaven. It is of surfeiting that the Son of God warns us to beware. Luke 21:34. There are a great many things in creation which God never designed for the use of man as food and drink. Temperance does not mean a moderate use of these things. Their use is wholly forbidden.

Again man may by certain processes change the natural into an unnatural and make it in opposition to God's law. Because man has not always had the glory of God as his object in eating, drinking, and clothing, but became intemperate in the things which he allows, many have through the lust of the flesh been led to indulge in things from which the Word of God and the laws of health demand total abstinence. The injurious indulgences are so many and various as to furnish subject enough for volumes. We can only mention briefly the ones that are most generally indulged in, and which are destroying soul and body.

ALCOHOLS.

All whiskies, rums, brandies, and fermented wines contain a certain amount of alcohol. It consists of hydrogen, carbon, and oxygen, and is a powerful antiseptic. It is the intoxicating ingredient found in distilled liquors. An appetite for spirituous liquors is unnatural. It is true this appetite may be inherited, but because the child apparently takes naturally to these strong drinks is no proof they are a natural drink.

The word alcohol is not used by any of the writers of the New Testament. Paul speaks of wine and says that the bishop must be a man "not given to wine" (1 Tim. 3:3; Titus 1:7), and of the deacon, "not given to much wine." ver. 8. To the church at Ephesus he says, "Be not drunk with wine, wherein is excess; but be filled with the Spirit." Eph. 5:18.

He recommends wine to Timothy: "Drink no longer water, but use a little wine for thy stomach's sake and thine often infirmities." 1 Tim. 5:23. There is nothing in this text for the consolation of the winebibber. The professed follower of Christ who loves to sip the wine-cup, and by this text persuades himself to believe he is not violating God's law, wrests it to his own hurt. That Timothy had some stomach trouble is very evident from this text. We are not ready to admit that it was fermented wine Paul advised him to use. It often happens that water, especially if it is not pure, will distress a diseased stomach. This wine was recommended as a hygienic law. When an individual is troubled with constipation he will find bread made from unbolted wheat flour to be much more healthful for him than bread made from fine white flour. We would not advise the use of this merely as a luxury, nor as a medicine, but as a common-sense law of health. The juice of the grape contains a considerable portion of water, so much that one can get all the water the system requires and not drink the sweet juice to an excess. From the text it is natural to conclude that water was hurtful to Timothy, since he is advised to drink no longer water.

In cities and certain countries travelers often find the water disagreeable and unhealthful to them. It would be wisdom to use unfermented wine, or boil the water and add the juice of a lemon or some fruit to make it palatable. It would be very unwise for us on such an occasion to justify ourselves in the use of narcotic and fermented drinks. They are as injurious to the stomach as impure water, and were we compelled to drink either, we would feel more in God's order to trust him to counteract the poison in the water rather than the poison of fermented wines and narcotic teas and coffees.

The drinking in moderation or "not to excess" of

unfermented wine is healthful, and in harmony with divine laws; but total abstinence from spirituous liquors is the command of God. While alcohol, whisky, and brandy are words not used in the New Testament their use is none the less objectionable and sinful. These ardent spirits produce an effect called drunkenness, and the Scriptures class drunkenness with the works of the flesh, and declare that they which do such things shall not inherit the kingdom of God. Gal. 5:19-21. The reader will only have to refer to any authentic medical or hygienic work to learn of the injurious effects of alcohol upon the human system.

"Wine is a mocker, strong drink is raging: and whosoever is deceived thereby is not wise." Prov. 20:1. "Who hath woe? who hath sorrow? who hath contentions? who hath babbling? who hath wounds without cause? who hath redness of eyes? They that tarry long at the wine; they that go to seek mixed wine. Look not thou on the wine when it is red, when it giveth his color in the cup, when it moveth itself aright [is fermented]. At the last it biteth like a serpent, and stingeth like an adder." Prov. 23: 29-32.

We would say again that in all things God has given us to sustain life and make us healthful, comfortable and happy he would have us to be temperate and "keep our body in subjection." But there are some things which he would have us "touch not, taste not; handle not." Col. 2:21,

TOBACCO.

Very few people, especially among the religious class, are not willing to admit that drunken debauchery and carousal is altogether outside the realms of Christianity, and can only be engaged in by those wholly devoid of the love and grace of God. It is however a source of astonishment to the pure-hearted child of God to find so many professing Christ, yet unwilling to admit that tobacco using is a lust of the flesh. Oftentimes when speaking to a man concerning the tobacco habit, he will say, The word tobacco is not mentioned in the Bible. This is true. As we have before said, the word alcohol is not found in the Scriptures, but its effects upon the human system are mentioned, and no one can thus affect his body without placing his soul in great danger.

Tobacco is not mentioned in the Scripture, but its effects are, and we are positively commanded to remedy such effects. Paul says, "Having therefore these promises, dearly beloved, let us cleanse ourselves from all filthiness of the flesh and spirit, perfecting holiness in the fear of God." 2 Cor. 7: 1. One effect of tobacco using is "filthiness," from which we are commanded to cleanse ourselves. But few people are not ready to admit that using tobacco is a filthy habit. Then since the Word of God condemns filthiness, the tobacco habit stands condemned. It is indeed a sin-seared and tobacco-stunned conscience that denies the use of tobacco being a lust of the flesh. It can be nothing else but a fleshly lust. How frequently the lust of the flesh is condemned in the Holy Scriptures. It wars against the soul. It is enmity against God. It lusteth against the Spirit.

Dear reader, will you listen to reason and truth? We are aware how difficult it is for man to see and acknowledge the truth when some cherished idol stands between him and the truth. It is not a difficult thing to help him to comprehend the sinfulness of some evil thing which his heart is not set upon, but he is blinded to any sin in the cherished object of his affections.

Recently there were in a meeting two middle aged ladies. One of them was fashionably dressed, while the other was uncommonly plain in her apparel. The lady in the plain dress was addicted to the habit of using snuff. The lady in the fashionable dress abhorred such a filthy practise. When the Word of God was read on the comeliness and plainness of female attire, the lady in the plain dress smiled and nodded assent. The lady whose heart was set on costly apparel, expressed a rejection of God's Word in her countenance and manner. In the discourse the subject was changed from the wearing of gay clothing to the practise of tobacco using. When the habit of using snuff was mentioned the plain lady's smile was turned to a sneer, and the fashionable lady's sneer was turned to a smile. Afterwards in conversation the fashionable lady said she believed it was a sin to use snuff, but she could not see any evil in wearing gay and fine clothing. The plain lady said she thought it was a sin to wear such plumed hats and beaded dresses, but she could see no harm in using snuff. This proved to us what we have before mentioned, that it is difficult for man to see any sin in his idol.

If you are not very careful you will be seeking to justify yourself in your indulgences, though they be wrong. So if you, dear reader, will lay down all prejudice, with a heart open to reason and truth, we will consider with you the use of tobacco. We claim, first, that tobacco is injurious to health. The Bible tells us that we are not our own, but are bought with a price; therefore we should glorify God in our body and spirit which are his. 1 Cor. 6: 19, 20. Also that whether we eat or drink, or whatsoever we do, we should do all to the glory of God. 1 Cor. 10: 31. We can not indulge in anything injurious to the health of the body without incurring the displeasure of God. Now we frequently meet strong looking, and apparently healthy men, who have used tobacco for several years. Such are often ready to say, "Tobacco does not hurt me." They are honest in this. Being strongly constituted the poison of tobacco has not as yet succeeded in affecting them to a noticeable extent. Sooner or later, however, it will make its awful sting to be felt. Some men may expose themselves to the most inclement weather for years and experience no visible injurious effects; however, slowly, but surely, such negligence is undermining the general health, and the pains of his old days will repay him for the foolhardiness of his youth.

We have read may works on hygiene, and never a one but what has without hesitancy pronounced tobacco and alcohol very injurious poisons. We have a few by us and will give you some short quotations.

"It tends to debilitate the organs, it weakens the memory. By the use of tobacco we entail upon ourselves a whole train of nervous maladies. It will bow down to the earth an intellect of giant strength and make it grind in bondage like Samson shorn of his strength."—*Hitchcock.*

"It impairs the functions of the brain, clouds the understanding, and enfeebles the memory."—*Dr. Stevens.*

"In whatever way it is used, tobacco is a narcotic and a poison. Its injurious effects are due to its active principle called "nicotine," which is of itself a narcotic poison. The extent to which the body may be injured by tobacco depends upon its moderate or excessive use. Even in moderate use it is hurtful to young persons, and by no means free from harm to adults. It produces an artificial exhaustion, as it were, of the nerve-centers. It certainly does no good, even when used in moderation. Tobacco produces functional derangement of the nervous system, palpitation of the heart, certain forms of dyspepsia, and more or less irritation of the throat and lungs. Sometimes after long smoking, a sudden sensation of dizziness, with a momentary loss of consciousness is experienced. At other times, if walking, there is a sudden sensation of falling forward, or as if the feet were touching cotton-wool. While the stomach is empty, protracted smoking will often produce a feeling of nausea, accompanied with a headache. The external application of tobacco to chafed surfaces, and even to the healthy skin, will occasion severe, and sometimes fatal results. A tea made of tobacco and applied to the skin has caused death in three hours. A tobacco enema has resulted fatally within a few minutes. The excessive smoking of tobacco has been known to produce violent and fatal effects. Nicotine is one of the most rapidly fatal poisons known. It rivals prussic acid in this respect. It takes about one minute for a single drop of nicotine to kill a fullgrown cat. A single drop has killed a rabbit in three minutes. The old tobacco-user is often cross, irritable and liable to outbursts of passion. The memory is also quite often impaired for the same reason. The narcotic principle, the deadly nicotine, has become soaked into the delicate nerve-pulp, retarding its nutrition. The nerve-centers are no longer able to hoard up their usual amount of vital energy."—*Young Folk's Physiology*.

Thus we could go on and quote volumes, if need be, but we will close our quotations with the words of Dr. Fowler, as quoted by W. J. Henry in "*Tobacco and Its Effects.*" "The actual loss of intellectual power which tobacco has hitherto occasioned, and is still causing in this Christian nation, is immense. How much so, it is impossible to calculate. Many a man who might have been respectable and useful has sunk into obscurity and buried his talent in the earth. This commands a consideration of deepest interest to every philanthropist, patriot and Christian in the land, and especially to all our youth. We live in a time and under circumstances which call for the exertion of all our intellectual strength, cultivated, improved and sanctified to the highest measure of possibility. Error, ignorance and sin must be met and vanquished by light and love. The eyes of the angels are upon us. The eye of God is upon us. Shall we fetter and paralyze our intellectual capabilities for the sake of enjoying the paltry pleasure of tasting the most loathsome and destructive weed in the whole vegetable kingdom?" Oh, for shame!

Tobacco is not a natural food. No one ever thinks of giving it to their children as a food. It is a habit, something to be acquired. Whatever God has given us as food for the sustenance of the body is natural with us and we do not have to become habituated to its use. Where is the individual that will deny that it is a habit? It must be, since it has to be acquired or learned. Who will say it is a good habit? Who will deny that it is a bad habit? Do you not think it much better that we as moral citizens, and much more as professed Christians, leave off our bad habits?

Who dare hope of going to heaven who will not forsake his bad habits? Reader, I appeal to your reason. You must answer me, Is it not a habit? Is it good or bad? What shall your answer be in the judgment-day? God will hold us responsible for the use we are making of the money he has permitted us to acquire in this world. He says, "Wherefore do ye spend money for that which is not bread?" Isa. 55:2. Does it not savor more of the principle and spirit of Christianity to use our money in feeding and clothing the poor, than in consuming it in this unhealthful, unsightly, unclean, and ungodly lust? Do you not believe that when you shall have come to that bright land beyond the grave, that you would have more treasures there if all the money you have spent for tobacco had been used to help the poor along the weary way of life? O fellow mortal, how can you chew and smoke and snuff and spit your money away, while thousands are starving for bread, and millions are going to an eternal wretchedness for the want of gospel light? Do not think that God will not punish you for your selfishness.

God will hold us responsible for the example we set before the youth of the land and the children of our home. Jesus says to the Christian, "Let your light so shine before men that they may see your good works and glorify your Father which is in heaven." Mat. 5:16. What kind of a light is the tobacco-user letting shine to this world? Can he say to all, "Follow me in this habit"? Would he advise the pure, innocent prattler upon his knee to chew or smoke the filthy thing? No man can indulge in one thing that he can not with clear conscience say to the whole world, "Follow me in," and stand clear and uncondemned before God in judgment. The Bible tells us, "In everything give thanks." Who feels like thanking God they have acquired the tobacco habit? The Bible tells us that "whatsoever you do in word or deed, do all to the glory of God." But very few have become so depraved as to say they can glorify God in tobacco using. Here we behold the sublime wonders of redeeming grace. This world lost in sin, mankind was bound by passions, appetites, desires and dispositions with which they could not glorify God, Jesus, full of grace and truth, came from heaven to cleanse man, to save him from everything with which he could not show forth his Maker's praise. Halleluiah!

We feel like giving you a bit of our experience before closing this subject. For several years we were bound hand and foot by the hideous monster—Tobacco. We repeatedly tried to extricate ourselves from his iron grasp, but tried in vain. Resolution upon resolution was made. The plug was frequently thrown away only to be shortly afterward searched for or replaced by another one. How the devil's power ground me beneath his hoof of steel. Awful slavery, terrible bondage! We often express our thankfulness for a free country, but who is free? Of all the many sins that lay upon my soul, none seemed so heavy as the tobacco sin. In a time of danger or fright our first thought would be of tobacco, and we feared and trembled before God. In a time of storm when the lightning would flash and the thunder roll we would vow to the Lord that if he would keep us through the storm we would use tobacco no more. But when the clouds had rolled away and the sun shone out so peacefully, our tyrannical master would scourge us beneath his heavy yoke, and we would yield to his demands. For several months we thus fought against this monster only to be conquered, until early one October morning when all alone we earnestly besought the God of heaven to come to our rescue. We confessed our sins to him and plead for mercy. He heard our prayer and blotted out all our transgressions. He filled our soul with such a wondrous glory that full two weeks had passed before we thought of tobacco, and when we did we loathed it more than we had ever loved it. Eight years have passed and still we are free. Since the day we were saved we have no more desired it than if we never had used it. "If the Son therefore shall make you free, ye shall be free indeed." John 8:36.

OPIUM.

The habit of eating opium is fast increasing. We are told that thousands of tons are used annually in smoking and chewing in different parts of the world. Over half a million pounds are consumed by the opium eaters of our own country. It is a lust of the flesh and classed among the things which if we do we can never enter heaven. It is because it is a sin that will bar you forever from the land of eternal rest, that prompts us to add a few words of warning.

Like alcohol and tobacco, the word opium does not appear in the Scriptures, but that it is a sinful lust but very few will deny. Opium is the dried juice of the white poppy. Morphine is a powder made from opium. Laudanum is made by soaking opium in alcohol. The custom of drugging infants and children with "Soothing Cordials" is shameful and sinful. The "soothing" effect is produced by the opium the drug contains. It is exceedingly dangerous. One writer has said that it is very certain that many infants annually perish from this single cause. Any work on hygiene or common school physiology will describe the effect of opium upon the human system.

But the injurious effects of these stimulants and poisons upon the physical health is not the primary cause for speaking against their use in this little work. It is because such is not a gospel light. No one can indulge in such practises and be a light in the world in this shining gospel day. Such sinful deeds of the flesh are but the works of darkness and denounced by the writers of the New Testament.

TEA AND COFFEE.

Like the other stimulants that bring the user into bondage, tea and coffee are not mentioned in the Word of God. That they are classed among the narcotic poisons is acknowledged by all medical authorities. "Tea and coffee," says an authentic writer, "weakens the action of the heart. They produce headache, heartburn, indigestion, constipation, and wakefulness at night. The peculiar beating of the heart or palpitation after much exertion is often due to tea and coffee, and produces what is known as the 'tea-drinker's heart.' "*

The greatest desire of the true, devoted Christian is to glorify God in all that he does. No one who is careless and unobservant about his manner of life can prosper in the things of God. He who is desirous of being a shining light for Jesus in this world is careful that all about him is to the glory of God. He will so govern or rule his life, by God's grace, he will so subject his appetites and passions, that his whole conduct in every respect will be an adornment of the doctrine of God his Savior. His or her dress will be in perfect accord with the Bible, no worldly air will linger in his behavior; even his eating and drinking will be such as is glorifying to God. You show me an individual that is careless about his diet, led by

*There is a little book entitled "Tea and Coffee as an Evil," published by the Gospel Trumpet Co., which gives the opinions, respecting these stimulants, of the best known men of medical science.

an unrestrained appetite in eating food highly seasoned and flavored with spices, cinnamons, peppers, and mustards, or freely eating of rich cakes, pastries and puddings, or in drinking of teas and coffees, and I will show you one in whom the ebb of spiritual life is very weak and low. It is true, to leave off eating condiments and drinking stimulants alone will not make you spiritual, but it is a certain fact that if you attain to any great degree of spiritual life you will abandon the use of these things. It is well known among the true children of God that the most spiritual, and those of the greatest faith do not use tea nor coffee.

Those who walk in close communion with God are careful to preserve their physical health. When one continues using a certain article of food and drink because it is pleasing to the taste, and yet hurtful to the body, he will soon by such selfishness destroy his spiritual life. "Whether therefore ye eat or drink, or whatsoever ye do, do all to the glory of God." 1 Cor. 10:31. "But I keep under my body, and bring it into subjection." 1 Cor. 9:27. "For if ye live after the flesh, ye shall die: but if ye through the Spirit do mortify the deeds of the body, ye shall live." Rom. 8:13. "Dearly beloved, I beseech you as strangers and pilgrims, abstain from fleshly lusts, which war against the soul." 1 Pet. 2:11. "This I say then, Walk in the Spirit, and ye shall not fulfil the lusts of the flesh." Gal. 5:16. "But put ye on the Lord Jesus

Christ, and make not provision for the flesh, to fulfil the lusts thereof." Rom. 13:14. The lust of the flesh as used in these and many other texts includes the use of alcohol, opium, tobacco, tea and coffee. So we have not departed from the Word of God, which is a lamp unto our feet and a light unto our path, when writing on these subjects. Those who most perfectly manifest the life of Christ, those who are the most brilliant spiritual reflectors, do not indulge in such narcotics. If you value your spiritual prosperity make these sayings subjects of earnest prayer before rejecting them.

SECRET VICE.

When we speak of secret sins many are ready to charge us with immodesty. It is those who indulge in those secret evils that blush the deepest when they are publicly mentioned. There are many habits and indulgences of man that the pure-hearted Christian feels it is a shame to speak of publicly, yet his love for fettered, perishing souls moves him to look up to God for a modesty and delicacy of speech that will not in any sense corrupt the mind of the pure, who may read, and yet in terms sufficiently plain to reveal these sins and bring deliverance to many. As we have before said, temperance is a law of heaven. For the propagation of the race, God has implanted in his creatures, male and female, a passion for sexual connection. This desire in the nature of mankind is really the highest and most sacred. By it this world is being populated with souls bound on toward an eternity. This passion legitimately indulged to the glory of God is one of the most sacred, holy and pure. Since it is the highest and noblest of all the faculties of our being, its abuse must be the very lowest and unclean in the depravity of man.

That this sacred passion has been most degradingly abused is witnessed to upon almost every hand. If man could behold in one scene the awful consequences of this abuse it would be the most beastly and hellish that could possibly be pictured. The misery, wretchedness and woe entailed upon mortals by these secret indulgences is untold. It is a lust of the flesh that brings disease upon the body, destroys the vitality of human life and sows the seeds of death in the soul, which shall be harvested in the eternal fires of torment. These sins of the dark have gone far to obscure the pure light of a Christian life. "Ye are the light of the world," can never be spoken of those who yield to the temptations of this monster vice. The Moon in her clear reflection of the Sun is unspotted by such evils. Young reader, have you any admiration for a pure life? Does there not slumber in the better faculties of your nature a love and esteem for the virtuous walks of life? What is nobler or more heavenly here upon the earth than a pure, untarnished soul? Oh, the sublimity of a Christian life! A youth or maiden with pure affections and holy desires, seeking after the character of God, is the admiration of angels. As God at one time said in the delight of his heart to Satan, "Hast thou considered my servant Job, that there is none like him in the earth, a perfect and an upright man, one that feareth God and escheweth evil?" so the lovely queen Virtue can say to the hideous monster Vice, "Hast thou beheld my admiring youth and maiden? There is none like them in all the earth, ones that love chastity and escheweth evil indulgences."

CHAPTER XV.

THE TRINITY.

The wonderful grace of God removes sin and its nature from the heart. It restores to man's heart holy and pure affections. It will turn away the love for sin and fill your soul with peace and purity and your mind with a train of holy thoughts.

That the New Testament teaches a trinity in the Godhead is made obvious in Eph. 4: 4-6. "There is one body, and one Spirit, even as ye are called in one hope of your calling; one Lord, one faith, one baptism, one God and Father of all, who is above all, and through all, and in you all." Also in Mat. 28: 19: "Go ye therefore, and teach all nations, baptizing them in the name of the Father, and of the Son, and of the Holy Ghost." And in 1 Pet. 1:2: "Elect according to the foreknowledge of God the Father, through sanctification of the Spirit, unto obedience and sprinkling of the blood of Jesus Christ." Jude 20, 21: "But ye, beloved, building up yourselves on your most holy faith, praying in the Holy Ghost, keep yourselves in the love of God, looking for the mercy of our Lord Jesus Christ unto eternal life." But the most indubitable text upon this subject is 1 John 5:7: "For there are three that bear record in heaven, the Father, the Word, and the Holy Ghost: and these three are one." Christ is the Word. John 1:1.

GOD THE FATHER.

Father is a title conferred upon the first person in the trinity. He is the Creator of all things. Much has been written in scholastic theology of God, but such is incongruous to this work. Since most men believe in the existence of God, the Creator and Father, our Scriptural quotations relating to him will be but few.

He is love. 1 John 4:8. It was God the Father that so loved this world as to give his only begotten Son to die for us that we might live. John 3:16.

He is eternal. "The eternal God is thy refuge, and underneath are the everlasting arms." Deut. 33:27.

He is omnipotent. "And when Abram was ninety years old and nine, the Lord appeared to Abram, and said unto him, I am the Almighty God; walk before me, and be thou perfect."

He is omniscient. "O Lord, thou hast searched me, and known me. Thou knowest my downsitting and mine uprising, thou understandest my thought afar off. Thou compassest my path and my lying down, and art acquainted with all my ways. For there is not a word in my tongue, but, lo, O Lord, thou knowest it altogether. Thou hast beset me behind and before, and laid thine hand upon me. Such knowledge is too wonderful for me; it is high, I can not attain unto it." Psa. 139: 1-6. "Known unto God are all his works from the beginning of the world." Acts 15: 18.

He is omnipresent. "Whither shall I go from thy spirit? or whither shall I flee from thy presence? If I ascend up into heaven, thou art there: if I make my bed in hell [Hades], behold, thou art there. If I take the wings of the morning, and dwell in the uttermost parts of the sea: even there shall thy hand lead me, and thy right hand shall hold me." Psa. 139: 7-10. "Am I a God at hand, saith the Lord, and not a God afar off? Can any hide himself in secret places that I shall not see him? saith the Lord. Do not I fill heaven and earth? saith the Lord." Jer. 23: 23, 24.

He is immutable. "For I am the Lord, I change not; therefore ye sons of Jacob are not consumed." Mal. 3: 6.

He is the source of all goodness. "And he said unto

him, Why callest thou me good? there is none good but one, that is, God." He dwells within the hearts of his saints: "And what agreement hath the temple of God with idols? for ye are the temple of the living God; as God hath said, I will dwell in them, and walk in them; and I will be their God, and they shall be my people." 2 Cor. 6:16.

He is capable of being grieved. "And grieve not the Holy Spirit of God whereby ye are sealed unto the day of redemption." Eph. 4:30. An influence can not be grieved. It is only a person that has feeling and affections.

God in olden time spoke audibly to his people. Such an order of things ended when Jesus came. His mission in that respect was accomplished. He came in the flesh as the Son, and conquering sin and the grave through death and resurrection, he ascended to the Father. His mission as a sacrifice was completed. He now comes in the Spirit. Christ in speaking of the Holy Spirit's coming, says, "I will come to you." John 14:18. Thus the Spirit is Christ or God in another personage. It is the Holy Spirit that now talks to men. He teaches, interprets, guides, comforts and reproves. The children of God once knew God by his audible voice. They know him now by the voice of the Holy Spirit. You show me a man that denies the Holy Spirit, and I will show you a man that does not know God. The terms Holy Ghost and God are used interchangeably. See Acts 5:3, 4. The attributes of

Deity are ascribed unto him as well as unto the Father and the Son.

He is eternal. "How much more shall the blood of Christ, who through the eternal Spirit offered himself without spot to God, purge your conscience from dead works to serve the living God?" Heb. 9:14. He is omnipresent. "Whither shall I go from thy Spirit?" Psa. 139:7. He is omniscient. "But God hath revealed them unto us by his Spirit: for the Spirit searcheth all things, yea, the deep things of God." 1 Cor. 2:10. He is omnipotent. "Through mighty signs and wonders, by the power of the Spirit of God." Rom. 15:19.

"And the angel answered and said unto her, The Holy Ghost shall come upon thee, and the power of the Highest shall overshadow thee." Luke 1:35. "For that which is conceived in her is of the Holy Ghost." Mat. 1:20. By this we understand the Holy Spirit to have the power of creation.

Some have erroneously taught that the Holy Spirit is the Word. How can they do so when the second person in the trinity declares he is the Word? John 1:1. "For there are three that bare record in heaven, the Father, the Word, and the Holy Ghost." 1 John 5:7. Is not this plain enough to stop the mouths of all such false teachers?

The office of the Holy Spirit. He is everywhere termed the Holy Spirit. It is true, Christ is holy, and God is holy, but this term is especially applied to the Spirit, because his particular mission is to restore mankind to holiness. Holiness and sanctification, so far as they apply to a state, are synonymous terms. The Holy Spirit is the sanctifier. Rom. 15:16. This is the especial mission and prime work of the Holy Spirit. Much is involved in the work of sanctification. In this is the destruction of carnality and division, and consequently the unifying of the children of God. The Holy Spirit is the agency in answering the prayer of the Savior: "Neither pray I for these alone, but for them also which shall believe on me through their word; that they all may be one." John 17:20, 21. Sanctification is the work which effects this oneness. "For both he that sanctifieth and they who are sanctified are all of one: for which cause he is not ashamed to call them brethren." Heb. 2:11. Holiness and unity accomplished by the Holy Spirit are the two most sublime themes in the New Testament. Nothing accomplished in the mission of the Holy Spirit is more glorifying to God.

GOD THE SON.

Jesus Christ, the second person in the trinity, is also called God. "And Thomas answered and said unto him, My Lord and my God." John 20:28. "In the beginning was the Word, and the Word was with God, and the word was God." John 1:1. He is God revealed in the flesh on a mission of love and mercy to this world. He came as a Redeemer or Savior. An angel of the Lord appeared to Joseph in a dream before the nativity of the holy child and gave him the name Jesus or Savior (see margin of Mat. 1:21), because he should save his people from their sins. He was both God and man. Born of a woman, he was human. Conceived by the Holy Spirit, he was divine. As God, he was not subject to temptation, "for God can not be tempted;" but as a man, he endured all the temptations common to mankind. In the beginning of his ministry he was forty days tempted of the devil.

He is one with God the Father. "I and my Father are one." John 10:30. Because of his divinity he is eternal. "I am Alpha and Omega, the beginning and the ending." Rev. 1:8. He is omnipotent. "I am Alpha and Omega, the beginning and the ending, saith the Lord, which is, and which was, and which is to come, the Almighty." He is able to subdue all things unto himself. Phil. 3:21. "All power is given unto me in heaven and in earth." Mat. 28:18. He is omnipresent. "For where two or three are gathered together in my name, there am I in the midst of them." Mat. 18:20. "Lo, I am with you alway, even unto the end of the world." Mat. 28:20. He is omniscient. "He saith unto him the third time, Simon, son of Jonas, lovest thou me? Peter was grieved because he said unto him the third time, Lovest thou me? And he said unto him, Lord thou knowest all things; thou knowest that I love thee." John 21:17. "Now we are sure that thou knowest all things." John 16:30. He is immutable. "Jesus Christ the same yesterday, and to-day, and forever." Heb. 13:8.

His mission to this world was to be offered as a sacrifice for the sins of this world. "So Christ was once offered to bear the sins of many." Heb. 9:28. God prepared a body for his Son which he could bring as a sacrifice for the sins of man. "But a body hast thou prepared me." Heb. 10:5. Truly, "without controversy great is the mystery of godliness: God was manifest in the flesh, justified in the Spirit, seen of angels, preached unto the Gentiles, believed on in the world, received up into glory." 1 Tim. 3:16. The writers of the Gospels record the event of his crucifixion. On the cross he cried, "It is finished." His mission was completed, the sacrifice was made, the blood was shed. The blood has a great atoning power, the devastation caused by sin is covered by the blood. It destroys the works of the devil.

Provision was made by the atoning blood for sickness as well as for sin. "When the even was come, they brought unto him many that were possessed with devils: and he cast out the spirits with his word, and healed all that were sick: that it might be fulfilled which was spoken by Esaias the prophet, saying, Himself took our infirmities, and bare our sicknesses." Mat. 8:16, 17. God manifested in the flesh is a perfect Redeemer, the conqueror of sin, sickness and death, the destroyer of Satan's works, and the light of the world.

GOD THE HOLY GHOST.

That the Holy Spirit is a personage many question. But the doubts and denials of a nation, or of a world, do not change the Word of God. He is the third person in the trinity without controversy. The Holy Spirit is not a mere emanation or influence, but a person or being, capable of works, or the performance of a mission. As a person he guides: "Howbeit when he, the Spirit of truth is come, he will guide you into all truth." John 16:13. He as a person teaches: "But the Comforter, which is the Holy Ghost, whom the Father will send in my name, he shall teach you all things, and bring all things to your remembrance, whatsoever I have said unto you." John 14:26.

This teacher and guide is not a mere influence, such as love. The Scriptures in speaking of the Holy Spirit use the personal pronoun. The Holy Spirit as the third person in the trinity is the special gift of God unto his children: "And, behold, I send the promise of my Father upon you." Luke 24:49. God gave this promise by the mouth of his prophet Joel, "And it shall come to pass afterward, that I will pour out my Spirit upon all flesh." Joel 2:28. This promise was the gift of the Holy Spirit. See Acts 2:17, 18, 38.

Upon whom this gift is bestowed is a subject of more controversy perhaps than any other Bible theme. There need be no confusion upon this point if all would take the plain statements and examples in the New Testament. Jesus declares the world can not receive the Spirit. John 14:17. The disciples enjoyed the experience of regeneration all through the Lord's ministry. Some will take issue with us here, but we have the whole of the Word on our side, or rather we are on the side of the Word of God. They preached, they cast out devils, they healed the sick, they rejoiced, they prayed, the Lord administered unto them the newly instituted ordinance of the Lord's Supper, and originated the precious ordinance of feet-washing. He told them their names were written in heaven. He said he had chosen them out of the world, and that they were not of the world, even as he was not of the world. He prayed God to keep them from the evils of the world, and said that the glory the Father gave him he had given them, and that he had kept them in his Father's name, and none of them was lost. What more proof do you require to convince you that they were not sinners? Some who endeavor to overthrow the doctrine of receiving the Holy Spirit as the sanctifier subsequent to regeneration, say that "the justification of the disciples was an Old Testament justification, and not a justification under the gospel, and Pentecost was the receiving of the New Testament justification." Did you ever hear of a justification under the law spoken of as the experience of the disciples was spoken of by the Savior? They were not like the other Jews that kept the law. They were separated from them and persecuted by them. Jesus said, "Ye have followed me in the regeneration."

Mat. 19:28. It was not a justification under the law, but a regeneration in Christ.

In John, seventeenth chapter, after telling the Father that he had chosen them out of the world and kept them in his name, that none of them should be lost, he then prays for their sanctification. After saying in the sixteenth verse, "They are not of the world, even as I am not of the world," in the next verse he prays the Father to sanctify them. In Mat. 9:2 Jesus says to the man sick of the palsy, "Son, be of good cheer, thy sins be forgiven thee." Was not this a gospel justification or pardon? There was no offering of the blood of animals to secure a justification by the law. This is to prove that Christ did give his followers the experience of the "new birth" before his crucifixion. I do not doubt that this man was present and received the Holy Spirit at Pentecost.

Another clear example set before us of the Christians in the morning of this gospel day receiving the Holy Spirit as the third person in the trinity after regeneration, is that of the brethren at Samaria, recorded in Acts, eighth chapter. Philip went down thither and preached Christ unto them, and they gave heed to the things he spake. ver. 5, 6. Do you not think this was a New Testament justification? The seventh verse says that unclean spirits were cast out and the palsied and lame were healed. Do you suppose that all this was done unto sinners? The fourteenth verse says they "received the word." James says, "Receive with meekness the engrafted word, which is able to save your souls." Jas. 1:21. The sixteenth verse of the eighth chapter of Acts says they were baptized in the name of Jesus. The seventeenth verse speaks of their reception of the Holy Spirit. Some are at this point ready to say that Simon believed Philip's preaching and was baptized, and yet not saved. This is very true. He was a hypocrite. The remainder were not, you know full well. Because they were sincere they received an experience, and were made fit subjects to receive the Holy Spirit. Because he was not saved he could not receive him.

A similar instance of the outpouring of the Holy Spirit upon the previously regenerated is that of Cornelius, recorded in the tenth chapter of Acts. We are often told that Cornelius was a devout man under the law like Moses, Isaiah, and other Old Testament prophets. This is only a supposition, and one without foundation. Cornelius was not a keeper of the law. He was a Gentile, a Roman centurion. He had heard of Jesus. ver. 36, 37. He had learned enough to believe on him for the salvation from sin, but wanted to be taught the way of God more perfectly. Under Peter's preaching they received the Holy Spirit. In the nineteenth chapter of Acts is preserved the experience of twelve men at Ephesus. They were disciples. The Jews under the law were never called disciples. A disciple is a follower or learner of Christ. Paul preached to them and laid hands upon them, and they received the Holy Ghost.

This is the dispensation of the Holy Spirit. As holy men were once led and spoken to by God directly, holy men are now led and spoken to by the Holy Spirit. The man who rejects the power, work and light of the Holy Spirit is like a blind man who does not believe the existence of a sun because he never saw the light. The Holy Spirit calls to the ministry. Acts 13:1-4. He leads them and directs them where to preach or labor. Acts 8:26, 29; 16:6, 7. He created the overseers. Acts 20:28. Men spake as moved by the Holy Spirit. They spake as the Spirit gave them utterance. God sets all the members in the body as pleases him. 1 Cor. 12:18. He does this through the agency of the Holy Spirit. 1 Cor. 12:13. Apostles and prophets and teachers and gifts of healing and miracles and tongues are all the gifts of the Holy Spirit. The whole work of God is now carried on by the Holy Spirit, the third person in the trinity.

CHAPTER XVI.

MISCELLANEOUS SUBJECTS.

WOMAN'S FREEDOM.

The Scriptural right for women to labor in the gospel as exhorters, teachers, preachers, etc., is questioned by many. To deny women such a privilege is contrary to the Christian spirit of equality, and a serious obstruction to pure gospel light. We (male and female) are all one in Christ Jesus. Gal. 3:28. In the kingdom of grace man and woman are on an equal footing so far as concerns the work of God. To explain some texts that seem to prohibit women from laboring in the gospel and to prove positively to you that women did so labor in the morning light of the church, we will transcribe an article written by Bro. Geo. Cole, and which appeared in the Gospel Trumpet.

"I commend unto you Phebe our sister, which is a servant of the church which is at Cenchrea." The church at Cenchrea was a local congregation or assembly. Phebe our sister—that this personage was a woman, no one disputes, and she was a servant of the church. Servant—*diakonos,* translated servant in the following texts: Mat. 23:11; Mark 9:35; John 12:26; Rom. 16:1. Translated deacon in Phil. 1:1; 1 Tim. 3:8, 12. Translated minister: Mat. 20:26, 28; Mark 10:43, 45; Rom. 15:8; 1 Cor. 3:5; 2 Cor. 3:6; 6:4; 11:15, 23; Eph. 3:7; 6:21; Col. 1:7, 23, 25; 4:7; 1 Thes. 3:2; 1 Tim. 4:6; Rom. 12:7; 2 Cor. 8:4; Mat. 25:44; 2 Cor. 3:3; Heb. 6:10; 1:14; 1 Pet. 1:12; 4:10, 11.

The extensive use of this word *diakonos* in the New Testament readily determines its meaning. That Paul conferred upon Phebe the church title *"diakonos"* is unquestionable, and as such it means minister or deacon. Liddell and Scott's lexicon comments on *diakonos* as used in the New Testament as follows: A servant, waiting man or woman, minister, a messenger, a minister of the church. Any one can see the above definition covers all the ground of elder. I will offer a few proof texts. "He that is greatest among you, shall be your servant [*diakonos*]." Mat. 23:11. "Whosoever will be great among you, let him be your minister [*diakonos*]." Mat. 20:26. "Ministers [*diakonos*] by whom ye believed." 1 Cor. 3:5. "Who also hath made us able ministers [*diakonos*] of the New Testament." 2 Cor. 3:6. "Thou shalt be a good minister [*diakonos*] of Jesus Christ." 1 Tim. 4:6. "In all things approving ourselves as the ministers [*diakonos*] of God." 2 Cor. 6:4. "Whereof I was made a minister [*diakonos*]." Eph. 3:7.

Thus we might swell the testimony that *diakonos* was the common term used in the New Testament signifying the ministerial office of minister, elder, preacher, etc. Therefore the evidences are in Phebe's favor that she was a minister or elder rather than a deaconess. If we consider Paul's commendation of her standing and the sending of his Roman epistle by her, as having some weight, this certainly favors the above conclusion.

PROPHECY.

Propheteuo—to prophesy publicly, to expound, to preach, etc. There were certain prophets and teachers in the church at Antioch, as Barnabas, Simeon, Lucius, Manaen, and Saul or Paul. Acts 13:1. They were public expounders of the Scriptures. Prophesy—to speak, to edify, exhort, and comfort. 1 Cor. 14:3. A few examples: Zacharias filled with the Holy Ghost prophesied. Luke 1:67-79. Compare this prophecy with Mary's words in Luke 1:46-55. "They spake with tongues and prophesied." Acts 19:6. "And Judas and Silas, being prophets also themselves, exhorted the brethren with many words, and confirmed them." Acts 15:32. "Mystery of Christ which in other ages was not made known unto the sons of men, as it is now revealed unto his holy apostles and prophets by the Spirit." Eph. 3:4, 5. Prophets were set in the church. "He gave some, apostles; and some, prophets." Eph. 4:11. "And God set some in the church, first apostles, secondarily prophets." 1 Cor. 12:28. And there were certain prophets and teachers in the church which was at Antioch. Acts 13:1.

Thus we see the prophets were identical with or a constituent part of the New Testament ministry; and it only remains for us to prove there were women prophets in the church and we have women identified with the ministry. Example: Philip the evangelist, which was one of the seven. "And the same man had four daughters, virgins, which did prophesy." Acts 21:8, 9. "But every woman that prayeth or prophesieth with her head uncovered dishonoreth her head: for that is even all one as if she were shaven." 1 Cor. 11:5. If there were no women prophets it were foolish to give directions for them while praying or prophesying.

Joel prophesied, "And it shall come to pass in the last days, saith God, I will pour out of my Spirit upon all flesh: and your sons and your daughters shall prophesy, and your young men shall see visions, and your old men shall dream dreams: and on my servants and on my handmaidens I will pour out in those days of my Spirit; and they shall prophesy." Acts 2:17, 18. We observe first, men and women were placed on equality as prophets; second, this was to be a characteristic feature or mark of the last days, or last dispensation; third, this was being fulfilled at that time, at Pentecost, as women were present. Acts 1:14. All were filled with the Holy Ghost, and spoke with tongues as the Spirit gave them utterance. Acts 2:1-4.

Paul speaks of the whole church coming together into one place. 1 Cor. 14:23. This includes both men and women. He says, "But if all [men and women] prophesy, and there come in one that believeth not, or one unlearned, he is convinced of all, he is judged of all." ver. 24. In verse 31 he says, "For ye may all prophesy one by one, that all may learn, and all may be comforted." This was an extended privilege to all, though not expected of all, as we see in 1 Cor. 12:29: "Are all prophets?" Paul expressly mentions those women which labored with him in the gospel. Phil. 4:3. See Rom. 16:1, 3, 7, 12. "Labored in the gospel." "Elders ... labor in the word and doctrine." 1 Tim. 5:17. This was exactly the kind of work that Paul was doing, and those women labored with him in the gospel. "In the gospel" signifies here, evangelizing, spreading or preaching the gospel, etc. Let us not confound ordinary testimony with prophesying. A person must have the gift of prophecy in order to prophesy; and it is this gift that constitutes a person a prophet. Proof texts, Rom.12:6; 1 Cor. 12:10, 28; 14:1, 3, 6, 12, 29, 39; Eph. 4:8-11. And we have before proved that women did possess this gift, hence were prophetesses or public expounders of the gospel, and hence they have a constituent part in the ministry, and as such are just as much elders in the church of God as men.

SILENCE IN THE CHURCH.

"Let your women keep silence in the churches." 1 Cor. 14:39. "Let him keep silence in the church." ver. 28. If these scriptures had no contexts to explain them we would all be silenced in the church. The context to the last quotation reads thus, "But if there be no interpreter, let him keep silence." This makes it clear. Context to the first reads, "For it is not permitted unto them to speak: but they are commanded to be under obedience, as also saith the law. And if they will learn anything, let them ask their husbands at home." What kind of speech is forbidden? Ans.—Asking questions in the church to learn, interrogative speech in the public congregation. The law did not prohibit women being prophets or prophesying. See Deborah, in **Judges 4: 4-14.** Miriam, Ex. 15: 20. Anna, Luke 2: 36. If the law did not prohibit women prophesying, Paul did not call in question the obedience of the law to prove that point. Thus the context explains itself without further comment. Does not the character of Jezebel "which calleth herself a prophetess" disapprove of women prophets? Rev. 2: 20. No! no more than Satan's ministers transforming themselves into the ministers of Christ would disapprove of the entire Christian ministry. The counterfeit proves there is a genuine. This is conclusive proof in itself that there were true prophetesses in the church in those days.

"Teach nor to usurp authority over the man" (1 Tim. 2: 12), is offered in argument against women prophets. Such argument betrays ignorance in the nature and spirit of prophecy. A woman filled with the Holy Spirit, prophesying, speaking unto men to edification, exhorting, and comforting, is not usurping authority over any one.

THE RESURRECTION OF THE BODY.

This chapter appears in Gospel Trumpet, written by H. F. Jackson.

1. Abraham. "Accounting that God was able to raise him up, even from the dead; from whence also he received him in a figure." Heb. 11: 19.

2. Moses. "Now that the dead are raised, even

Moses showed at the bush, when he called the Lord the God of Abraham, and the God of Isaac, and the God of Jacob. For he is not a God of the dead, but of the living: for all live unto him." Luke 20:37.

3. Job. "For I know that my Redeemer liveth, and that he shall stand at the latter day upon the earth: and though after my skin worms destroy this body, yet in my flesh shall I see God: whom I shall see for myself, and mine eyes shall behold, and not another; though my reins be consumed within me." Job 19:25-27.

4. Isaiah. "Thy dead men shall live, together with my dead body shall they arise. Awake and sing, ye that dwell in dust: for thy dew is as the dew of herbs, and the earth shall cast out the dead." Isa. 26:19.

5. Daniel. "And many of them that sleep in the dust of the earth shall awake, some to everlasting life, and some to shame and everlasting contempt. And they that be wise shall shine as the brightness of the firmament; and they that turn many to righteousness as the stars forever and ever. But go thou thy way till the end be: for thou shalt rest, and stand in thy lot at the end of the days." Dan. 12:2, 3, 13.

6. Hosea. "I will ransom them from the power of the grave; I will redeem them from death: O death, I will be thy plagues; O grave, I will be thy destruction: repentance shall be hid from mine eyes." Hos. 13:14.

THE DOCTRINE DERIDED AMONG THE GREEKS.

"Then certain philosophers of the Epicureans, and of the Stoics, encountered him. And some said, What will this babbler say? other some, He seemeth to be a setter forth of strange gods: because he preached unto them Jesus, and the resurrection. And when they heard of the resurrection of the dead, some mocked: and others said, We will hear thee again of this matter." Acts 17: 18, 32.

PAUL'S DEFENSE OF THE DOCTRINE.

"Now if Christ be preached that he rose from the dead, how say some among you that there is no resurrection of the dead?" 1 Cor. 15: 12. "But if there be no resurrection of the dead, then is Christ not risen: and if Christ be not risen, then is our preaching vain, and your faith is also vain. Yea, and we are found false witnesses of God; because we have testified of God that he raised up Christ: whom he raised not up, if so be that the dead rise not. For if the dead rise not, then is not Christ raised: and if Christ be not raised, your faith is vain; ye are yet in your sins. Then they also which are fallen asleep in Christ are perished. Else what shall they do which are baptized for the dead, if the dead rise not at all? . . . and why stand ye in jeopardy every hour?" 1 Cor. 15: 13-18, 29, 30.

DEATH TO REIGN UNTIL THE RESURRECTION.

"The last enemy that shall be destroyed is death." 1 Cor. 15:26.

THE RESURRECTION OF CHRIST ENSURES THAT OF HIS FOLLOWERS.

"If in this life only we have hope in Christ, we are of all men most miserable. But now is Christ risen from the dead, and become the first-fruits of them that slept. For since by man came death, by man came also the resurrection of the dead. For as in Adam all die, even so in Christ shall all be made alive. But every man in his own order: Christ the first-fruits; afterward they that are Christ's at his coming." 1 Cor. 15:19-23.

CHRIST'S PROMISE TO RAISE HIS FOLLOWERS.

"And this is the Father's will which hath sent me, that of all which he hath given me I should lose nothing, but should raise it up again at the last day. And this is the will of him that sent me, that every one which seeth the Son, and believeth on him, may have everlasting life: and I will raise him up at the last day." John 6:39, 40.

THE ORDER OF THE RESURRECTION.

1. The dead will first be raised. "But I would not have you to be ignorant, brethren, concerning them which are asleep, that ye sorrow not, even as others

which have no hope. For if we believe that Jesus died and rose again, even so them also which sleep in Jesus will God bring with him. For this we say unto you by the word of the Lord, that we which are alive and remain unto the coming of the Lord shall not prevent them which are asleep. For the Lord himself shall descend from heaven with a shout, and with the voice of the archangel, and with the trump of God: and the dead in Christ shall rise first." 1 Thes. 4: 13-16.

2. Living saints will be caught up. "Then we which are alive and remain shall be caught up together with them in the clouds, to meet the Lord in the air: and so shall we ever be with the Lord. Wherefore comfort one another with these words." 1 Thes. 4: 17, 18.

THE GLORY OF THE CONSUMMATION.

"Behold, I shew you a mystery; we shall not all sleep, but we all shall be changed, in a moment, in the twinkling of an eye, at the last trump: for the trumpet shall sound, and the dead shall be raised incorruptible, and we shall be changed. For this corruptible must put on incorruption, and this mortal must put on immortality. . . . Then shall be brought to pass the saying that is written, Death is swallowed up in victory. O death, where is thy sting? O grave, where is thy victory? The sting of death is sin; and the strength of sin is the law." 1 Cor. 15: 51-56.

THE MOSAIC LAW.

There is recorded in the Old Testament the account of God giving a law to govern his people Israel. This is called a covenant, and was to serve as a schoolmaster to lead its subjects to Christ. This law was a shadow of good things to come; that is, it contained types and shadows of something real in the blessed day of gospel grace. The blood of the animals that was shed could not take away sins, but is typical of the blood of Jesus, who in the end of the world appeared to put away sin by the sacrifice of himself. There is no power in the blood of animals to redeem man from sin, but we are redeemed with the precious blood of Christ, as of a lamb without blemish and without spot. The unblemished lamb offered in sacrifice under the Jewish economy was typical or a shadow of the spotless Christ, slain for the sins of the world. The types and shadows of the law all center in Christ. When he the substance is come the shadow of necessity vanishes away. When the shadow meets the substance the shadow has an end. The redemption which we have in Jesus not only redeems us from sin, but also from the bondage of the Sinaitic law. "But when the fulness of the time was come, God sent forth his Son, made of a woman, made under the law, to redeem them that were under the law, that we might receive the adoption of sons." Gal. 4:4, 5. "Christ hath redeemed us from the curse of the law, being made a curse for us." Gal. 3:13.

There is no salvation to be obtained by the observance of any part or the whole of the law of Moses including the ten commandments. Salvation or redemption is only found in Christ and the gospel. "Neither by the blood of goats and calves, but by his own blood he entered in once into the holy place, having obtained eternal redemption for us." Heb. 9:12. "For what the law could not do, in that it was weak through the flesh, God sending his own Son in the likeness of sinful flesh, and for sin, condemned sin in the flesh." Rom. 8:3. It is not through the law we obtain salvation, but through the gospel. "For I am not ashamed of the gospel of Christ: for it is the power of God unto salvation to every one that believeth; to the Jew first, and also to the Greek." Rom. 1:16. "Wherefore lay apart all filthiness and superfluity of naughtiness, and receive with meekness the engrafted word, which is able to save your souls." Jas. 1:21. "Being born again, not of corruptible seed, but of incorruptible, by the word of God, which liveth and abideth forever." 1 Pet. 1:23. In Rom. 1:16, Gal. 3:28, Rev. 5:9, and many other texts, we learn that all are accepted by God unto salvation through Christ. This necessitates an end of the law, since the law is given to the Jew only. There is no shift or revision made of the law in Christ to include both Jew and Gentile; it is simply done, and the gospel succeeds.

The apostles very clearly and decidedly teach an

abolition of the ancient faulty Sinaitic law. Paul says, "Having abolished [destroyed—Webster] in his flesh the enmity, even the law of commandments contained in ordinances; for to make in himself of twain one new man, so making peace." Eph. 2:15. The enmity here spoken of is the enmity or separation made between the Jew and Gentile by the Mosaic law. This law of the Jews stood as a partition wall between the Israelite and the Gentile world. In Jesus this wall was torn down, and the Gentile as well as the Jew was offered salvation. In verse fourteen Paul says, "For he is our peace, who hath made both one [Jew and Gentile], and hath broken down the middle wall of partition between us." The Jewish ordinances and laws that stood as a mighty wall between the Gentile and the Jew were broken down and all the world of every kindred, nation and tongue was given equal rights under an entirely new order of things.

The coming of Christ was the fulfilling of the law. The law was only given to serve until Jesus came. When he came its object or purpose was fulfilled and had an end. "But before faith came, we were kept under the law, shut up unto the faith which should afterwards be revealed. Wherefore the law was our schoolmaster to bring us unto Christ, that we might be justified by faith. But after that faith is come, we are no longer under a schoolmaster." Gal. 3: 23-25. This is plain, positive language. After faith or Christ has come we are no longer under a schoolmaster, which is the law. This accords with Rom. 6:14: "For sin shall not have dominion over you: for ye are not under the law, but under grace."

As we have before mentioned, the law did not deliver us from the power of sin; but after grace came by Jesus Christ we are not under the law, but under grace, and where sin once abounded, that is, had power or dominion, grace now much more abounds; therefore sin has no dominion over us. In Rom. 7:4 the apostle tells us we have become dead to the law by the body of Christ.

In the seventh verse, still speaking of this law, to which we become dead by the body of Christ, he quotes one of the ten commandments, thereby teaching us that by the body of Christ we are no longer under the ten-commandment law. The ten-commandment law simply as the ten-commandment law is no more in force and effect than if it were never given. Some of the principles embodied in the ten commandments are embodied in the New Testament. These are in effect, not because they are principles of the ten commandments, but because they are principles of the New Testament. Must I as a Christian refrain from committing adultery because it is forbidden by one of the ten commandments? We answer, No. But as a Christian in this dispensation of the gospel I must refrain from such acts because it is forbidden in the New Testament. We must live in the spirit of the gospel. We could live without violation of this seventh commandment, and yet commit adultery according to the New Testament and be wholly destitute of the grace of God. Jesus says that "whosoever looketh on a woman to lust after her hath committed adultery with her already in his heart." Mat. 5:28. The salvation of the gospel removes such unholy desires from the heart.

"Tell me, ye that desire to be under the law, do ye not hear the law? For it is written, that Abraham had two sons, the one by a bondmaid, the other by a freewoman. But he who was of the bondmaid was born after the flesh; but he of the freewoman was by promise. Which things are an allegory: for these are the two covenants; the one from mount Sinai, which gendereth to bondage, which is Agar. For this Agar is mount Sinai in Arabia, and answereth to Jerusalem which now is, and is in bondage with her children. But Jerusalem which is above is free, which is the mother of us all." Gal. 4:21-26. Here the apostle uses the two sons of Abraham allegorically. They represent the two covenants or testaments. See margin. The one by the bondmaid he uses to represent the testament or covenant given from Sinai. The one by the free woman, the covenant given by Christ, or the New Testament.

The apostle goes further and tells us what disposition to make of the two sons or testaments. "Nevertheless what saith the scripture? Cast out the bondwoman and her son: for the son of the bondwoman shall not be heir with the son of the freewoman. So then, brethren, we are not children of the bondwoman, but of the free." Gal. 4: 30, 31. The mission of the Sinaitic law is completed. It has finished its course. We are in the glorious freedom of the New Testament. Paul adds in the next chapter, "Stand fast therefore in the liberty wherewith Christ hath made us free, and be not entangled again with the yoke of bondage." ver. 1.

He speaks further of the two covenants in the eighth chapter of Hebrews, and says, "For if that first covenant had been faultless, then should no place have been sought for the second. For finding fault with them, he saith, Behold, the days come, saith the Lord, when I will make a new covenant with the house of Israel and with the house of Judah: not according to the covenant that I made with their fathers in the day when I took them by the hand to lead them out of the land of Egypt; because they continued not in my covenant, and I regarded them not. saith the Lord." What was the covenant that God made with Israel when he led them out of the land of Egypt? It was the entire law given at Sinai, including the ten commandments. Whoever would here make a division in the covenant, and say only the ceremonial law is included in the covenant mentioned in these texts simply makes the assertion to sustain some adopted views of his creed. There is no foundation here for any division. This first covenant is the whole covenant, and it was faulty. In verse thirteen he says it waxeth old and is ready to vanish away. Continuing in the ninth chapter the apostle speaks of the ordinances of the first covenant, which stood in meats and drinks and divers washings. ver. 10. These ordinances of the first covenant were imposed upon them until the time of reformation. We are to understand by this that at the bringing in of the reformation they "vanished away." In the Colossian letter he mentions those ordinances together with some others as being blotted out at Calvary. We will quote his words: "Blotting out the handwriting of ordinances that was against us, which was contrary to us, and took it out of the way, nailing it to his cross." Col. 2:14. In the sixteenth verse he tells us what ordinances were blotted out: "Let no man therefore [since they are nailed to the cross] judge you in meat or in drink, or in respect of a holy day, or of the new moon, or of the sabbath days." The Jew was denied by the law the privilege of eating certain kinds of meat. Such restrictions were nailed to the cross, and since Calvary nothing is "common or unclean." Their holy days and solemn assemblies at certain stages of the moon find no place in the New Testament. The keeping of the Sabbath as commanded on the tables of stone was also nailed to the cross, therefore let no man judge us or bind these things upon us.

The Sabbath of the ten commandments had its

mission. It was a shadow of good things to come. It was typical of the rest which is found in Jesus. Of all the types and shadows of the Sinaitic covenant, none is more beautiful than the keeping of the Sabbath. It foreshadows the rest or peacefulness of Christ's kingdom. Jesus says, "Come unto me, all ye that labor and are heavy-laden, and I will give you rest. Take my yoke upon you, and learn of me; for I am meek and lowly in heart: and ye shall find rest unto your souls." Mat. 11:28, 29. The Old Testament prophets beheld the rest that was to be obtained in Jesus: "And in that day there shall be a root of Jesse, which shall stand for an ensign of the people; to it shall the Gentiles seek: and his rest shall be glorious." Isa. 11:10.

That the seventh-day Sabbath kept by the Jews is the Christian day of worship is a heretical doctrine, being taught at the present day. To make clear to your understanding that the Sabbath of the ten-commandment law is not the Christian day of worship is our object in showing you it was only a type. If it was a type then certainly when we have reached the antitype the type has an end. Since the Word of God is so plain we feel confident we can make it clear and comprehensive to you. We will first quote from Heb. 4:4-11: "For he spake in a certain place of the seventh day on this wise, And God did rest the seventh day from all his works." (See Gen. 2:1-3.) "And in this place again, If they shall enter into my rest." See third verse. "Seeing therefore it remaineth that some must enter therein, and they to whom it was first preached entered not in because of unbelief: again, he limiteth a certain day, saying in David, To-day, after so long a time, as it is said, To-day if ye will hear his voice, harden not your hearts. For if Jesus had given them rest, then would he not afterward have spoken of another day. There remaineth therefore a rest to the people of God. For he that is entered into his rest, he also hath ceased from his own works, as God did from his. Let us labor therefore to enter into that rest, lest any man fall after the same example of unbelief."

We now wish to briefly review this quotation. In the fourth verse it is said that God rested on the seventh day from all his works. This is recorded in Gen. 2:1-3. This is the "place" that the seventh-day rest is spoken of. But this day of rest is only a shadow of another day of rest. He speaks of another day. See seventh and eighth verses of quotation; also Psa. 95: 7, 8, "To-day if ye will hear his voice, harden not your heart." "For if Jesus had given them rest." Rotherham says, "For if unto them Joshua had given rest." See also margin of common version. Joshua led the children of Israel across the Jordan into the land of Canaan. This land is also typical of a restful state in the kingdom of grace. Had Joshua given them rest he would not have spoken of another day of rest. But they did not enter into his rest, therefore there remaineth another day of rest to the people of God. What day is it? It is the gospel day. The marginal rendering of the word "rest" is the "keeping of a Sabbath." "Hence there is being left over a sabbath keeping for the people of God."—Rotherham. Like as God did cease from his own works and rest on the Sabbath, and as the Jews kept it strictly as a day of rest, so we in Jesus find rest and have ceased from our own works. It was all works under the law, but we have ceased from such works in Jesus. Therefore the Jewish Sabbath day of rest only typifies the blessed rest of the day of salvation by grace, and not by works.

Under the New Testament we keep as one of the early church fathers has said, "The day on which our Lord arose." The writings of church history frequently make mention of Sunday (the first day of the week) as being the Christian's day of worship in commemoration of the resurrection of our Lord, in whom we are a new creation. The weekly meeting together of the Christians as recorded in the New Testament was always on the first day of the week. See Luke 24:33; John 20:19, 26; 1 Cor. 16:2; Acts 20:6, 7. There is not one text in the New Testament recording a Christian meeting on the seventh day. Here are four texts recording meetings held on the first day. The Sabbath, as well as the whole of the ten-commandment and ceremonial law, finds an end when we have come to "another day"—the day of salvation, wherein we are a new creation. 2 Cor. 5:17.

We will close this subject by quoting 2 Cor. 3, beginning at verse five: "Not that we are sufficient of ourselves to think anything as of ourselves; but our sufficiency is of God; who also hath made us able ministers of the New Testament; not of the letter, but of the Spirit: for the letter killeth, but the Spirit giveth life. But if the ministration of death, written and engraven in stones, was glorious, so that the children of Israel could not steadfastly behold the face of Moses for the glory of his countenance; which glory is to be done away: how shall not the ministration of the Spirit be rather glorious? For if the ministration of condemnation be glory, much more doth the ministration of righteousness exceed in glory. For even that which was made glorious had no glory in this respect, by reason of the glory that excelleth. For if that which is done away is glorious, much more that which remaineth is glorious. Seeing then that we have such hope, we use great plainness of speech: and not as Moses, which put a vail over his face, that the children of Israel could not steadfastly look to the end of that which is abolished: but their minds were blinded: for until this day remaineth the same vail untaken away in the reading of the Old Testament; which vail is done away in Christ. But even unto this day, when Moses is read, the vail is upon their heart. Nevertheless when it shall turn to the Lord, the vail shall be taken away."

It is with reluctance that we refrain from comment

on the above, however we believe the abolition of the whole Mosaic system to be so plain to every unprejudiced heart as to render comment unnecessary.

GOOD WORKS.

Christians possess a light; they are "children of light," and are commanded to "let their light shine." How can Christians shine the light of the gospel and of God? By their good works. Jesus says, "Let your light so shine before men, that they may see your good works, and glorify your Father which is in heaven." Mat. 5:16. God has ordained that in Christ we should perform good works. "For we are his workmanship, created in Christ Jesus unto good works, which God hath before ordained that we should walk in them." Eph. 2:10. By the apostle Christians are exhorted to be careful to mantain good works. "This is a faithful saying, and these things I will that thou affirm constantly, that they which have believed in God might be careful to mantain good works." Titus 3:8. Then adds, "These things are good and profitable unto men."

We have proven by the Word elsewhere that salvation from sin is not attained by good works alone, but after we are saved by grace we retain the grace by a strict and faithful performance of all Christian duties. The first neglect to perform a known duty is the first step the Christian takes on his return to the "beggarly elements of the world." We are commanded to "search the scriptures." By looking into this perfect "law of liberty," and conforming our lives to the glorious truth taught there, we will be led into the beautiful walk of Christian virtue and duty. "All scripture is given by inspiration of God, and is profitable for doctrine, for reproof, for correction, for instruction in righteousness that the man of God may be perfect, thoroughly furnished unto all good works." When a house is "thoroughly furnished" we understand it is furnished in every room up-stairs and down. The Scriptures are given us that by searching them and receiving of their corrections, reprovings, and instructions we may be furnished in every department of our capabilities with good works. If man obeys the voice of the inspired Word of God he will be "a vessel unto honor, sanctified and meet for the Master's use, and prepared unto every good work." Christians should be rich in good works. "That they do good, that they be rich in good works, ready to distribute, willing to communicate." 1 Tim. 6:18.

Saints should be fruitful in good works. "That ye might walk worthy of the Lord unto all pleasing, being fruitful in every good work, and increasing in the knowledge of God." Saved people in some texts of Scripture are likened unto good trees. They are a tree that is abounding with the fruit of every good work. Christians are admonished to be ready to every good work. "Put them in mind to be subject to principalities and powers, to obey magistrates, to be ready to every good work." Titus 3:1. They should be established in them. "Now our Lord Jesus Christ himself, and God, even our Father, which hath loved us, and hath given us everlasting consolation and good hope through grace, comfort your hearts and stablish you in every good word and work." 2 Thes. 2:16, 17. They should abound to all good works. "And God is able to make all grace abound toward you; that ye, always having all sufficiency in all things, may abound to every good work." 2 Cor. 9:8.

The apostle prayed that they should be made perfect in every good work. "Now the God of peace, that brought again from the dead our Lord Jesus, that great Shepherd of the sheep, through the blood of the everlasting covenant, make you perfect in every good work to do his will, working in you that which is well-pleasing in his sight, through Jesus Christ: to whom be glory forever and ever. Amen." Heb. 13:20, 21. This is a most precious text. "Working in you" in the margin is rendered "doing." All the good things a Christian does is not him doing it, but it is God doing it in him, so he is not found going about telling what he has done.

Saints should provoke each other to good works. "And let us consider one another to provoke unto love and to good works." Heb. 10:24. We know of no better way to provoke others to good works than by setting a good example before them. All their good works should be done in wisdom and meekness or humility. "Who is a wise man and endued with knowledge among you? let him shew out of a good conversation [or conduct] his works with meekness of wisdom." Jas. 3:13.

The people of God do not adorn themselves with gold and pearls and costly array to appear beautiful, "but with good works." 1 Tim. 2:9, 10. What can be more lovely than a character beautified by the ornaments of every good work in the meekness of wisdom? Glory to the name of Jesus! My soul feels like crying, "Lord, work more of thy good works in the hearts of thy people." Man's works shall be brought into judgment. "For we must all appear before the judgment-seat of Christ; that every one may receive the things done in his body, according to that he hath done, whether it be good or bad." 2 Cor. 5: 10. "For God shall bring every work into judgment, with every secret thing, whether it be good, or whether it be evil." Eccl. 12:14.

That will be an awful hour when we are called before the tribunal of God and there have to unfold to the incomprehensible One our true character. Oh, what will it be worth in that day to hear him say, "Come, ye blessed of my Father, inherit the kingdom prepared for you from the foundation of the world: for I was an hungered, and ye gave me meat: I was thirsty, and ye gave me drink: I was a stranger, and ye took me in: naked, and ye clothed me: I was sick, and ye visited me: I was in prison, and ye came unto me." Mat. 25:34-36.

CHRISTIAN GIVING.

The cheerful giving of our worldly goods to help the needy or for the furtherance of the cause of Christ is a work very commendable in the sight of the Lord. "But this I say, He which soweth sparingly shall reap also sparingly; and he which soweth bountifully shall reap also bountifully. Every man according as he purposeth in his heart, so let him give, not grudgingly, or of necessity: for God loveth a cheerful giver. And God is able to make all grace abound toward you; that ye, having all sufficiency in all things, may abound to every good work: as it is written, He hath dispersed abroad; he hath given to the poor: his righteousness remaineth forever." 2 Cor. 9:6-9.

To quote from the writings of a Christian friend will be sufficient on this subject, we think, to enable the reader to see the beauty and blessings in giving unto the needy and the cause of Christ as unto the Lord.

"We find both in prophecy and in the New Testament much about giving. In Amos, chapter four, we read, 'Hear this word, ye kine of Bashan, that are in the mountain of Samaria, which oppress the poor, which crush the needy, which say to their masters, Bring, and let us drink. The Lord God hath sworn by his holiness, ... I also have given you cleanness of teeth in all your cities, and want of bread in all your places: ... also I have withholden the rain from you, when there were yet three months to the harvest. ... I have smitten you with blasting and mildew: when your gardens and your vineyards and your fig-trees and your olive-trees increased, the palmer worm devoured them. ... I have sent among you the pestilence, ... yet have ye not returned unto me, saith the Lord.'

"Dear ones, has such been your experience? Have your crops failed in this manner, and suffered for want of rain? Let us read further: 'Return unto me, and I will return unto you, saith the Lord of hosts. But ye said, Wherein shall we return? Will a man rob God? Yet ye have robbed me. But ye say, Wherein have we robbed thee? In tithes and offerings. Ye are cursed with a curse: for ye have robbed me, even this whole nation. Bring ye all the tithes into the storehouse, that there may be meat in mine house, and prove me now herewith, saith the Lord of hosts, if I will not open you the windows of heaven, and pour you out a blessing, that there shall not be room enough to receive it. And I will rebuke the devourer for your sakes, and he shall not destroy [corrupt, margin] the fruit of your ground; neither shall your vine cast her fruits before the time in the field, saith the Lord of hosts.' Mal. 3:7-11.

"Bring in the tithes and offerings, that God may be

pleased with you, and bless your labors that they be profitable. Before we proceed further, let us notice what offerings are accepted with God. 'But to do good and to communicate [share] forget not: for with such sacrifices God is well pleased.' Heb. 13:16. To whom shall we communicate, or with whom shall we share? 'Let him that is taught in the Word communicate unto him that teacheth in all good things. ... And let us not be weary in well-doing: for in due season we shall reap, if we faint not.' Gal. 6:6-9. Here is one class. Share with those who teach you in the Word. 'Distributing to the necessity of saints; given to hospitality.' Rom. 12:13. Distribute to needy saints, and God will never let you come to want for so doing. There is yet another class. 'As we have therefore opportunity, let us do good unto all men, especially unto them who are of the household of faith.' Gal. 6:10.

"We will now look into the New Testament Scriptures to see what God has promised there. These are Jesus' own words: 'Give, and it shall be given unto you; good measure, pressed down, and shaken together, and running over, shall men give into your bosom. For with the same measure ye mete withal it shall be measured to you again.' Luke 6:38. Surely if any one is needy, he had better begin giving and receive the hundredfold. No danger of coming to want with such a promise from the great God hanging over you. Move out and no longer fear; for 'my God shall supply all your need according to his riches in glory by Christ Jesus.' Phil. 4:19. 'Yes,' says some one, 'you ministers and gospel workers can depend upon God for what you need, but we must work for what we get.' Will you please turn to Phil. 4:9 and read on down very carefully. You will see that Paul was writing to them concerning giving; telling them how once and again he had received their gifts, and how he is still encouraging them to give more. He says, 'Not because I desire a gift: but I desire fruit that may abound to your account.' ver. 17. And that he had received 'the things which were sent from you, an odor of a sweet smell, a sacrifice acceptable, well-pleasing to God.' [Giving to the poor and needy, or sending the gospel to those who sit in darkness, is an odorous sacrifice to God. How beautiful! The remembrance of our deeds of charity and hospitality being a sweet odor unto God must make such offerings a delight—*Auth.*] Then he gives them this great promise that God would supply all their needs. He was not talking to preachers at all, although we can rest upon this promise, but to the church at Philippi. And the same Lord is rich unto all who call upon him. Praise his name!

"Now, you who are at home laboring in temporal things, and can not go yourselves to minister the Word of God to others, just let go of everything and get down before God and ask him how much you can give to help this work along. Here is an opportunity to do good to all men. And 'as ye have therefore opportunity, do good unto all men,' then you can take these promises for your own and depend upon God to supply all your needs. You can and need to be just as much given up to God, and just as dependent upon him as the ministry is. Who will help now, by means and prayers, to send the gospel to every creature and every land?''

Good works do not cease with giving. There are many opportunities for all to do good that God might be glorified. Even the poor will find many opportunities for doing something that will benefit some fellow creature, exalt the name of Jesus and bring a blessing to their own soul. There are the sick and the discouraged to be visited and prayed with. There are kind and sympathetic words that need to be spoken to lighten the burden of some weary heart. All around us are opportunities for loving deeds and good works that can be done as unto Jesus, which are precious treasures being laid up for us in the glory world.

EATING OF MEATS.

Many are the arguments on this subject from the pulpit and the press, from the wise and not wise; and many have been deceived and led to believe that to eat or refuse to eat certain kinds of meat is a duty they either owe to themselves or to God. Many professed gospel preachers spend much time in discussing this subject of meats, and would have their followers believe that the eating of certain kinds of meat is an offense against God, and through their selfishness and ignorance endeavor to prove their arguments from the law of Moses, which was absolutely done away with when Christ died on the cross as a sacrifice for the sins of the world. I have no more to do with the law of Moses than I have with any law that has been repealed by the last act of Congress. It is disannulled and taken away by the one that succeeds it. Paul says, "Christ the end of the law for righteousness to every one that believeth." Rom. 10:4.

The law was merely a temporary form of government until Christ should come, to whom the promise was made. It served as a schoolmaster to bring us to Christ, but when Christ came we were no longer under a schoolmaster. Gal. 3:19, 24.

"Christ is become of no effect unto you, whosoever of you are justified by the law; ye are fallen from grace." Gal. 5:4. "That no man is justified by the law in the sight of God, it is evident: for, The just shall live by faith." Gal. 3:11. "Christ hath redeemed us from the curse of the law." Gal. 3:13. These scriptures show plainly that the law of Moses can not be taken as proof of the righteousness which Jesus Christ established; for, says the apostle, "The law was given by Moses, but grace and truth came by Jesus Christ." John 1:17. So then the law was neither grace nor truth as regards matters pertaining to you and me.

The New Testament Scriptures settle most questions beyond all doubts, and leave no room for discussion. Paul speaks very lightly of this matter of eating meats, and his language shows it to be of no importance whatever. He says, "Meats for the belly, and the belly for meats: but God shall destroy both it and them." 1 Cor 6:13. "For the kingdom of God is not meat and drink; but righteousness, and peace, and joy in the Holy Ghost." Rom. 14:17. The apostle means to set forth the idea that the kingdom of God has nothing to do with meat and drink, and such trifling things as dieting ourselves is not taken into consideration. But the kingdom of God is righteousness, peace, and joy in the Holy Ghost; it is a spiritual, not a physical existence. I may eat all kinds of meat and be in the kingdom of God, or I may eat no meat and be in the kingdom of God.

Christ said, "There is nothing from without a man, that entering into him can defile him; but the things which come out of him. . . . Are ye so without understanding also? do ye not perceive that whatsoever thing from without entereth into the man it can not defile him; . . . because it entereth not into his heart, but into the belly, and goeth out into the draught, purging all meats." Mark 7:15, 19. "That which cometh out of the man, that defileth the man. For from within, out of the heart of men, proceed evil thoughts, adulteries, fornications, murders, thefts, covetousness, wickedness, deceit, lasciviousness, an evil eye, blasphemy, pride, foolishness: all these evil things come from within and defile the man." Mark 7: 20-23.

Paul says, "Let not him that eateth despise him that eateth not; and let not him which eateth not judge him that eateth: **for God hath received him.**" Rom. 14: 3. "I know and am persuaded by the Lord Jesus, that there is nothing unclean of itself: but to him that esteemeth anything to be unclean, to him it is unclean." Rom. 14: 14. And again, "Let no man therefore judge you in meat, or in drink, or in respect of an holy **day, or of the new moon, or of the sab**bath days." Col. 2: 16. Paul says, "The Spirit speaketh expressly [notice he says the Spirit speaketh *expressly*], that in the latter time some shall depart from the faith, giving heed to seducing spirits, and doctrines of devils: speaking lies in hypocrisy: having their conscience seared with a hot iron; forbidding to marry, and commanding to abstain from meats which God hath created to be received with thanksgiving of them which believe and know the truth. For every creature of God is good, and nothing to be refused, if it be received with thanksgiving: for it is sanctified by the Word of God and prayer." 1 Tim. 4: 1-5.

Now note carefully the apostles language. Those who forbid to marry and command to abstain from meats are classed with those who hold forth the doctrine of devils, and speak lies in hypocrisy. It is the doctrine of devils to say that any meat is unclean; for said he, God created them and they are his creatures. Then he goes on to say to Timothy, "If thou put the brethren in remembrance of these things, thou shalt be a good minister of Jesus Christ, nourished up in the words of faith and of good doctrine, whereunto thou hast attained." 1 Tim. 4: 6. If any kind of meat is offensive to me, there is no law either natural or divine that says I must eat. I have a right to abstain from it if I choose. It is no sin for me to do that, but I have no right to say to others, It is a sin for you to eat pork or any other kind of meat.

THE SIN AGAINST THE HOLY GHOST.

"Wherefore I say unto you, All manner of sin and blasphemy shall be forgiven unto men: but the blasphemy against the Holy Ghost shall not be forgiven unto men. And whosoever speaketh a word against the Son of man, it shall be forgiven him: but whosoever speaketh against the Holy Ghost, it shall not be forgiven him, neither in this world, neither in the world to come." Mat. 12: 31, 32.

"Verily I say unto you, All sins shall be forgiven unto the sons of men, and blasphemies wherewith soever they shall blaspheme: but he that shall blaspheme against the Holy Ghost hath never forgiveness, but is in danger of eternal damnation: because they said, He hath an unclean spirit." Mark 3: 28-30.

"And whosoever shall speak a word against the Son of man, it shall be forgiven him: but unto him that blasphemeth against the Holy Ghost it shall not be forgiven." Luke 12: 10.

From these texts of Scripture we learn that all manner of sin is pardonable, save one, the blasphemy against the Holy Ghost. There is no crime too great, or sin too deeply dyed to be forgiven, except the one designated in these scriptures. Well might it be asked, What is that sin? It is evident that the Holy Spirit (which is the same as the Holy Ghost) is no more supreme or important than others of the trinity; so therefore why should all blasphemy against the Father or Son be pardonable, and the blasphemy of the Holy Spirit be unpardonable. The answer will be found to lie in the nature and office work of the Holy Spirit, as being different from that of the Father or Son. Of course the Father, Son, and Holy Spirit are all one; yet they might well be considered as three, when we speak of their respective offices. The Father, the grand author of all good, the Creator of the world, the one who holdeth all things in his control, the designer of the glorious plan of redemption of fallen man. The Son, the one on whom that redemption depended, who only was found worthy to open the book and loose the seals of the divine plan, and thus make salvation possible. The Holy Spirit, the one who, after the Father and Son had perfected their work, was sent to reprove the world of sin, of righteousness, and of judgment. He it is that strives with men by way of a kind of inherent knowledge, testifying to them of salvation's waters flowing free, and that they should forsake sin and plunge therein. By the Holy Spirit is God's way of manifesting himself to men, convicting them of sin, righteousness, and judgment. True, as Paul says, God "hath in these last days spoken unto us by his Son;" but notice, it is *"hath spoken."* The Son has done his part, we have his words on record, and he is at the right hand of the Father; and he has himself said that he would go away, that the Comforter (Holy Spirit) might come. And now we are living in the special dispensation of the Holy Spirit.

The sin against the Holy Ghost, as it is commonly called, is also known as the "unpardonable sin," and the "sin unto death." See 1 John 5:16. As we before said, the answer to the question, Why is it unpardonable, lies in the very nature of the Holy Spirit's relationship to man. Are we to suppose that it is some sin too heinous to be forgiven? or that God has decided that this sin is one that bears too heavily against his willingness to forgive? or, in other words, that his great love is not sufficient, were it weighed in the balance with this sin? Nay; that is not the light in which it is to be regarded. This is a sin that is different in its effects from other sins. It is one by which man unprivileges himself to be saved.

He disconnects himself, so to speak, from all possible operations or strivings of the Spirit of God with him. He might blaspheme God, or the Son, and it would be the same as any other sin. But he blasphemes the Spirit whenever he takes action against (and casts out, so to speak) that inherent principle in him which tends to draw him to God. By so doing he places himself outside the realm of possibilities, as regards his own salvation; for he severs all possible communication from God to him, unless it be what is manifest by the presentation of awful fear of approaching damnation.

It will be seen that in committing this sin a man by choice wilfully places himself in such a position, in reference to the inner dictations of the Spirit, that the latter is killed or destroyed. He can blaspheme God, and the convictions of the Spirit in him be unaffected, save that continual so doing might lessen them; but when he blasphemes the Spirit—it being so interwoven as to be, in a sense, a part of himself—he involves his own soul, by taking a stand against himself, as it were, thereby unfitting and unqualifying himself to be further affected by the Spirit. He drowns, dissolves, annihilates the inner strivings of the Spirit.

If we examine carefully the quotation from Mark, we see by verse thirty that the reason Christ said what he did about blasphemy against the Holy Ghost was because certain scribes said he had an unclean spirit, and cast out devils by Beelzebub, the prince of devils. Now whether they thereby committed the blasphemy of the Spirit, we do not know; but from Christ's words that followed, a strong inference could be drawn that they did. It was at least a close step to it, and depended on the degree of inherent knowledge they had that Jesus was the Christ. If they did it ignorantly, it was not blasphemy.

In the sixth chapter of the Hebrews, verses four to eight, the apostle speaks of such as have been partakers of the Holy Ghost, and were enlightened, etc., who, if they shall "fall away," directly disinherit themselves of the privilege of being renewed unto repentance, and "crucify *to themselves* the Son of God afresh, and put him to an open shame." By so doing they virtually do violence to the Spirit's convictions to such an extent that they blaspheme the Spirit. We are persuaded that Paul here had no reference to a person being overcome of the devil in some great temptation so as to commit sin, while at the same time the soul protests against sin. That would not be *falling away* (as here meant) from the love, neither the faith of God. Indeed, it is the very love of God, as well as the Spirit's convictions, that causes such a one to have immediate sorrow for the sin committed, and causes the soul to quickly flee to God again. But what the apostle meant by "falling away" was to forsake the Lord, give up the faith, walk no more in the truth or with God's children, and be content to live in sin. But take notice of the standard which he gives, from which "falling away" may be considered. He says, "those who were once enlightened," had "tasted of the heavenly gift," were "partakers of the Holy Ghost," had "tasted the good word of God, and the powers of the world to come;" if such fall away—forsake the Lord and choose to live in sin—they soon become incapable of being affected by any manifestation of the Spirit or any inducement held out to them—a deplorable, lost condition! bearing only thorns and briers! whose end is to be burned! Now we ask, Who ever saw any one come back to God who was content to remain away from God, after having had the experience described in Heb. 6:4, 5? We have seen some who exactly correspond to the description Paul gives here, but we have never known any such to come back to the truth. May we use this, as the apostle intended it, as a warning against unfaithfulness to God.

In Heb. 10:26-29 the apostle makes mention of the same conditions, only in a different way. Here he speaks of *sinning wilfully* "after that we have received the knowledge of the truth." Of course, all sin, to be sin, is done more or less wilfully; but the apostle can not have reference to a sin committed on account of a spiritual lack, while the soul meaningly presses on in the race for God. We know that such a sin does not unfit one to become pardoned again, the Holy Spirit is not blasphemed, and therefore the sacrifice (Christ) still remains, to which the soul may flee. To "sin wilfully" here means more, as is unmistakably implied in verses twenty-eight and twenty-nine. He illustrates by one who despised Moses' law, as though he now means one who is despising the law of Christ; and he explains himself in verse twenty-nine, where we see he has reference to one "who hath trodden under foot the Son of God, and hath counted the blood of the covenant, wherewith he was sanctified, an unholy thing, and hath done despite unto the Spirit of grace." Here "sin wilfully" comprehends the blasphemy of the Spirit, and he evidently means, by the term, a wilful turning again to a life of sin, a deliberate giving up of the faith, and choosing sin instead. This is also used as a stimulus to the saints to exhort one another, and neglect not the assembling of themselves together, or the provoking unto love and good works, etc.

From these two places in the Hebrews it might be supposed that to be in an unpardonable condition a person must have once been saved. But the apostle in both places is necessarily addressing saved people, and holds up such a condition as a warning against unfaithfulness. He deals in what is applicable to them. But this does not prove that a man who has never known the way of truth may not also place himself where he is unpardonable.

It is safe and Scriptural to take the stand that a person is pardonable so long as he is capable of being sorry for his sin, for God's sake, or of having a real desire to love and serve God. The promise and privilege is to "whosoever will." This is as broad as broad can be, and whoever wills can know assuredly that salvation is for him, notwithstanding the disputations of the devil to the contrary. In Heb. 12:16, 17 one would infer from the apostle's illustration of Esau that a person can be in a condition where repentance may be earnestly desired, even with tears, yet impossible to be found. But genuine repentance is not implied here. The margin has it, "He [Esau] found no place to change his mind," instead of "no place for repentance." A person may commit the unpardonable sin and still desire to change his condition or lot; he may through fear of eternal damnation desire rather the position of a Christian: but he never repents, he can not repent, it is not "in him" to repent, he will not meet the conditions for salvation, and no one can get him to do so. He may bewail his condition and stand in dread of the judgment, from a feeling of selfish protection; he may be sorry for his sins as a criminal may be sorry for his crime when he is sentenced to be punished: but he has no inclination to godly sorrow; in fact, the spirit of the man and the Spirit of God are incompatible; he has placed himself where the Spirit of God can in no way bring itself to bear upon him. Oh, how awful is such a state! But he is not conscious of any awfulness from having offended God;

his awfulness proceeds from a sense of his being eternally lost. The only impulses that might draw such a one to seek the Christian state are those of the selfish kind, just as a man may desire salvation from a belief that it would be conducive to his selfish interest. A person will never get an experience of salvation through such motives; and in the case of the one who has committed the blasphemy of the Spirit, he may have such motives, but he can never have the genuine kind, or in other words, be drawn of the Spirit. Such a sin need not be prayed for. 1 John 5:16. It is certainly a sin unto death.

In conclusion we would say that the unpardonable sin is not to be regarded as some particular sin, singled out from all others, as though it were some form of murder, lying, or stealing, more heinous than the rest. But it lies in the nature of the sin committed, as affecting the relationship with the Holy Spirit. A person may have committed a whole list of the blackest crimes, and yet not have committed the unpardonable sin; or vice versa, a person may have a good standing in point of morality, and yet have blasphemed the Spirit, and severed himself from all possibility of repentance. We would say to every despairing soul seeking salvation, that if you are capable of having the least godly sorrow on account of your sin, or a real, inward desire to serve God, you can rest assured that you have not committed the unpardonable sin. If you feel the Spirit of God telling you that you ought to be saved, then salvation is for you. The unpardonable sin deprives a person of the desire to will to love and serve God and obey the truth. So in the language of Scripture we continue to hold out the blessed invitation—"Whosoever *will*, let him take the water of life freely." Amen.

THE CONSCIENCE.

When we behold the mechanism of man, we are made to exclaim with the Psalmist, "I am fearfully and wonderfully made; marvelous are thy works; and that my soul knoweth right well." Man is so constituted as to experience a feeling of joy when a desired object is obtained, or a feeling of disappointment if it is not obtained. When danger approaches he intuitively seeks to avert it, and experiences a feeling of gladness if he succeeds. Among the elements of man's moral nature the highest and most important, perhaps, is the conscience. Conscience is a principle which God has placed in man's moral being to teach him what is right and what is wrong. Some have said that conscience is the "voice of God in the soul." It is a voice that is inaudible to the ear, but we feel it speaking in us, saying, "This action is right," or, "That action is wrong." We believe that Solomon was referring to the conscience when he said, "The spirit of man is the candle of the Lord, searching all the inward parts of the belly." Prov. 20:27.

Where there is no known law, conscience becomes

our guide and the standard by which we are judged. For proof of this we will quote Rom. 2: 14, 15: "For when the Gentiles, which have not a law, do by nature [a kind of intuitive knowledge of right] the things contained in the law, these, having not the law, are a law unto themselves; which shew the work of the law written in their hearts, their conscience also bearing witness, and their thoughts the meanwhile accusing or else excusing one another." In many circumstances of life we have no written law of God to guide our actions, consequently must be directed by reason and conscience, which are highly analogous. To be perfectly and properly directed by the conscience necessitates a close walk with God. "Keeping in touch with God" is God in our conscious being, impressing us with proper actions, and leading us in the right way, and showing us the relationship existing between the pure soul and the Deity. Where there is no written law of God to direct the actions in a certain circumstance, those who experience a close connection with God will always act the most wisely; because the "candle of the Lord" (the conscience) is a light in them, impressing them with feelings of right in the matter.

The conscious principle in the moral nature suffered greatly in the fall of man, and is seriously impaired by violation of the known laws of God, or laws of conscience. There is a beautiful harmony between truth and a correct conscience. Obedience to the truth is always approved by an unimpaired conscience. When a known truth is violated, a searing influence is introduced upon the conscience, which grows with every violation, until the conscience becomes seared as with a hot iron. Dangers of delusion lie in the fact that after a succession of violations, the conscience becomes so morbid that it fails to be a correct judge of action. After a time a man can violate a plain truth without experiencing any sting of conscience; therefore he concludes his actions are right, because he experiences no condemnation, though they are in opposition to the truth. There is great beauty in the thought, and gratification in the knowledge, that by obedience to the truth we can obtain a sound moral condition, whose conscientious principles are so acute that there is a timely warning at every approach of error.

To possess a purged, pure, and undefiled conscience is our privilege in the economy of grace. See Heb. 9:14; 1 Tim. 3:9; Titus 1:15. To possess an unimpaired conscience and then so meet all our obligations to God and man is to have a conscience void of offense. What implicit confidence we can have in God when in a normal moral condition, and have an uncondemned heart. Enoch walked with God and had the witness (consciousness) that he pleased the Lord. What can bring greater happiness to the heart of man? The man who, having an undefiled moral being has a conscience void of offense toward God and man, experiences a satisfaction and a happiness unsurpassed by any mortal being.

THE TWO FAMILIES.

The Scriptures talk of two classes of people on the earth. The inhabitants of this globe are by the Word of God divided into two great families. One family is termed the righteous, and the other the unrighteous. One is the godly, the other the ungodly. One is the holy, the other the unholy. The righteous family is likened unto or called sheep, the unrighteous family, goats. Mat. 25:32, 33. They are interspersed throughout the earth. When the Son of man is come they shall be separated. One family shall be admitted into an eternity of bliss, the other into an eternity of punishment. One family is represented by a good tree, the other by an evil tree. In the parable of the sower the Savior likens one family unto wheat, and the other unto tares.

Since there are two families there are, of course, two fathers. God is the Father of one of these families (2 Cor. 6:18), and Satan is the father of the other. John 8:44. These fathers are sometimes called masters. "One is your Master, even God." Now every individual on the globe is either in servitude to one or the other of these masters—never to both. "No man can serve two masters." "His servants ye are to whom ye obey, whether of sin unto death or of obedience unto righteousness."

The Scriptures so plainly locate the dividing line between these two families that all can very well know to which family they belong. Those who are born into God's family do not commit sin. 1 John 3:9; 1 John 5:18. Those belong to the devil's family who do commit sin. 1 John 3:8. This is very plain. None need be mistaken. Those who do not commit sin are the wheat or good seed, and are children of the kingdom. Those who do commit sin are the tares or children of the wicked one. Mat. 13. Those who do not commit sin have their names written in heaven. But those who sin do not have their names written there (Ex. 32:33), therefore are not members in the family of God.

It is said that some people are mistaken as to which family they belong, but it is "not every one that saith, Lord, Lord, that shall enter into the kingdom of heaven." God's family are righteous, they are holy, they are pure, they are saints. Satan's family are unrighteous, they are unholy, they do not believe in purity, they commit sin. The Savior has gone to prepare a place for his own so that where he is there they may forever be—glory! glory! Those who live and die in sin can not go to that pure and happy place. John 8:21. Dear friend, get ready. Live a pure, holy life and spend an eternity in the blissful presence of our dear Redeemer. God bless you, is my sincere prayer.

THE TWO WAYS.

This earth is only man's transitory home. He lives here a few years, then goes to an eternity. There are two abodes or dwelling-places for man in that eternity. One is called heaven, the other is called hell. One is a place of peace and joy, the other a place of torment and woe. One place is called eternal life, the other is called eternal death.

As man enters upon his journey of life two ways are set before him. Deut. 30: 15, 19. One way leads to heaven, and is called the way of life and good. The other way leads to hell, and is called the way of death and evil. The way to heaven is denominated the holy way, where walk the redeemed. The ransomed ones go singing on this way with crowns of joy upon their heads. This way shines more and more, brighter and brighter, as it nears the end.

The way to hell is denominated the way of the transgressor. It is a hard way. There is no peace there, no rest. The darkness becomes more dense, and fears increase as it nears the end. The way to everlasting life in heaven is called a narrow way. Mat. 7: 14. There are few that walk this way. The way that leads to destruction is a broad way. Mat. 7: 13. There are many who are walking in that way. Dear reader, will you not choose the way of life and make heaven your eternal and happy home?

CONCLUSION OF PART FIRST.

We have now reached the conclusion of the first division of the Gospel Day, namely, The Morning. We have not given the reader our opinion, or our interpretation of the Scriptures, but we have given the pure, simple Bible truths as taught by Christ and the apostles. It is not our doctrine, but the doctrine of him that sent us. What we have taught is in perfect accord with the Bible, and who can gainsay it?

To believe, experience, and live the truths of God's Word is to be a light in the world. To disbelieve any part, to come short of any part in practical life, is to be to the same extent in darkness. Christ was a light because he was the Word. The early church and apostles were a light because they believed, experienced and practised in life the whole Word. The Bible was written in their hearts as well as in the book. The Bible never changes, God never changes, the nature of faith and grace never changes, and true gospel light never changes. What created light in the first century of this Christian era will create light in any other century, and nothing but what was light in the primitive days of Christianity will be light at any other time. Whatever may be claimed to be light, if it is not the light of Christ, is a false light.

May God help people to see the true light. Oh, glorious light of the morning! Christ and his church in all humility, gentleness, spotlessness and love. In their lowly, inoffensive walk with God, holy, harmless, undefiled, unblamable, separated from and unspotted by the world, persecuted, rejected, and despised by men. Enduring all without a murmur, contented in any and every circumstance of life; counting everything joy, glorying in tribulation, patient in imprisonments, in stripes, in tumults, in hunger, in fastings, in necessities, in afflictions, in distresses, always rejoicing. When reviled, they reviled not again; when they suffered they threatened not, but showing all meekness and gentleness unto all men, loving and praying for their enemies, feeding them when they hungered and giving them drink when they thirsted, preaching the gospel without money and without price, led exclusively by the Holy Spirit, having power with God over devils to cast them out, to heal the sick and lame, to restore sight to the blind and hearing to the deaf, to give speech to the dumb, and to raise the dead. Wonderful light of the gospel morning! Dear reader, we invite you to look upon the picture. See it in its beautiful transparent effulgent light. Pure as heaven, holy as a band of angels, peaceful as the silent, flowing river, harmless as the gentle dove, in a oneness equal with the holy trinity, and conquerors of sickness, sin and Satan. Such was the pure virgin bride of Christ—the church—when she was the light of the world.

> O Moon—so fair in the rosy morn,
> Reflecting the light of Christ—the Sun,
> So spotless and pure in robes of white,
> Beautiful, wonderful city of light.

PART II
THE NOONDAY:
or,
THE DOCTRINES OF AN APOSTATE RELIGION OBSCURING THE GOSPEL LIGHT.

The prophet Isaiah said, "The morning cometh, and also the night." Isa. 21:11, 12. A dark night succeeded the morning of this gospel day. Jesus said to his disciples, "But in those days, after that tribulation, the sun shall be darkened, and the moon shall not give her light." Mark 13:24. The tribulation here spoken of was the siege and destruction of Jerusalem, the city of the Jews, by the son of Vespasian, A. D. 70, in which eleven hundred thousand persons perished. Josephus says of this time, "The sufferings indeed of the devoted inhabitants are such as humanity shudders to contemplate, and over which pity is glad to throw a veil." This is the tribulation of which our Lord spoke. The darkening of the sun and moon was the fading away of the gospel light.

About the year 96 A. D. the writings of the New Testament were closed. From that time we have only history to tell us of Christianity and its light in the life of men. That the noontime of this gospel day was dark, is unquestionable. To ascertain as near as possible the date of the close of the morning light and the beginning of the dark noonday we must resort to history. No one can rightly object to this. We assure you we will extract nothing that will conflict with the inspired and infallible Word of God. Where the Word of truth is silent and we can gain information from authentic history it must certainly be proper and right. Historical facts only verify and explain the truthfulness of the Scriptures.

CHAPTER I.

THE DATE OF THE BEGINNING OF NOONDAY.

SABINE'S ECCLESIASTICAL HISTORY.

In speaking of Constantine's expedition to Rome in the year 311, when there appeared supernaturally a cross above the sun, he says: "During the vicissitudes in the state, the church exhibits nothing peculiarly great. Among the common people there were doubtless many truly devoted in the spirit of their mind, and among them many that loved the divine

Savior above life itself; but among the bishops and pastors nothing like what we saw in the past century. Indeed the principal events in the internal department of the church are rather more to its disgrace than its honor."

Speaking further of this time in another chapter he says: "The pagan temples were pulled down or converted into Christian churches; the exercise of the old priesthood was proscribed and the idols destroyed; elegant structures for Christian worship were raised, and those already erected, enlarged and beautified; the episcopacy was increased and honored with great favors and enriched with vast endowments; the ritual received many additions; the habiliments of the clergy were pompous, and the whole of the Christian service at once exhibited a scene of worldly grandeur and external parade. What a mighty change! But a short time since, and Christianity was held in sovereign contempt: now she is a favorite at court, and the companion of princes. Alas! such is the change, that it scarcely affords ground for triumph. The kingdom of our God and his Christ is become a kingdom of this world, and the church of Jesus reduced to a mere worldly sanctuary. The glory is departed, the gold is become dim, and the fine gold is changed.

"Indeed prelatical pride had been rising very high for a century before this. The pastors had forgotten their Master's instruction, 'Be ye not called Rabbi; for ye are brethren.' Lord bishops and archbishops and all the spirit of such distinction had been long enough upon the advance to congratulate such an emperor as Constantine. The materials for a hierarchy having been prepared it was no difficult thing for a set of worldly-minded bishops, countenanced by a prince, to put them together. Under all these circumstances, real religion was not likely to be bettered by such a reverse in external affairs, and so the event proved. The ancient contest, which was for the faith once delivered unto the saints, declined apace, and a strife for worldly honor, fleshly gratification, and spiritual dominion substituted in its stead."

Such was the true condition of things in the year 311. Surely there had been a change, the kingdom of God had become the kingdom of the world, the glory was gone, strivings for worldy honor, fleshly gratification, and spiritual dominion had taken the place of "striving for the faith once delivered to the saints." What a change from the humble, self-denying, flesh crucifying days of Christ and the apostles. Truly we can say sometime before this the morning light had dimmed and died, and darkness intervened. The historian does not fix this date (311) as the beginning of the dark noonday. (The reader already begins to see, no doubt, why it was dark at the noontime.) He says in a preceding chapter, "About A. D. 264, a considerable stir was made by Paul of Samosata, bishop of Antioch. 'Great was the falling off in this church since the renowned Ignatius. The principles of Paul were exceedingly loose, and his practise was correspondent.' He rejected the divinity of the Son and substituted his own reason for the light of the Spirit. The way in which he lived fully proved that he was a man of the world."

The historian proceeds to tell more of this bishop's wicked life. The Scriptural qualifications of a bishop are, blamelessness, the husband of one wife, vigilant, sober, of good behavior, given to hospitality, apt to teach; "not given to wine, no striker, not greedy of filthy lucre; but patient, not a brawler, not covetous; one that ruleth well his own house, having his children in subjection with all gravity." 1 Tim. 3: 3, 4. The seventh verse adds: "Moreover he must have a good report of them which are without." Such a bishop must be, in the very strictest sense, to be a light in the world. Here was a bishop, of perhaps the strongest Christian congregation in the world, almost everything to the contrary. How true the Savior's prophecy: "The moon shall not give her light, and the stars of heaven shall fall." Paul, of Samosata, became so wicked he was deposed from his office and became a "fallen star."

Sabine speaking of divisions and their causes says: "In this century the general church was rent in twain. This century also produced a train of other officers (beside bishops and deacons), such as subdeacons, who were all to the deacon what the presbyter was to the bishop; acolytes, persons to attend at service time on the ministers; ostiaries, doorkeepers; readers, men who were appointed to read the Scriptures in public; exorcists, officers of weak and superstitious appointment, whose business was to pretend to expel the devil from the candidate for baptism. All these encroachments and changes mark, strongly mark, a great decline in the spirit and power of primitive Christianity.''

All of these things, and many more similar ones, were occurring in the latter part of the third century.

In the year of our Lord 248 Cyprian was ordained a presbyter in the church at Carthage. Ten years later he laid down his life for Jesus. It is said of him that he "displayed a benevolent and pious mind and evinced much of the character of the Christian pastor in the affectionate solicitude with which he watched over his flock. In epistle eleven he says: "It must be owned and confessed that the outrageous and heavy calamity which hath almost devoured our flock, and continues to devour it to this day, hath happened to us because of our sins, since we keep not the way of the Lord, nor observe his heavenly commands, which were designed to lead us to salvation. Christ our Lord fulfilled the will of the Father, but we neglect the will of Christ. Our principal study is to get money and estates; we follow after pride, we are at leisure for nothing but emulation and quarreling, and have neglected the simplicity of faith. We have renounced this world in words only, and not in deed. Every one studies to please himself and to displease others."

This account of professed Christianity at this time by Cyprian is confirmed by the testimony of Eusebius, who was nearly contemporary with him. "Through too much liberty they grew negligent and slothful, envying and reproaching one another, waging, as it were, civil wars among themselves, bishops quarreling with bishops, and the people divided into parties. Hypocrisy and deceit were grown to the highest pitch of wickedness. They were become so insensible as not so much as to think of appeasing the divine anger; but like atheists they thought the world destitute of any providential government and care, and thus added one crime to another. The bishops themselves had thrown off all concern about religion, were perpetually contending with one another, and did nothing but quarrel with and threaten and envy and hate one another; they were full of ambition and tyrannically used their power."—*Eusebius' History*, Book VIII, Chap. I, as quoted in *Jones' Church History*.

RUTER'S CHURCH HISTORY. (THIRD CENTURY.)

"With the opinions, the Christian teachers had adopted the habits and manners of the philosophic school. They assumed the dress of the pompous sophist, and delivered the plain doctrines of the gospel with strained and studied eloquence."

"This season of external prosperity was improved by the ministers of the church for the exertion of new claims and the assumption of powers with which they had not previously been invested."—p. 52.

"Several alterations in the form of church government appear to have been introduced during the third century. Some degree of pomp was thought necessary to render so singular an institution respectable to the minds of a gross multitude who are only capable of judging from external appearances. As their numbers increased their labors became proportionally greater, and it was necessary to provide assistance and more agreeable to good order to assign to each his proper function. Inferior ministers were therefore instituted, who derived their appellations from the office they filled.

"These ministers probably derived their emoluments, not merely from the precarious bounty of the society, but from a certain proportion of the fixed revenues of the church. The principal of them had obtained before the close of this century the possession of several considerable estates, which had been bequeathed or presented to the church. The external dignity of the ministers of religion was accompanied by a still greater change in its discipline. The simple rules prescribed by the apostles for the preservation of good order in the church branched out into so many luxuriant shoots that it was difficult to recognize the parent stem."—p. 53.

"A regular form of discipline began to take place during the third century in every matter which fell within the cognizance of the church." p. 51.

Following this, Ruter gives an account of the penitents seeking salvation who had to proceed step by step. The first degree was to prostrate themselves in the avenues of the church building. Here they were called *flentes*. In the second degree they were allowed to enter the building and hear the sermon. Here they were called *audientes*. In the third degree they were allowed to unite in prayers offered in their own behalf. Here they were called *genuflecientes*. In the fourth degree they were allowed to approach the altar and were called *consistentes*. In the taking of these degrees the penitents were compelled to appear in sackcloth and ashes, and in some places the men were obliged to shave their heads and the women to wear veils. The duration of their penitence was regulated by the bishop. He could make the time of taking these degrees short, or extend it to any length. This was called an indulgence.

This is shocking in the extreme. Where in the humble acts of Jesus and his apostles do you hear of such an order of things? Truly at this time the sun was darkened, and the moon did not give her light, and the stars had fallen. How true now appears the prophecy of Isaiah: "The people of thy holiness have possessed it but a little while: our adversaries have trodden down thy sanctuary." Isa. 63:18. Jesus says, "Lay not up for yourselves treasures upon the earth," and Paul says to the bishop to be "not greedy of filthy lucre"; and Peter says, "Taking the oversight not for filthy lucre's sake"—and here before the close of the third century we find the bishops coming into possession of large estates through the revenues of the church, and as Cyprian has said of the bishops of this time, "Our principal study is to get money and estates."

We have before us Mosheim's Church History. In speaking of the internal history of the church in the third century he says that "the bishops of Rome, Antioch and Alexandria had a kind of preeminence over all others, and particularly the bishop at Rome." There was a change in the form of government and this change was followed by a train of vices. "Many of those who had the administration of the church affairs were sunk, he says, "in luxury and voluptuousness, puffed up with vanity, arrogance and ambition; possessed with a spirit of contention and discord. They appropriated to their evangelical function the splendid ensigns of temporal majesty: a throne, surrounded with ministers, exalted above his equals, the servant of the meek and humble Jesus. ... The titles of sub-deacons, acolythi, ostairii, readers, exorcists, copiatæ, would never have been heard of in the church if its rulers had been assiduously and zealously employed in promoting the interest of truth and piety by their labors and their example." He gives an account of the trouble in the church of Rome between Cornelius and Novatian, in the year 250, who were aspirants for the Roman See.

Eusebius tells of the increasing vices, schisms, quarrelings of the bishops, of their greed for money and preeminence in the last half of the third century. In speaking of the bishops and pastors who had the administration of church government in the year 260, he says: "But some that appeared to be our pastors, deserting the law of piety, were inflamed against each other with mutual strifes, only accumulating quarrels and threats, rivalship, hostility and hatred to each other, only anxious to assert the government as a kind of sovereignty for themselves." Then he adds, "As Jeremiah says, 'The Lord in his anger darkened the daughter of Sion [the church or moon], and hurled from heaven to earth the glory of Israel.'"

By this we learn that Eusebius would place the darkening of the church, or the beginning of the dark noonday, near the year 260 A. D. Quotations could be transcribed from Coleman, Marsh, Waddington and others, in which they all place the close of the morning light and the rise of the apostasy or dark noonday between the years 260 and 280 A. D. To our knowledge, Joseph Milner is the only non-contemporary historian that fixes the date to any definite time. He says, "I know it is common for authors to represent the great declension of Christianity to have taken place only after its external establishment under Constantine. But the evidence of history has compelled me to dissent from this view of things. In fact we have seen that for a whole generation previous to the persecution, few marks of superior piety appeared. Scarce a luminary of godliness existed, and it is not common in any age for a great work of the Spirit of God to be exhibited but under the conduct of some remarkable saint, pastor and reformers. This whole period as well as the whole scene of the persecution is very barren of such characters. Not but that many precious children of God suffered in much patience and charity. But those who suffered with very much of a different spirit, found no pastor to discountenance their self-will and false zeal: a sure sign that the true spirit of martyrdom was less pure than it had formerly been. Moreover the prevalence of superstition on the one hand, and the decay of evangelical knowledge on the other, are equally apparent. Christ crucified, justification purely by faith, and the effectual influences of the Holy Ghost, ... were ideas at least very faintly impressed at that day on Christian minds. It is vain to expect Christian faith to abound without Christian doctrine. Moral and philosophical and monastical instructions will not effect for men what is expected from evangelical doctrine. And if the faith of Christ was so much declined (and its decayed state ought to be dated from about the year 270) we need not wonder that such scenes as Eusebius hints at without any circumstantial detail took place in the Christian world."—*Century IV,* p. 31.

After searching history we find no objection in making use of the year 270 A. D. as the date of the *beginning of the dark noontime.* Milner says at this time, "Scarcely a luminary of godliness existed. The great luminaries, or lights, were eclipsed and darkness reigned. Some of our contemporary writers have fixed upon this year as the date of the rise of the beast power, which created this darkness. "The real papacy was set up, not at the Nicene Council, A. D. 325, as some affirm; but we find vivid traces of the very same beast authority as early as A. D. 270."—*Biblical Trace of the Church.* In the city of Nice in Bithynia, A. D. 325, was held what is called "The First General Council." There was present at this council the Emperor Constantine, as the historian says, "Like an angel of God exceeding all his attendants in size, gracefulness and strength, and dazzling all eyes by the splendor of his dress, showing the greatest humility, seated in a chair covered with gold." There were present at this meeting three hundred and eighteen bishops, and a number of deacons and subdeacons, amounting in all to two thousand and forty-eight persons. Here was drawn up a creed, declaring to be the **only true and orthodox** faith. It bears the title of Nicene. This creed was at once confirmed at Rome by two hundred and seventy-five bishops, and was the setting up of the **Roman hierarchy.** This council can not however with propriety be said to be the true setting up of the beast power. Nearly all the forms and doctrines of this creed had been observed and taught by the bishops and pastors for several decades. The most sensible date, and most consistent with revelation, *for the bringing in of the dark noontime of the gospel day is A. D. 270.* We feel confident that no one can rightfully object to us making use of this date for this work. Those who do so must do it through prejudice or ignorance.

CHAPTER II.

SCRIPTURAL PREDICTIONS OF AN APOSTASY.

Who has not wondered, as they read of the Savior's and the apostles' warnings of "false teachers," grievous wolves, delusive powers, and deceptive lights, what it all could mean? These things certainly are not without meaning. Jesus says, "And many false prophets shall rise, and shall deceive many. And because iniquity shall abound the love of many shall wax cold. For there shall arise false Christs, and false prophets, and shall show great signs and wonders; insomuch that, if it were possible, they shall deceive the very elect." Mat. 24:11, 12, 24. The Son of God foretells the arising of false prophets and teachers. He tells us how they may be known. "Beware of false prophets, which come to you in sheep's clothing, but inwardly they are ravening wolves. Ye shall know them by their fruits." Mat. 7:15, 16.

By the pen of the apostle John we learn something of the fruit of these false, deceiving prophets. "For many deceivers are entered into the world, who confess not that Jesus Christ is come in the flesh. This is a deceiver and an antichrist. Look to yourselves, that we lose not those things which we have wrought, but that we receive a full reward. Whosoever transgresseth, and abideth not in the doctrine of Christ, hath not God. He that abideth in the doctrine of Christ, he hath both the Father and the Son. If there come any unto you, and bring not this doctrine, receive him not into your house, neither bid him Godspeed: for he that biddeth him Godspeed is partaker of his evil deeds." 2 John 7-11. The fruit of a false prophet is a false doctrine. A doctrine in opposition to the plain, simple doctrine of Christ is the principal characterizing feature of a deceiver. The doctrine of Christ is light. All who abide in the doctrine of Christ are a light in the world. Any doctrine contrary to the doctrine of Christ is darkness, and its propagator, a deceiver and an antichrist. This same apostle in his first letter, cautions us to "try the spirits [and doctrines], whether they are of God: because many false prophets are gone out into the world. Hereby know ye the Spirit of God;

Every spirit that confesseth that Jesus Christ is come in the flesh is of God: and every spirit that confesseth not that Jesus Christ is come in the flesh is not of God: and this is that spirit of antichrist, whereof ye have heard that it should come; and even now already it is in the world." 1 John 4: 1-3.

We feel like it would be justice to the reader to here explain how we can confess that Christ is come in the flesh, and how we can deny that he has so come. That this does not refer to his personal coming in the flesh, as a sacrifice for sin, is evident. But few but what confess that Christ was here in the flesh as recorded in the Gospels, yet many of them are not of God. Jesus says, "We will come unto him and make our abode with him." "Know ye not that ye are the temple of God?" "For ye are the temple of God; as God hath said, I will dwell in them, and walk in them; and I will be their God, and they shall be my people." "At that day ye shall know that I am in the Father, and ye in me, and I in you." John 14: 20. That day spoken of is when the Holy Spirit would come and teach them all things. That was at Pentecost. Then they knew that Christ was in them. This then is Christ come in the flesh.

Now it is not every one either that confesses by the word of mouth that Christ dwells in them that are of God. A Scriptural confession is not by word only, but by the deed, or life. Every one who confesses by their life that Christ is come in the flesh or dwells in them must and will abide in the whole doctrine of Christ, and live just as he lived. Such a one is of God, and is a light even as Christ was a light. Whoever rejects any of the Savior's doctrine, and does not, and will not, experience and practise it in his life, the same is an antichrist, however much he may profess to be of God. Try all doctrines and spirits by the doctrine of Christ, is the infallible rule.

THE PROPHECY OF PAUL.

"For I know this, that after my departing shall grievous wolves enter in among you, not sparing the flock. Also of your own selves shall men arise, speaking perverse things to draw away disciples after them. Therefore watch, and remember, that by the space of three years I ceased not to warn every one night and day with tears." Acts 20: 29-31. Paul saw the awful apostasy from the simple faith of Christ arising. The shadows of the dark noonday were slowly and surely creeping on. He beholds it with tears. This was not really some heathenish foreign power, but he says it should be men of their own selves arising, speaking perverse things. He saw that the leaders and overseers of the flock (see ver. 28) would become greedy of worldly gain, contentious, followers after pride, filled with envy, loving preeminence, speaking things contrary to the doctrine of Christ. It had begun to work already in his day. "The mystery of iniquity doth already work." 2 Thes. 2: 7.

John says these false prophets "even now already are in the world." Even before the apostles had closed their labors they saw this dark power working. Year after year, decade after decade, it developed and grew. Star after star had fallen until by the middle of the third century there was "scarcely left a luminary of godliness in existence."

Paul seeing the great crisis coming, is in fear. "But I fear, lest by any means, as the serpent beguiled Eve through his subtilty, so your minds should be corrupted from the simplicity that is in Jesus. For if he that cometh preacheth another Jesus, whom we have not preached, or if ye receive another spirit, which ye have not received, or another gospel, which ye have not accepted, ye might well bear with me. . . . For such are false apostles, deceitful workers, transforming themselves into the apostles of Christ. And no marvel; for Satan himself is transformed into an angel of light. Therefore it is no great thing if his ministers also be transformed as the ministers of righteousness; whose end shall be according to their works." 2 Cor. 11:3, 4, 13-15. Thus Paul gives warning to the Corinthians of false apostles and deceitful workers. All of this certainly is not without meaning. He foresees great danger. He earnestly exhorts the Thessalonian brethren to be not soon shaken, saying: "Let no man deceive you by any means: for that day shall not come, except there come a falling away first, and that man of sin be revealed, the son of perdition; who opposeth and exalteth himself above all that is called God, or that is worshiped; so that he as God sitteth in the temple of God, showing himself that he is God. Remember ye not, that, when I was yet with you, I told you these things? And now ye know what withholdeth that he might be revealed in his time. For the mystery of iniquity doth already work: only he who now letteth will let until he be taken out of the way. And then shall that wicked be revealed, whom the Lord shall consume with the spirit of his mouth, and shall destroy with the brightness of his coming: even him, whose coming is after the workings of Satan with all power and signs and lying wonders." 2 Thes. 2: 3-9.

This is indeed a wonderful and an awful prophecy. Surely a dark image or power called a "man of sin" and "son of perdition" shall arise and eclipse the sun (Christ) and the moon (the church) and cause the stars (the holy ministry) to fall. "There shall come a falling away first." This has direct reference to the corruption of God's professed people led by an exalted, selfish, greedy and blinded ministry. "The falling away" is translated from the Greek *apostasia,* and means a departure. Lexicographers define the word as meaning "an abandonment of what one has professed." In this text it means an abandonment of the true principles and doctrines of Christianity.

That "man of sin," "son of perdition," or, as in Rotherham's translation, "man of lawlessness," and "son of destruction," is what arose and obscured the sunlight. This epithet is given to Judas Iscariot, the betrayer of Christ, in John 17:12. This "man of sin" is a betrayer of Christ and his pure doctrine. This "man of lawlessness," no doubt, has reference directly to the pope of Rome as the prime factor in the apostasy; but in its broadest sense it includes the whole of the beast religion, both Romanism and Protestantism. This "man of sin" is a manism, or a power under the government of man, and is identical with the beast power of Rev. 13. This "son of destruction" "opposeth and exalteth himself above all that is called God." He opposes or denies, and perverts the doctrines of God that are not congenial to his desires. He denies in a measure the divine authority, and forms creeds and laws for the government of God's people, thus arrogating to himself what properly belongs to God. They take upon themselves such titles as "Father," "Holy Father," "Vicegerent of the Son of God," "Doctor of Divinity," "Reverend," etc. These are titles or distinctions belonging to God only. "Call no man your Father," is the command of Jesus; and, "Be ye not called Rabbi."

Vicegerent is one acting in the place of another. The pope's claim was that God had ceased to reign and had delegated all power unto himself—the power to forgive sins and to grant indulgences. An indulgence is an act of the Roman pontiff, wherein men by making certain vows and paying certain sums of money receive pardon of their sins. By the payment of certain amounts they can commit most any crime and their purchased indulgence absolves them from guilt.

THE PRICE OF PARDON.

Below we will give an extract from page 263 of "The Master Key to Popery," by Anthony Gavin, formerly one of the Roman Catholic priests at Saragossa, Spain. He says: According to a book called the "Tax of the Roman Chancery," in which are contained the exact sums levied for pardon of each particular sin, we find some of the fees to be thus:

Robbing a church	$ 2.25.
Simony	2.25.
Perjury	2.00.
Forgery and lying	2.00.
Robbery	3.00.
Burning a house	2.75.
Eating meat in Lent	2.75.
Killing a layman	1.75.
Striking a priest	2.75.
Procuring abortion	1.50.
Priest to keep a concubine	2.25.
Ravishing a virgin	2.00.
Murder of father, mother, brother, sister or wife	2.50.
Nun for fornication in or out of the nunnery	5.00.
Marrying on a day forbidden	10.00.
Adultery committed by a priest with nuns and others	10.00.
Absolution of all crimes together	12.00.

Following this we will give a few of the secret instructions of the Jesuits as revealed by Z. T. Griffin:

"A Christian (Romanist) may deliberately discard his Christian character and act like other men in those things which are not properly Christian. By the command of God it is lawful to murder the innocent, to rob and commit all lewdness because he is Lord of all things, and thus to fulfil his mandate is our duty.

"It is lawful to kill an accuser whose testimony may jeopardize our life and honor.

"If an adulterous priest, aware of his danger, having visited an adulteress is assailed by her husband, kills the man in his own defense, he is not a criminal.

"Papist children may accuse their parents of heresy, although they know their parents will be burned.

"A priest may kill those who hinder him from taking possession of any ecclesiastical office.

"Servants may secretly steal from their masters as much as they judge their labor is worth more than the wages which they receive.

"A woman may take her husband's property to supply her spiritual wants and to act like other women.

"A witness is not bound to declare the truth before a lawful judge, if his deposition will injure himself or his posterity, or if he be a priest; for a priest can not be forced to testify before a secular judge.

"Priests may kill the laity to preserve their goods, etc."

Such appears extremely shocking to a man of integrity and principle. Such laws and tolerations and the direct sale of indulgences brings a blush of shame to a moral man, and much more to the Christian. The sale of indulgences is not true of Romanism only. Throughout the realms of Protestantism there is a shameful sale of these indulgences in an indirect way. Wicked and designing men are tolerated and fellowshiped by the sect ministry because of their liberality to the church. It is true it matters not if a man does occasionally get drunk, or if he does defraud his neighbor, or commit adultery, abuse his wife, attend theaters, and such like sins, if he is a liberal contributor to their treasury, he is smiled at, welcomed and encouraged to be faithful.

While in the papacy we find such titles as "Holy Father," etc., in Protestantism we find the "D. D." and "LL. D." and "Reverend." They who assume such honorary titles set themselves up to be equal with God. The word "reverend" is from the Hebrew "*yare,*" and means "to be feared." So man is thus setting himself up as one to be feared, when the Word of the Lord tells us to "fear not man, but fear God." "Holy and reverend is his name." God alone is to be revered, and for man to prefix such a title to his name is to sit as God in the temple of God.

Popes and bishops are found in the councils and conferences framing laws and passing resolutions for the government of their membership and for the qualifications of a minister, like as if God had ceased to reign and there was no Bible and they alone were invested with power to govern and control the kingdom of heaven. The qualifications of a minister in some of the popular denominations of to-day are a certain number of years in school and a certain number of histories and commentaries mastered. The qualifications as given by Paul are almost wholly ignored. The profession of the ministry in the sect world has been dragged down to a level with the professions of the world. A young man decides to be a physician. He goes to school and learns his profession. He receives his diploma, comes out and practises what he was taught at school, and makes his living thereby. Another young man decides to be a lawyer. He studies for that profession, is admitted to the bar, practises, and makes his living thereby. Another young man decides to be a preacher. He goes to school and learns his profession. He is licensed, comes out and preaches, and makes his living thereby.

"For the mystery of iniquity doth already work." This is the spirit of antichrist, of which John says, "even now already is it in the world." This antichrist, apostate spirit is a mystery. It contains a hidden mysterious power that has blinded and deceived millions of souls. Even in Paul's time it began its hidden mysterious working. The Roman Catholic sect arose and met this description of the "man of sin" as given by Paul. The Waldenses in the thirteenth century looked upon the church at Rome as the "whore of Babylon," and the "man of sin." Those blinded by the mysterious, delusive spirit of iniquity considered such language against the "holy church" as blaspheming against God. Protestantism to-day with its great bishops and reverends and D. D.'s and creeds and systems, forms and ceremonies, almost as perfectly meets the description of the "man of sin" as does the Roman hierarchy. The same hidden mysterious delusive spirit has so intoxicated its subjects that they consider such speech as blasphemy.

This "man of sin" is described as coming with signs and lying wonders. The lying wonders of this dark reign of the "son of perdition" are almost innumerable. It is said that a milkwhite dove descended from heaven with a phial of oil at the baptism of Cloris.

A Sicilian hermit had a revelation from heaven in which was revealed that the prayers of the monks of Clugny would be effectual for the deliverance of the departed spirits from the expiatory flames of a middle state.—*Mosheim's Church History.*

A woman named Julian pretended she had a revelation from God in which it was disclosed to her to be the will of God that a peculiar festival should be held annually in honor of the real presence of Christ in the holy sacrament. She said that as often as she addressed herself to God or to the saints in prayer she saw a full moon with a small defect, and the spirit informed her that this defect was the want of this annual festival. This festival was established by Clement V in 1311 A. D.

The fables of the removal of the chapel of Loretto, the wandering Jew, the visions of Stockius and Sims, and St. Anthony's obliging an ass to adore the sacrament as related by Mosheim, are astonishing lying wonders and ridiculous inventions. The Protestant daughters of mystic Babylon are not free from lying wonders to this present day. The book of Mormon contains fabulous stories; the spiritualists' work is freighted with many satanic wonders, and frequently we hear of visions and revelations that when tried by the immutable Word of God are proven to be lying wonders. Our God is able to perform wonders, and of a truth, wonderful are his doings at this present time, but all that he does is in decency and in order, and contains nothing of the fabulous.

Paul says, "Now the Spirit speaketh expressly, that in the latter times some shall depart from the faith, giving heed to seducing spirits, and doctrines of devils; speaking lies in hypocrisy; having their conscience seared with a hot iron; forbidding to marry, and commanding to abstain from meats." 1 Tim. 4:1-3. You will only have to read the history of the Roman Catholic sect, of its fabulous inventions, of its awful tyranny, its superstitions, its rites and ceremonies, to find the fulfilment of this prophecy. It is extremely astonishing that men of intelligence would be the supporters of such a dark institution. It only shows the seductive power of demon spirits. The doctrines of devils that have been originated both in Romanism and Protestantism are almost without number, some of which we will speak of in our next chapter. The hypocritical lies that have been invented and the persecutions and contentions and quarrelings and fightings against one another can only be carried on by men whose conscience is seared by a hot iron. The Catholics abstain from eating meat on certain days and at certain times. A certain law sect, called the Seventh Day Adventist, teaches abstinence from pork. The papists forbid the marriage of the clergy. Neither is this unscriptural prohibition confined to the papacy alone, but some of her harlot daughters have patterned after her, and even gone beyond her in this respect.

In the time of this apostasy it is said by the apostle that "they will not endure sound doctrine; but after their own lusts shall they heap to themselves teachers, having itching ears; and they shall turn away their ears from the truth, and shall be turned unto fables." 2 Tim. 4: 3, 4. Where shall we look for a fulfilment of this prophecy? Who does not know that we have now come to that time? The sound doctrine which if obeyed will make men a light in the world is not endorsed in the circle of the papacy, neither in the Protestant denominations. To-day the generality of mankind, even in professed Christianity, do not care to hear the practical truths of the gospel as we have recorded in part first of this work.

Theories and speculative opinions have taken the place of sound doctrine in the Protestant pulpit of this present day. The congregations in general have become so proud and vain in their imaginations, and so spoiled through philosophy, that they heap to themselves teachers having the wildest speculative opinions. Their itching ears have an insatiable desire for fine essays, amusing stories, and historic tales. The proud, arrogant pulpit orator of this present day makes it a study how best to calm the fears, gild the sins, and strew with flowers the iniquitous path of his passionate congregation.

Protestantism presents a most deplorable picture to those who have escaped her ruinous walls. Many a bishop and lord is bewailing his sad spiritless, powerless state, and crying, "Whither are we drifting?" Where will you have to go to-day but to Protestantism to find a fulfilment of Paul's prophecy in 2 Tim. 3:1-5? "This know also, that in the last days perilous times shall come. For men shall be lovers of their own selves, covetous, boasters, proud, blasphemers, disobedient to parents, unthankful, unholy, without natural affection, truce-breakers, false accusers, incontinent, fierce, despisers of those that are good, traitors, heady, high-minded, lovers of pleasure more than lovers of God; having a form of godliness, but denying the power thereof: from such turn away."

Paul here speaks of a religious people. They have "a form of godliness." While the "last days" and "last time" often include the whole of this gospel day, yet this prophecy particularly relates to the nearing of the end of time. Jesus says, "As the days of Noe were, so shall also the coming of the Son of man be. For as in the days that were before the flood they were eating and drinking, marrying and giving in marriage, until the day that Noe entered into the ark." Mat. 24: 37, 38. Let us considerately review this prophecy.

"Lovers of their own selves." Such a disposition of heart will manifest itself. Such people have more concern for their own welfare than for their neighbor's. They will look out for their own best interest. In the ministry it would be manifested in seeking places of ease, luxury, honor, and wealth.

"Covetous." A desire for worldly gain, loving money. By their conversation and general manner they manifest a strong desire for wealth, resorting to festivals and fairs to gain money.

"Boasters." Placing a high estimate on their own personal worth and accomplishments. As a man recently remarked of a stained window in a meeting-house: "See that window! Is not that fine? That cost one hundred dollars. That is my window, I put that in. These others only cost seventy-five dollars. See, here are my initials."

"Proud." Studying to make a fine appearance,

striving to excel in pulpit oratory, advertising the work they have done—so many have been converted through my labors, etc. All these works are indications of a proud heart.

"Blasphemers." To speak lightly of sacred things, to ridicule any portion of God's Word. Many professors of Christianity of to-day when asked if they believe in the ordinance of feet-washing will make some such answer as, "If your feet are dirty, you ought to wash them." The doctrines of holiness and divine healing are often impiously spoken of. Jesus Christ is sometimes charged with being a freemason, and recently a man said that the Savior went to school and studied for the ministry.

"Disobedient to parents." Is there not many a young lady and young man in apostate Protestantism, trampling under their feet the commands and wishes of their parents? The "old man," or the "old woman" (as they often speak of their parents), they say, "is not going to rule me."

"Unthankful." Murmuring when reverses come: complaining if their financial undertakings are unsuccessful; dissatisfied and discontented. These are evidences of an unthankful and ungrateful heart.

"Unholy." Those who dispute the doctrine of holiness, of purity or sinless perfection. They confess that they commit sin, and their life bears evidence that their confession is true. Or should they profess holiness and yet not live a true holy life they are classed with the great dark apostasy.

"Without natural affection." Many times the love of self, the love of pleasure, the love of the world, and sin in general destroys the natural affection. Mothers in their heart regret their children were born, because it prevents their entering society as they would like. They bewail the state of pregnancy for the same reason, and resort to murderous means for the privilege of enjoying more of the pleasures of sin and the world. Children also often betray a great lack of natural affection by their treatment of parents and one another.

"Truce-breakers." Having but little regard for a promise or obligation; violating obligations and promises to God and to man.

"False accusers." Slandering those who do live and obey the whole Word of God.

"Incontinent." Those who are living in the lust of the flesh; controlled by a depraved appetite.

"Fierce." Getting angry and becoming quarrelsome; all that is the opposite of gentleness and kindness.

"Despisers of those that are good." Because a man lives a good, pure, consistent Christian life it puts a rebuke upon the hypocrite, and for this reason he despises the good man.

"Traitors." Actually denying and renouncing portions of the Holy Bible, which they profess to believe. They are traitors to God and to Christianity.

"Heady." They are unteachable. No matter what

the Bible says, they know they are all right if they do indulge in things that are wrong.

"High-minded." So lifted up in themselves that the humble doctrines of the Savior are beneath their observance. These humble truths of the Bible are considered as nonessentials by the heady and high-minded.

"Lovers of pleasure more than lovers of God." Take more real comfort and delight in the party or festival than they do in worship. A sermon of thirty minutes is about as long as they can endure. Reading the Bible is an unpleasant task, therefore the good old book lies unused; but they can spend hours in the place of revelry.

Where do we have to look for such doings and characters as we have described? They abound in great numbers in the various denominations of to-day. Adam Clarke in his comentary in speaking of this prophecy, says: "This description the papists apply to the Protestants. The Protestants in their turn apply it to the papists. There have been both teachers and people in every age of the church and world to whom these words may be most legitimately applied. Both Catholics and Protestants have been lovers of their own selves," etc., "having a form of godliness, but denying the power thereof." How often the sectish lords lament the deadness of their congregations, and also grow weary of their own spiritless, formal prayers and sermons.

Bishop Weaver of the United Brethren denomination uses the following language, as quoted by a holiness periodical:

"POWER VERSUS FORM.

"The pulpit ought to be a center of power. But is it? God said to Jonah, 'Preach the preaching I bid thee.' Jesus said, 'Preach the gospel.' Paul said, 'Preach the Word.' Again he said, 'We preach Christ.' Philip 'preached Jesus.' All this means the selfsame thing. Christ is the soul of the gospel as well as the substance of all doctrine. Much of the preaching, reading or talking—whatever you please to call it—is Christless and powerless. Of course, this is a refined age, and the people are away up, but the devil can appear as refined as a saint. Nothing suits him better than to get the preacher away from the gospel on to some fine topic and then get some one to tell him (the preacher) that he made a fine effort. The pulpit should proclaim the great, fundamental doctrines of the Bible. But does it? The people are often treated to a well-written essay or dissertation on some abstract question that does not contain an ounce of pure gospel. There is neither lightning nor thunder in it. One reason why Paul was not ashamed of the gospel of Christ was because it was the power of God unto salvation. But it was no more the power of God unto salvation then than it is now. It is the same eternal truth, yesterday, to-day, and forever.

"In Hosea we read, 'Like people, like priest.' In Isaiah we read, 'As with the people, so with the priest.' There is a great deal of harmony between the pulpit and the pew. Everything goes along in an orderly manner. All services must be short or the people can not stand them—short prayers, short sermons, short everything. Oftentimes the service is gone through with, and nothing in it but an out-and-out performance; no life, no spirit, no power. Protestants often speak disparagingly of the ritualistic services gone through with by the Roman Catholic church, but if you come right down to it you will find about as much spirit and power in the one as the other. The result is that scores and hundreds of men, and women, and children are being gathered into the Protestant church who have not an ounce of Christian experience. If reformation was necessary in the times of Luther and Wesley in Europe, and Otterbein and Asbury in America, it is scarcely less necessary now. But some one may say this is putting it too strong. What are the facts? Is it not a fact that the church is drifting away from the more spiritual to the social and intellectual? If the religion of Jesus Christ is what the Bible represents it to be, then the church in general is far below the standard. Where is the spiritual power that was breathed into the apostolic church? Peter's sermon on the day of Pentecost was not what the people of to-day would call brilliant, but the people were pricked, not in the head, but in the heart.

"What did it? Two things. First, he preached the gospel straight. Second, the Holy Spirit quickened the Word spoken and made it powerful. What would the people do if there should be such an uproar in some of our congregations to-day? It would scare some of them half to death, and many would run for dear life. But we have the same gospel Peter had, and the same Holy Spirit to accompany the Word. What is the matter? The people do not want it that way, neither does the devil. Thousands of church people instead of praying for the baptism of the Holy Spirit, are asking such questions as these: Is it wrong for a Christian to dance? to go to the theater? to visit places of amusement? to play progressive euchre? etc. Why don't they ask such questions as these: Is it wrong to pray? to go to church? to take the sacrament? etc. The fact is, a man or woman filled with the Spirit of Christ knows without asking any questions whether a thing is right or wrong.

"But some may say that the writer is getting old and feeble, and has fallen far behind in the race, all of which is readily granted; but the fact remains that we have the same gospel, which is as changeless as the throne of God. If in the days of the Son of man and his inspired apostles it was necessary that a man should be 'born again,' 'born of the Spirit,' 'made a new creature,' and be 'cleansed from all sin,' it is necessary now. If there ever was a time when men were born into the kingdom of grace by the power of the Holy Ghost, it remains the same to-day. What under the heavens is the use for preachers and people to go whining around, and winking at this and that when they know it is out of harmony with the plain teaching of God's Word? It is all well enough to be nice and orderly in the house of God, but there is no substitute for the power of the Holy Spirit. Jesus Christ is the advocate between God and man, and the Holy Spirit is the executive officer in the holy trinity. If the church with its splendid machinery were endued with power as it might and ought to be, there is no telling what might be done in the next ten years. But what good is all this machinery, with no power to run it? What good is an engine without steam? I saw Engine 999. It was beautiful to look at. Everything was as near perfect as it could well be. But it was standing stock-still. Why? There was no steam; no power to move a wheel. That represents a good many congregations. The machinery is there, but no power to run it. In Ezekiel's vision he saw a marvelous vehicle, which moved with great rapidity. But it did not move itself. The spirit of the living creature was in the wheels; but for that it would not have moved at all. So it is with the church. If the Spirit of the living God is not in it, it will not and can not move forward. Oh, this spiritless, powerless performance called worship. How it detracts from the usefulness of the church!''

Such a description as given by Paul in the above

prophecy, and by this bishop, is true of sect Babylon of to-day. Such graceless, spiritless, Christless institutions are dark enough to obscure the beautiful light of the gospel.

The *Christian Advocate,* the organ of Methodism, a few years ago said: "We are approaching a crisis in church life. Gradually, but surely, disregard for the Bible, for the Sabbath, for the church, and for God, is taking possession of Christians. Teachers whose reputation for scholarship gives them wide influence, give it as their opinion that the Bible is not inspired at all, except as other great books are inspired. This poison has penetrated all our churches. The virus of skepticism has entered the pulpits in our own denomination."

Who can take issue with this editor? We very heartily agree with him. If any one is disposed to doubt that the virus of skepticism has entered the Methodist pulpits, he will only have to read the account of the meeting of four hundred of the leading ministers of New York and vicinity, including Bishop Edward G. Andrews. Below we give an account of the meeting as published in the *Atlanta Journal.*

METHODIST MINISTERS QUESTION THE BIBLE.

At a meeting of Methodist ministers last Monday morning in New York City, the validity of many of the stories of the Bible was questioned. Rev. S. P. Cadman urged at that meeting that the Bible could not be accepted as the sole rule of faith any longer. He pointed out alleged discrepancies in it, and said people could find truth only at its fountain head, Christ. The other ministers applauded him.

"That the inherency and infallibility of the Bible are no longer possible of belief among reasonable men."

This proposition, the acceptance of which will tear away the fundamental pillar of Methodist theology, was urged in all force, sincerity, and enthusiasm by the Rev. Cadman, pastor of the Metropolitan Temple, before the regular weekly meeting of the Methodist ministers of New York.

Four hundred of the leading ministers of New York and its vicinity, including Bishop Edward G. Andrews, were present when Mr. Cadman's paper was read. He was applauded when he arose to read it, and applauded again when he got through.

Mr. Cadman's paper was one of a series on Bible criticism. A paper taking practically the same ground was read before the ministers on the Monday evening before last, another paper on the subject will be read next Monday.

This bold portentous utterance, involving the most radical departure from accepted tenets of the Methodist church since its very foundation, was made before the most representative body of Methodist clergy in America. It included the vast majority of the preachers of Greater New York. It is the first announcement of an impending controversy, which may shake the Methodist church to its very foundation stones.

The acceptance of Dr. Cadman's proposition, heard with respect and applause by the New York ministers, is comparable to the adoption of a new constitution for the United States. It places the Bible on the basis of historical works on other than divine subjects; it rejects the authenticity of all parts of Holy Scripture which are repugnant to human reason.

Some of the details of the Bible that these ministers find fault with are:

That the earth was created in six days.

That Methuselah died at the age of 969 years.

That a whale swallowed Jonah, in whose belly he lay three days.

That the Red Sea was divided in order to permit the passage of the children of Israel out of Egypt.

That a snake tempted Eve in the Garden of Eden.

That Joshua commanded the sun to stand still, and that it obeyed him.

The tower of Babel narrative.

The turning of Lot's wife into a pillar of salt.

The story of Noah, the flood, and the ark.

That God spoke to Moses out of a burning bush.

That Aaron turned his rod into a serpent.

That Moses tapped a rock, and that water gushed forth.

That Moses drew forth his hand and that it was "leprous, white as snow."

THE LIGHT OF CHRISTIANITY. 409

That Elijah was translated to heaven in a chariot of fire.

That Elisha threw the mantle of Elijah across the Jordan, causing it to dry up and allow him passage.

That the earth opened and swallowed Achan and his companions.

That Shadrach, Meshach, and Abednego walked in a fiery furnace unharmed.

That Daniel stayed unhurt in the lions' den.

Wm. S. Breakey, of New York, in a letter to the editor of the *Revivalist* spoke concerning the above meeting and Methodism as follows: "I enclose a clipping from the *New York Herald* of recent date. It needs no comment, and explains the lack of spiritual power in the M. E. church of to-day. The attitude of the listening ministers and bishop, and their approval (of a majorty at least) of the sentiments expressed by the speaker and indicated by the applause shows the extent to which this so-called liberal element has permeated the M. E. church. This man is the leader of the so-called forward movement of the M. E. church in New York City, a movement consisting of short popular sermons, pleasant hours, Sunday evening concerts, lectures, united choir, and the innumerable fandangoes to entertain the people and keep the church crowded.

This is the Methodism of to-day in a leading metropolis of the country. It makes my soul—and, I believe, the soul of every one jealous for the glory of God and the honor of the Holy Spirit and the eternal welfare of human souls being led into the ditch of eternal night by these blind, reason-exalting leaders—cry out, 'How long, O Lord, how long,' must the followers of the life of Jesus Christ endure these things and by their silence be charged (by implication) with endorsing the present condition of things and methods of church work?"

We are often told by those who know no better, that this world is becoming more Christianized. The Bible says, "But evil men and seducers shall wax worse and worse, deceiving, and being deceived." 2 Tim. 3: 13. People are more advanced in invention and education than in former years, we frankly admit. There are not the inhuman wars and barbarous massacres and bloody persecutions that once were, and by hasty external view of political governments and educational interest one may conclude that the world is growing better. But where matters are growing worse and things becoming more deceivable is to be found in "mystery Babylon the great" and her harlot daughters; namely, Catholicism and the Protestant sects. They are becoming more worldly and covetous, more proud and popularity-loving. They are denying much of the Bible, turning their meeting-houses into concert halls and opera-houses. In a village where we resided until recently the Methodist meeting-house was called by the community in general the Methodist theater.

The paper by Mr. Cadman as quoted above is a specimen of how they deny the Bible. They almost unanimously deny the unity of the Bible, divine healing, holiness and some of the ordinances. But in the decade to come you will see much more astonishing things. The sectarian world is now just setting sail upon such a sea of revelry, banqueting, money getting, lewdness, and idolatry, as we have not seen before. Her awful sins will reach unto heaven, yea, for some years past have been crying out against her, but each year growing worse. Where is the aged man or woman but who remembers the day when Methodists had a plain, unassuming, consecrated ministry? The laity went plainly and modestly dressed. They had real Holy Ghost revivals, but those days are gone. To-day she is intoxicated with the spirit of worldliness. Every effort is being put forth, every nerve strained, the power and energy of intellect used to dazzle the world by oratory, and pompous show. O God, as we behold the awful sins of sectarianism we feel in our soul like Jeremiah when he wrote his Lamentation.

"Mine eyes do fail with tears, my bowels are troubled, ... because the children and the sucklings swoon in the streets of the city." "How is the gold become dim! how is the fine gold changed! the stones of the sanctuary are poured out in the top of every street." "The kings of the earth, and all the inhabitants of the world, would not have believed that the adversary and the enemy should have entered into the gates of Jerusalem. For the sins of her prophets, and the iniquities of her priests, that have shed the blood of the just in the midst of her, they have wandered as blind men in the streets, they have polluted themselves with blood, so that men could not touch their garments." "God will visit thine iniquity, he will discover thy sins."

The sins of Protestantism are sufficient cause to wring tears and prayers and fastings from every Christian heart. Who will not consecrate his time, talent, and means for the deliverance of God's beloved from their captivity?

THE PROPHECIES OF PETER.

"But there were false prophets also among the people, even as there shall be false teachers among you, who privily shall bring in damnable heresies, even denying the Lord that bought them, and bring upon themselves swift destruction. And many shall follow their pernicious ways; by reason of whom the way of truth shall be evil spoken of. And through covetousness shall they with feigned words make merchandise of you: whose judgment now of a long time lingereth not, and their damnation slumbereth not." 2 Pet. 2:1-3.

Here the inspired apostle foretells the coming of false teachers, who shall bring in damnable heresies. Heresy is translated from the Greek word *hairesis*.

The word "sect" is translated from the same Greek word. The word "damnable" is from the Greek *apoleia*, and means destruction. So the rendering of Rotherham, "parties of destruction," and of the German, "destructive sects," corresponds with the original. Protestant teachers will readily tell you that these "false teachers" and "destructive sects" refer to the heresies that sprang up in the first few centuries of this Christian era. We admit that sects and parties arose in those primitive days. We see something of this spirit in 1 Cor. 3: 1-5.

But are sects damnable in one age of the world and commendable in another? We conclude that if partyism, sectarianism, schisms, divisions, and heresies were destructive and brought destruction upon their adherents in the first centuries, it will do likewise in the last centuries. Paul says, "I beseech you, brethren, by the name of our Lord Jesus Christ, that you all speak the same thing, and that there be no divisions [schisms, margin] among you; but that ye be perfectly joined together in the same mind and in the same judgment." 1 Cor. 1: 10.

Many shall follow in the pernicious ways of these heresies. Is not this true at this present time? By them the way of truth shall be evil spoken of. There is scarcely a sectarian in the universe but will speak evil of some portion of the truth. These false teachers shall with feigned words make merchandise of their followers, because of their covetousness. This is really more true of present day sectarian preachers than it was of the false teachers in the first centuries. Does not the ministry of the present day resort to the telling of amusing stories, and touching incidents, and fabulous tales to amuse and allure the people, and are they not making merchandise of them? Are they not receiving large salaries? And no matter how poor you may be you must pay your preacher or else you have no hearty welcome to membership. The preacher can sit in his easy chair with folded arms while you labor and strive for his support. He can spend his evenings in luxury and pleasure while you are tossing upon your bed thinking and planning how to clothe and feed your little ones and get money to pay your church dues; for you know full well if you do not pay you will be snubbed and rejected and finally cut off and made believe, if possible, that you are on your way to hell.

The remainder of this chapter, beginning with the twelfth verse is a vivid description of the hireling ministry of these days. For the benefit of the reader we will quote and number each verse and give brief comment. 12. "But these as natural brute beasts made to be taken and destroyed, speak evil of the things they understand not, and shall utterly perish in their own corruption."

They are not governed by the Bible, but as "brute beasts" follow their covetous ways, speaking evil of the holy commandments of God, which they do not understand. They are the "blind leaders of the blind."

13. "And shall receive the reward of unrighteousness, as they that count it pleasure to riot in the daytime. Spots they are and blemishes, sporting themselves with their own deceivings while they feast with you."

The excursions of sightseeing and pleasure, the picnics and parties they count great pleasure. Characters that engage in such revelry and worldliness are spots and blemishes to Christianity. We are commanded to keep ourselves unspotted from the world. "Sporting themselves with their own deceivings while they feast with you." They will teach their young members that it is no harm to go to the party, to attend the shows and fairs, the suppers and entertainments, to play cards for amusement, and many like things; and with their own deceivings they will feast with them in such sports.

14. "Having eyes full of adultery, and that can not cease from sin; beguiling unstable souls: a heart they have exercised with covetous practises; cursed children."

Their hearts are inclined to evil ways and filled with fleshly desires; loving the things of the world and often confessing, "We can not live in this world without committing sin." By their evil example and false teachings they are beguiling many unstable souls. Their covetous heart is scarcely ever satisfied.

The prophet Isaiah speaks of these prophets saying, "They are all ignorant, they are all dumb dogs, they can not bark; sleeping, lying down, loving to slumber. Yea, they are greedy dogs which can never have enough." Isa. 56: 10, 11. This is a lazy, ease-loving greedy ministry. If they are getting $500.00 a year they will want $600.00. If they are receiving $1,000.00 they will want $1,200.00, and go wherever they can get the most. "Cursed children."

15. "Which have forsaken the right way, and are gone astray, following the way of Balaam the son of Bosor, who loved the wages of unrighteousness."

These false teachers have known a better way. The Lord showed Balaam the right way, but he was seduced by the reward offered by Balak. So with these teachers; they once knew a more righteous way, but have turned aside for the wages of unrighteousness.

16. "But was rebuked for his iniquity: the dumb ass speaking with man's voice forbad the madness of the prophet." As Balaam was rebuked by the dumb ass, so these false teachers in their madness for worldly honor, gain and wisdom are rebuked by the humble ignorant Christians, whom they consider as dumb ignorant creatures.

17. "These are wells without water, clouds that are carried with a tempest; to whom the mist of darkness is reserved forever."

Salvation is often spoken of as the "water of life." These false teachers are wells without water. Their preaching does not feed and water their flock. Their empty forms and stale essays contain no spiritual food. For this reason there is a famine throughout Babylon. "Behold, the days come, saith the Lord God, that I will send a famine in the land, not a famine of bread, nor a thirst for water, but of hearing the words of the Lord." Amos 8:11. From the pulpit we hear lectures, stories, and history, and not the pure gospel; this is the cause of this famine. "Clouds they are carried with a tempest." When there is some appearance of rain or water from these teachers, and you have hopes of hearing some of the Word of God, behold some false wind of doctrine for personal advantage carries away every sign of rain.

18. "For when they speak great swelling words of vanity, they allure through the lust of the flesh, through much wantonness, those that were clean escaped from them who live in error."

They preach in sublime style, and speak great words of vanity, almost incomprehensible to common people, and by touching incidents and sympathetic stories they allure, and those who were really converted are often led into error and formalism by these vain teachers.

19. "While they promise them liberty, they themselves are the servants of corruption."

From the pulpit they speak in elegant, flowery language of Jesus and heaven, and give great promises of blessings to their hearers, while they themselves are walking in sin and under bondage to the flesh.

It is not difficult for all who are not entombed in the mystic fogs of Babylon delusion to locate the fulfilment of this prophecy. Were Peter living to-day and should look over the Catholic and Protestant ministry he could not pen a better description of them than he has here done.

THE PROPHECY OF JUDE.

"Likewise also these filthy dreamers defile the flesh, despise dominion, and speak evil of dignities." ver. 8.

"But these speak evil of those things which they know not: but what they know naturally, as brute beasts, in those things they corrupt themselves. Woe unto them! for they have gone in the way of Cain, and ran greedily after the error of Balaam for reward, and perished in the gainsaying of Core. These are spots in your feasts of charity, when they feast with you, feeding themselves without fear: clouds they are without water, carried about of winds; trees whose fruit withereth, without fruit, twice dead, plucked up by the roots; raging waves of the sea, foaming out their own shame; wandering stars, to whom is reserved the blackness of darkness forever." ver. 10-13.

"These are murmurers, complainers, walking after

their own lust; and their mouth speaketh great swelling words, having men's persons in admiration because of advantage." ver. 16.

We believe that comment here is unnecessary since commenting on Peter's prophecy. In verses seventeen and eighteen Jude tells us these are the mockers of Christianity that should come in the last time, who should walk after their own ungodly lust. Jude foresees the great dark beastly manism that was to darken the earth in the clear day, the same as was seen by the Savior, Paul, and Peter.

When quoting the twelfth verse the Spirit of the Lord referred us to the wonderful prophecy of Ezekiel: "Son of man, prophesy against the shepherds of Israel, prophesy, and say unto them, Thus saith the Lord God unto the shepherds; Woe be to the shepherds of Israel that do feed themselves! should not the shepherds feed the flock? Ye eat the fat, and ye clothe you with the wool, ye kill them that are fed; but ye feed not the flock. The diseased have ye not strengthened, neither have ye healed that which was sick, neither have ye bound up that which was broken, neither have ye brought again that which was driven away, neither have ye sought that which was lost; but with force and with cruelty have ye ruled them." Ezek. 34: 2-4.

These shepherds feed and clothe themselves. They are more concerned for their own personal gain than for the souls of the people. If they do not receive an ample salary they will leave the souls to perish. They are unlike Paul, who labored with his own hands for his support while he fed starving souls upon the words of life. He was a light in the world, and the covetous, greedy shepherds are creators of darkness. These prophecies are all true of the present day sectarian ministry. They are the hireling shepherds that flee when they see the wolf coming. When poverty comes, they flee to a place where they are better supported. The prophecies concerning the apostasy are more particularly against the ministry than the laity, because the ministers are the leaders, leading their followers on in darkness.

THE REVELATION OF JOHN.

The prophecies of the book of Revelation have long been a mystery to the people. Occasionally some honest soul, laboring under the confusing mists of sectish night, has attempted to reveal the secret things of this book. His interpretations were so obscure and erroneous that he has only added confusion to confusion and mystery to mystery. However in the past few years as we are nearing the "time of the end," God by his Spirit has made clear these prophecies unto his humble, devoted people. Trusting in God to give the proper interpretation by his Spirit we will ask the reader to consider with us some of the prophecies of this book,

Chapter 13.

Ver. 1. "And I stood upon the sand of the sea, and saw a beast rise up out of the sea, having seven heads and ten horns, and upon his horns ten crowns, and upon his heads the name of blasphemy."

"Beast" means a fleshly, human, or mannish power. "Sea" is often used to represent trouble, upheaval, and commotions. History abounds with accounts of the upheavals in the ecclesiastical heavens between bishops in the third century. Out of these contentions and strivings and confusions arose in the year 325 A. D., a beastly or mannish form of ecclesiastical government; namely, the Roman Catholic church.

The "seven heads" have by some writers been interpreted to be the seven mountains on which the city of Rome is situated. For proof of this interpretation they quote Rev. 17:9. How that inanimate, literal mountains can represent heads, since the head contains the power of intellect and authority, lies beyond our comprehension.

That the ten horns are the ten kingdoms spoken of by Daniel (chap. 7, ver. 24) is, we consider, unquestionable. Now it may be a little obscure why the Revelator will make use of ten stately kingdoms to represent the ten horns of an ecclesiastical government. It is because this ecclesiastical government is human the same as a state government; and because the beastly Romish church was supported, and became what they were pleased to call both church and state.

The seven heads are seven supreme forms of government. These seven heads are seven mountains (not literal) and the seven mountains are seven kings. Rev. 17:9, 10. History tells us there were seven distinct forms of government in the Roman empire. The first, a royal or kingly government, continued about 428 years. The second was republic in form under the administration of dictators. This form of government continued eighty and eight years. The third form of government was under the absolute control of ten magistrates called decemvirs, and are also called prætors. The duration of this form of government exceeded three hundred years. In the year 336 B. C., the third form of government came to an end by the Latins being conquered by the Romans, and the consulate government succeeded, which continued until about the year 50 B. C. The fifth form of government was under the control of three men, and therefore called a triumvirate. The triumvirate form of government came to an end before John's vision of these heads. These are the five "fallen ones." Rev. 17:10. The power that then was, which was the sixth head of the beast, was the imperial power of the Cæsars, which continued more than four hundred years. The seventh power was the patriciate, which continued about fifty years.

These are the seven heads and ten horns—the seven forms of government, and the ten kingdoms out of which grew the eleventh horn which Daniel saw, or the beast which John saw. Thus we have the beast with its seven heads and ten horns.

Ver. 2. "And the beast which I saw was like unto a leopard, and his feet were as the feet of a bear, and his mouth as the mouth of a lion: and the dragon gave him his power, and his seat, and great authority."

Sins and worldliness are termed spots by the Bible. The leopard is a spotted beast, so no other animal could better represent the Romish sect with its dark spots of sin and crime. The bear makes use of the foot to deal the deadly blow upon an enemy. The papacy with its tyrannical feet has trodden down all that would dare rise against it. Great thunderings and loud roarings proceed out of the mouth of the lion in his strength and glory. So this beast fitly represents the Catholic church in her boasted strength, power, and authority.

The dragon that gave this ecclesiastical beast its authority and seat was the Roman state. In connection with this we will consider the first three verses of the twelfth chapter of Revelation. "And there appeared a great wonder in heaven; a woman clothed with the sun, and the moon under her feet, and upon her head a crown of twelve stars." ver. 1. The woman is the church. By believing or standing upon the Word a soul is brought into the church by the Spirit. Thus the church stands upon the moon (the Word of God), clothed by the sun (the Spirit).

This is no disagreement with a former use we have made of the sun and moon as symbols. An object may be used to symbolize different things in different prophecies.

"And there appeared another wonder in heaven; and behold a great red dragon, having seven heads and ten horns." ver. 3. This dragon is the same as the dragon that gave power to the beast of Rev. 13:2; namely, the Roman state. The Roman empire, pagan as it was, endeavored to devour the church as is said of the dragon in Rev. 12:4.

We will now return to Rev. 13:3: "And I saw one of his heads as it were wounded to death; and his deadly wound was healed: and all the world wondered after the beast."

As we have before observed, the seven original heads were the seven principalities, or forms of government, which gave rise to the Roman empire. A head or an ecclesiastical form of government in Romanism received a wound. The world wondered after the beast. This beast religion—manism—the Catholic sect, was now looked upon as the church. It was considered the only way to heaven. There was no salvation outside her walls. The true church was hidden. The sun, moon and stars were eclipsed. Christ had given his authority over to the pope, so it was believed, and the Romish sect stepped into the place of the true church. Christ and his church—the lights of the world—were no longer seen. The pope and his church stood up in their sins and abominations, and the world looked upon them as the church. This is certainly sufficient cause for darkness at the noonday.

Ver. 4. "And they worshiped the dragon which gave power unto the beast: and they worshiped the beast, saying, Who is like unto the beast? Who is able to make war with him?"

The people worshiped not only the church of Rome, but both church and state; for they were now consolidated. So the people worshiped the dragon and the beast, and boasted of their greatness.

Ver. 5. "And there was given unto him a mouth speaking great things and blasphemies; and power was given unto him to continue forty and two months."

From this text there opens a wide field before us, which we will enter for a while, and then return again to the further consideration of this chapter.

The pope's claims of power to forgive sins, to be infallible, to be the vicegerent of the Son of God, to have power to deliver from purgatory, and a number of other shameful pretensions, are certainly shocking blasphemies. Power was given him forty and two months.

In Rev. 12: 6, the woman (the church) is described as fleeing into the wilderness prepared for her of God, there to be fed a thousand two hundred and three score days. Here we learn that the woman fled from before the dragon and was protected of God (or fed) from the dragon's power for a thousand two hundred and three score days. This is virtually the same power; namely, the Romish state and church, that continued forty and two months as spoken of above.

In Rev. 11:3 we have another allusion made to the church of God at this period. "And I will give power unto my two witnesses, and they shall prophesy a thousand two hundred and three score days, clothed in sackcloth." A day in Scripture is used in different texts to represent different lengths of time. In some texts quoted in the introduction of this work a day is used to represent the whole of the Christian dispensation. Again it is said that "one day is with the Lord as a thousand years, and a thousand years as one day." In Rev. 11:11, a day is used to represent one hundred years; and in Ezek. 4:6, we learn that a day is often used to represent one year. A day in Rev. 11:3 and 12:6 signifies one year. Forty and two months (as mentioned in Rev. 13:5) are equal to 1260 days, allowing 30 days to the month. Here also a day signifies a year. Thus the beast supported by the dragon had power 1260 years. While this beast was in authority the woman was in obscurity, which was 1260 years. While the beast was in power and the woman in silence the two witnesses could only testify in sackcloth, which was 1260 years. These two witnesses in the church of God are the

Word of God, and the Spirit of God. A sackcloth dress is one donned in a time of grief or lamentation. The Word and Spirit of God, because of the sad state of the church, were draped in mourning or sackcloth.

We have before learned that the date of the rise of the apostasy was 270 A. D. By these prophecies made plain by the Holy Spirit we clearly understand the first beast as seen in the apostasy was to continue 1260 years, which added to 270 years will bring us down to 1530 A. D. At this date we have the Lutheran reformation, when the power of Catholicism as a universal state church was broken. The world as a whole no longer looked upon that dark, ungodly institution as the only way to heaven. They saw there was salvation outside the pales of Romanism.

Now we will return to Rev. 13th chapter. Ver. 6. "And he opened his mouth in blasphemy against God, to blaspheme his name, and his tabernacle, and them that dwell in heaven."

We have already spoken of how the papacy uttered blasphemy against God and his name, his church and his true people.

Ver. 7. "And it was given unto him to make war with the saints, and to overcome them: and power was given him over all kindreds, and tongues, and nations."

Catholicism numbers her slain by the thousands. If your human heart can endure the reading of a book on martyrdom and the tortures of the inquisition, you would there learn that it was the Romish sect that made war with and overcame the saints. To her was granted power over kings and nations. While the state gave her her power, she in turn rose to power and rule over the state.

Ver. 8. "And all that dwell upon the earth shall worship him, whose names were not written in the book of life of the Lamb slain from the foundation of the world."

Ver. 9. "If any man have an ear to hear, let him hear."

Ver. 10. "He that leadeth into captivity shall go into captivity: he that killeth with the sword must be killed with the sword. Here is the patience and the faith of the saints."

All worshiped the papacy except those who were really spiritual, and those were slain. The tenth verse is a prophecy against her; as she killed with the sword, so she shall be killed with the sword (the Word of God).

Ver. 11. "And I beheld another beast coming up out of the earth: and he had two horns like a lamb, and he spake as a dragon."

Here appears upon the scene another beast. A human ecclesiasticism, a manism. Protestant authors who brand the first beast as the Roman hierarchy are confounded at the appearance of this second beast. By these two beasts we understand the apostasy to be under two forms. We have no hesitancy in branding this second beast as Protestantism. In the church of God all is controlled exclusively by the Holy Spirit. There is no manism in the church of God, therefore it is not animal or beastly. All sectism is controlled largely by man, therefore is a beast power. At first Protestantism had a mild, gentle, lamb-like appearance compared with Catholicism.

The two horns are two state powers that gave support to the beast. Germany and England supported Protestantism, therefore are the two horns. The dragon spoken of in this eleventh verse is, like in the second verse and also in chapter 12:3, a state power.

This second beast "exercised all the power of the first beast before him." See ver. 12. Was this not true in England, where the king was head of both church and state? Consequently we see that the second beast or man religion spoken of was authorized by a dragon or state power. In verse thirteen it is said he doeth great wonders, so that he maketh fire come down from heaven on the earth. Throughout the reign of Protestantism there has been frequent spiritual revivals and reformations. God really sent the Holy Spirit fire upon the honest efforts of men, and wonders were accomplished betimes in the name of Jesus.

In the fourteenth verse it is said that he deceived them that dwell on the earth by the means of those miracles which he did. Each reformation in the past three centuries was begun by holy men, upon whom God sent the holy fire; but others rising up subsequently, who were devoid of spirituality, built upon their foundation, and now deceive the people in making them believe that they and their sect institutions are of God because God manifested himself to their predecessors. In this verse we also learn that an image was made unto the first beast. Upon the work of each reformer a sect institution was organized, which was fashioned after the Roman Catholic sect, the mother of all sects.

According to the words of the fifteenth verse these images will in some future day, which the Lord knows, find a consummation in one great image, unto which all bow and pay homage or else suffer martyrdom. To receive the mark of the beast as spoken of in verse sixteen is to receive the ceremonies and customs and doctrines peculiar to each respective sect. Any one acquainted with the customs and doctrines of the different denominations can to-day determine to what denomination a stranger belongs by his dress or manner of speech. The number six hundred sixty-six refers to the number of leading religious denominations.

We will now, briefly as possible, consider the first eight verses of the seventeenth chapter of Revelation. In verse one John speaks of seeing a great whore sitting upon many waters. In verse two he speaks of the kings of the earth becoming drunk on the wine of her fornication. This has all been true in the papacy. There is in this hierarchy an enchanting, delusive spirit that has intoxicated her subjects. This is the real secret of her power.

In Rev. 17:5 the apostasy is termed "Mystery, Babylon the Great, The Mother of Harlots and Abominations of the Earth." Here we see again the apostasy in two forms or generations. The mother is the first, and is identical with the first beast of Rev. 13:1. The harlot daughters are the second, and are identical with the second beast of Rev. 13:11. We consider it needful to enquire what is meant by the term

BABYLON.

There is the natural world and the spiritual world. Babylon has existed under both. There are many references made to it in both the Old and New Testaments. In the Old Testament we find the origin and final doom of literal Babylon. In the Apocalypse we find the origin and final doom of spiritual Babylon, the antitype. In the days of Noah the world became very wicked and God destroyed all save Noah and his family. For a time after the flood the people were righteous and the whole earth was one language and one speech. Gen. 11:1. God's people in those days all spoke the same language and understood each other, because they understood truth as it was.

"And it came to pass, as they journeyed from the east, that they found a plain in the land of Shinar;

and they dwelt there. And they said one to another, Go to, let us make brick, and burn them thoroughly. And they had brick for stone, and slime had they for mortar. And they said, Go to, let us build us a city and a tower, whose top may reach unto heaven; and let us make us a name, lest we be scattered abroad upon the face of the whole earth.'' Gen. 11:2-4.

God's people started on a pilgrimage in the order of God, but they tarried, they ceased to ''go forward.'' Had God's people continued on Babylon would never have been built. This has its spiritual import. When God's spiritual people cease to advance, when they get out of God's order, they will soon seek some other way to heaven.

This ancient city of Babylon grew until it became a mighty, resistless, universal empire. For a time in its history it held the people of God in captivity. The day came, however, when this mighty city passed away forever. The only dwellers among its lonely ruins are wild beasts and hissing serpents. The Babylon mentioned in Revelation is the spiritual antitype. The great tower of ancient Babel finds its antitype in mystery Babylon, the mother, and the diversified city at its feet finishes its antitype in the multiplicity of sects and creeds, where they speak a different spiritual language, as they cluster around their mother's knee. In this great apostate Babylon the true children of God have long been taken captive, but the day comes when God's own make their escape and return to spiritual Jerusalem, their native home. The Revelator beholds spiritual Babylon in a fallen condition, inhabited only by foul, devilish spirits, and unclean and hateful birds. Rev. 18:2.

There are many prophecies in Daniel and other chapters of Revelation relating to the dark apostasy of the noonday, which we reluctantly forbear to consider in this work, but are compelled to do so lest our volume swell to too great proportions.

In the conclusion of this chapter we desire to make a few quotations from other authors concerning mystery Babylon and her harlot daughters.

"This woman (popery) is called the mother of harlots and abominations. Who are the daughters? The Lutheran, the Presbyterian, and the Episcopalian are all branches of the Roman Catholic. Are not these demonstrated harlots and abominations in the above passage? I so decide. I could not, with the stake before me decide otherwise. Presbyterians and Episcopalians compose a part of Babylon. They hold the distinctive principles of papacy in common with papists."—*Tennessee Baptist*.

"I think Christ has a true church on earth, but its members are scattered among the various denominations, and are more or less under the influence of mystery Babylon and her daughters."—*Bible Doctrine*, p. 249.

"Is antichrist confined to the church of Rome? The answer is readily returned in the affirmative by Protestants in general, and happy had it been for the world were that the case. But although we are fully warranted to consider that church as the mother of harlots, the truth is that by whatsoever arguments we succeed in fixing that odious charge upon her, we shall by parity of reasoning be obliged to allow other national churches to be her unchaste daughters, and for this plain reason, among others, because in their very constitution and tendency they are hostile to the nature of the kingdom of Christ."—*Encyclopedia of Religious Knowledge.*

"The writer of the book of Revelation tells us he heard a voice from heaven saying, 'Come out of her, my people.' If such persons are to be found in the mother of harlots, with much less hesitancy it may be inferred that they are connected with her unchaste daughters, these national churches, which are founded upon what are called Protestant principles."—*Encyclopedia of Religion.*

"If she be the mother, who are the daughters? It must be the corrupt national established churches that came out of her."—*Lorenzo Dow.*

CHAPTER III.

FALSE TEACHINGS OF THE APOSTASY.

This is subject enough for volumes. There is scarcely a text in the Bible but what has been perverted by some one confused by the fogs of Babylon,

Perhaps you can not find two individuals in the whole of sectism that see "eye to eye" upon the whole truth. To mention all the erroneous teachings of apostates would be almost impossible. However we believe it to be compatible with this work and to the glory of God to mention and refute a few of the false doctrines that have been most effectual in obscuring the light of the sun and moon.

We will quote from an unknown author the following unscriptural dogmas of the Romish sect, and the date of their origin:

Prayers for the dead .... A. D. 200.
Worship of saints, angels and martyrs ......350.
Worship of Virgin Mary developed .... 431.
Worship in unknown tongue .... 600.
Papal supremacy .... 606.
Worship of images and relics imposed ...... 788.
Baptism of bells .... 965.
Obligatory celibacy of priests ....1000.
Infallibility of church ....1076.
Sale of indulgences ....1190.
Transubstantiation officially decreed ....1215.
Auricular confession officially imposed ......1215.
Cup kept from laity officially sanctioned ....1415.
Purgatory officially recognized ....1430.
Romish tradition put on level with Scripture .1540.
Immaculate conception proclaimed ....1864.
Papal infallibility proclaimed ....1870.

These dogmas are without Scriptural authority. They are only the traditions of men, and is it any wonder that the pure light of the gospel of the Son of God was dimmed when such blasphemous doctrines were substituted? Besides these, in the papacy originated many other erroneous superstitious doctrines that have been handed down and perpetuated through Protestantism. One of the most general is that of

INFANT BAPTISM.

This ceremony is wholly without Scriptural foundation. We have previously shown the true object and mode of baptism, and who are proper candidates. We asked a mother recently, whose babe had just been "christened," as she termed it, by a Methodist preacher, "What benefit has your child derived from this ceremony?" Her answer was like this: "None at all, but I had it done because others do it." And so it is with many other traditions and customs of men. Many a parent has their babe "christened" merely because it is a custom, or the preacher has said so, never searching the Word of God to know the reason why. Had she searched the Word of the Lord to know something of this doctrine she never would have found the object of her search. As we look upon the "christening" of an infant we are reminded more of heathendom than of the kingdom of grace.

The word "christen" we have not been able to

find in the Bible. Nowhere since the ordinance of baptism was instituted have we a commandment to baptize infants, and nowhere in all the evangelistic work of the apostles is there an instance of infant baptism recorded. If it is as important as some teach, even the child's eternal destiny depending upon it, do you not think there would have been some plain commandment in the teaching of Jesus and his apostles to that end? One command would be sufficient, but we have none. Infant baptism originated in the confusions of the apostasy. John refused to baptize some because they bore no fruit of repentance. Repentance, therefore, must precede baptism. This was plainly taught by Peter. "Then Peter said unto them, Repent, and be baptized every one of you in the name of Jesus." Acts 2:38. A little child can not repent, and needs no repentance.

Does baptizing an infant prepare it for heaven? If so, give one text as proof. If an unbaptized infant dies, will it be damned? If so, give one text as proof. Does baptism make the child any more religiously inclined, and will it not go into sin the same as unbaptized children? Give one text showing what is effected by infant baptism. Thousands are having their children baptized, and they do not know the reason why any more than that it is a custom. Thus we behold the meaninglessness, looseness, and carelessness of professed Christians. Just doing things because others do them. They have no conviction from

God nor the Bible. God wants us to be able to give a Scriptural reason for all we do in our form of worship.

Some have taught that circumcision of the Old Testament typifies infant baptism. This is a gross error. The circumcision of the Mosaic law is typical of a broken, penitent heart. "For he is not a Jew, that is one outwardly; neither is that circumcision, which is outward in the flesh; but he is a Jew, which is one inwardly; and circumcision is that of the heart, in the spirit, and not in the letter; whose praise is not of men, but of God." Rom. 2: 28, 29. A man was made a Jew under the old law by circumcision. He is made a spiritual Jew by the circumcision of the heart under the New Testament. It was only the male children that were circumcised according to the law of Moses. If circumcision be typical of infant baptism, it is only the boy infant that would be Scripturally baptized. You may ask, "What harm can result from such ceremony, even if it accomplishes no good?" It leads the child into error, and blinds his understanding to the true mode and object of baptism. To be a light in the world is to be and do just as Jesus did. To be in error concerning any doctrine of the Bible is to be to that extent in darkness.

The baptism of infants is wholly without Scriptural foundation, and is one of the erroneous teachings of the apostasy, a doctrine that aided in darkening the pure light of the gospel.

SPRINKLING AND POURING.

These forms of baptism originated among the heretics of the second century. *"Ego men baptizo humas en hudati."* Mat. 3:11. To give this a true literal translation, we have: "I indeed immerse you in water." Immersion is a mode of baptism, and the only Scriptural one. We have no account of sprinkling and pouring until the third century. The Novatians practised it in the third century. When we understand the true object of baptism, and what it represents, we find that sprinkling and pouring would be altogether inappropriate.

TRINE IMMERSION.

This is another doctrine of the apostasy. We have before stated that baptism represents a burial. Rom. 6:4. We can at once see the inappropriateness of three immersions. So far as we know all trine immersionists immerse forward. This does not fitly represent a burial. The baptismal formula of Mat. 28:19 is the trine immersionists strongest proof-text. "In the name of the Father, and of the Son, and of the Holy Ghost." These three, we are told, are one. 1 John 5:7. There are three personages in the Godhead, but these three are one. It does not require three acts of faith for pardon, yet we are told to believe in God, and to believe on the Lord Jesus Christ, etc. To be baptized in the name of the Lord Jesus

Christ is to be baptized in the name of the full triune God, because in him dwelleth all the fulness of the Godhead. Col. 2:9.

The disciples well understood the Savior in his commission in Mat. 28:19. They baptized under his direction before the commission. One act in the name of the Lord Jesus is all we can find them practising. "And he commanded them to be baptized in the name of the Lord." Acts 10:48. "When they heard this, they were baptized in the name of the Lord Jesus." Acts 19:5. "They were baptized in the name of the Lord Jesus." Acts 8:16.

Tertullian in the third century in writing on the subject of baptism says, "We solemnly profess that we disown the devil and his pomp and his angels. Hereupon we are thrice immersed, making a somewhat ampler pledge than the Lord has appointed in the gospel."—*The Crown.*

Trine immersionists make use of such historical records to establish the doctrine of trine immersion. Instead of being in its favor, it is against them. They were at this time under the delusions of a heresy. Apostate teachers had elected exorcists in what they called the church, whose business it was to expel the devil from the candidate for baptism. This is an awful heresy. Those of whom Tertullian writes disown the devil under the hand of these exorcists and are then thrice baptized. Tertullian understands, however, that this heresy is performing more than the Lord Jesus had appointed. Sprinkling, pouring, and trine immersion originated under the apostasy. Single immersion is the only Scriptural mode of baptism.

CHURCH ORGANIZATION.

To-day the teachers in Babylon and their subjects are in darkness concerning church organization. The election of officers and their framing of laws, and the location of the ministers by the annual conference are all human authority, and belong to the apostasy. The Holy Spirit is the sole organizer in the church of the Bible. There are a few texts in which the Holy Spirit is spoken of as working in conjunction with man, or using man as an agency. This is very limited. Conferences claim to work in conjunction with the Holy Spirit, but we have no such instances in the Scripture. One minister told me he trusted the Holy Spirit to direct conference to give him the proper appointment. This is popish—man not able to be directed by the Holy Spirit himself, but has a mediator.

Our space will prevent our telling of the adding of tradition to the Scripture, and of the rejection of much of the Word of God. Catholicism and Protestantism largely deny the doctrine of holiness. Some of the Protestant teachers teach holiness to a degree, but very few, or none of them, teach true Bible holiness. By far the large majority of sectarians reject the doctrine of Christian perfection, heart purity, or freedom from sin. Is it any wonder they are a great object of darkness when they are living in and can not be free from the very element of darkness? There is no light in them. The vast majority of the beast worshipers reject the doctrine of divine healing. As plainly as it is recorded in the Bible, they in the darkness comprehend it not. The whole of the sectarian world denies the unity of God's people as taught by the Savior, and as experienced by the church in the morning light. Nearly the whole of mystery Babylon and her harlot daughters reject the sacred ordinance of feet-washing. Some of them deny all the ordinances, and the others have misused and misapplied them so as to make them without meaning. But few sects that practise the lifting up of holy hands, and the greeting with a holy kiss.

The humble ordinances of feet-washing and greeting with a holy kiss are very repugnant to the generality of proud-hearted sectarians. They look upon these ordinances as being degrading to morality. They call it an "act which public decency abhors." Here they are mistaken: it is not public decency that abhors it; it is a proud heart. A holy kiss is not indecent, whether it be public or private.

Proud, sensual hearts have very depraved ideas of what is true decency. We will here give an authentic newspaper account of a scene which all the pure in heart consider a public indecency, moral degrading, Christian disgracing, and soul damning.

"Buffalo, Feb. 4.—A lively row is in progress at Burns, a little town about twenty miles from Buffalo, growing out of a new money-making scheme, introduced at a church social held there in the Lutheran church parlors. The church is heavily in debt, and the ladies advertised a social in the church to raise money to pay the preacher and buy some coal. The men of the congregation had all been seen and informed that the women had a big surprise for them.

"Across one end of the room was a curtain. For an hour the guests chatted after the old-fashioned church social style. Then the curtain was suddenly withdrawn. There in a row stood six of the prettiest women in the congregation, blushing and smiling, each bearing upon her bosom a placard, on which were the words: 'You may kiss me for 25cts.'

"It was fifteen minutes before the device began to work; but when it did, the silver quarters fairly showered into the young ladies' circle. Old and young rushed eagerly to the front to exchange coins for kisses. The show lasted only a short time, when the curtain was drawn. Then the storm burst. The women were jealous of their husbands, and a dozen or more family fights were started at once."

Similar scenes, and still more degrading ones, are occurring daily in the aristocratic religious denominations. The sect parties and socials, the fashionable balls, the obscene theatrical performances, are enjoyed, and admired, and applauded, by thousands so low in morality that they feel no shame. Their hearts are so naturalized and inclined to lewd ways that sin can scarcely bring a feeling of shame. It is only holy and pure things that are repugnant to their dispositions and inclinations.

A large majority of the sectarian world reject the scriptures that teach plainness of dress, that condemn revelry and fleshly lusts. There is not a sect upon the earth but what rejects some portion of God's Word, and taking them all together, probably there is not a text in the Bible but what is rejected or perverted by them. Sectism to-day presents a deplorable picture.

I would ask the reader to look at the plain, simple truths of the Bible as taught by the Savior and the disciples. Picture to your mind, by what knowledge you have of Scripture, the life of Christ and the apostles and the church in their day. Notice their humility, their equality, their care for souls, their privations, their persecutions, their holiness, their faith for healing the sick, their oneness, their unselfishness, their love for each other, their separation from the world, and their belief of the whole truth. Alongside of this place a picture of the religious denominations of to-day with their proud, highly educated and high-salaried ministry, rejecting much of the Bible, denying holiness and the humble ordinances, no healing faith, assuming proud titles, building fine temples, living in ease and luxury, joined to the world, free from persecution—their greed for money, their revelry, the pomp and show—and, oh, what do you see of the church of God? Truly, this great dark beastly sect religion has darkened the pure church of God.

We can scarcely forbear mentioning and exposing many other false teachings of the denominational world, but will console ourself with the hope that the reader will thoroughly acquaint himself with the Word of God and try every spirit and doctrine by the same. There remains yet one almost universal false and dangerous doctrine, which we deem but justice to the reader to refute. I refer to the doctrine of the

MILLENNIUM.

This is not a Bible word, nor a Bible doctrine. It is a word and teaching of the apostasy. The word is used to denote a thousand years. The most general teaching of the millennialist is that there will be a personal reign of Christ upon this earth of a thousand years after his second coming. There are very many theories respecting the millennium. This of itself is enough to make the doctrine very questionable. If there is such a doctrine in the Bible it should be so sufficiently clear as to not admit of so much disagreement. The millennial doctrine as taught by sectarian teachers we emphatically declare to be wholly without Scriptural foundation. It is a purpose of

Satan to cause man to place what should be a present realization to some time in the past or future.

In the days previous to the coming of Christ the Jews were in great expectation concerning the kingdom of God. They looked forward with great joy and anticipation to the coming of Christ, their King, who should set up a kingdom which should never be destroyed. They expected him to reign in a pomp and splendor that excelled the Cæsars. The kingdom of God came, but their proud hearts and high minds overlooked it altogether. The same is true to-day. The cold formal professors in Babylon see in the Bible a glowing description of the kingdom of God, and they, failing to come to its present and blessed realizations, have come to the conclusion that it must be in an age to come.

With perfect confidence we say there is not one text in the Bible speaking of the glory of Christ's kingdom but what is fulfilled here in salvation or in the eternal glory world above. There is no intervening state of peace and righteousness. We will briefly notice some of the principal texts used by millennial teachers, and we will find almost every one, if not every one, refers to the wonders of salvation here in this life. Mr. Talmage, in a sermon in October 1898, said in referring to Isa. 35:6: "In the millennial the lame man shall leap as an hart." Where can we behold a greater exposition of Bible ignorance? There is not a sentence in the whole of this chapter but points to the blessings of grace in this gospel day. Did not the lame man leap as an hart in the days of Christ and the apostles? Why will man be so unfair or so blind as to place the fulfilment of such prophecies in a millennial, when every word has been fulfilled, and is being fulfilled to-day, in those who are possessing the fulness of Christ's kingdom?

A text quoted by millennial teachers everywhere is found in Isa. 11: 6-8: "The wolf also shall dwell with the lamb, and the leopard shall lie down with the kid; and the calf and the young lion and the fatling together; and a little child shall lead them. And the cow and the bear shall feed; their young ones shall lie down together: and the lion shall eat straw like the ox. And the sucking child shall play on the hole of the asp, and the weaned child shall put his hand on the cockatrice' den." In the next verse you will learn where this peacefulness shall reign.

"They shall not hurt nor destroy in all my holy mountain." It is in God's holy mountain where they shall not hurt nor destroy. What is God's holy mountain? It is Zion, the church. "And it shall come to pass in the last days [the gospel days] that the mountain of the Lord's house shall be established in the top of the mountains, and shall be exalted above the hills; and all nations [both Jew and Gentile] shall flow unto it. And many people shall go and say,

Come ye, and let us go up to the mountain of the Lord, to the house of the God of Jacob; and he will teach us of his ways, and we will walk in his paths: for out of Zion shall go forth the law, and the word of the Lord from Jerusalem." Isa. 2:2, 3.

This is surely too plain to need comment. Zion is the Lord's mountain. The wolf dwelling with the Lamb is figurative language, and never will be literally fulfilled, but has been spiritually and figuratively fulfilled throughout the whole of this Christian dispensation. It shows the wonders of God's grace. Jesus called Herod a "fox." Luke 13:32. He certainly did not mean that he was truly a fox, but that he had a thieving, dishonest, foxlike disposition. Paul says, "Beware of dogs." Phil. 3:2. He is not giving us a warning against this literal animal, but against men that have a fierce and doglike nature. Jesus again says, "Beware of false prophets, which come to you in sheep's clothing, but inwardly they are ravening wolves." Mat. 7:15. Here we learn that men are inwardly ravening wolves; that is, they have a devouring, wolflike disposition. Thus we could continue.

In Isa. 35:9 it says that no lion shall be in the highway of holiness. In a Christian's holy life there is no lionlike nature. God's salvation saves men from such dispositions. And the whole of Isa. 11:6-8 is a prophecy relating to this present time, when the salvation of Jesus saves men from all wolf, bear, lion, and leopardlike natures, and fills all with a peaceable nature, that an innocent child shall lead them.

Please read the first verse of this chapter. Do we not find its fulfilment in Christ? Also read the tenth verse. Does it not point to the Savior? It all relates to the time when Christ shall come and the Gentile can be saved as well as the Jew. The ninth verse is often misquoted. Many say that in the millennium "righteousness shall cover the earth as the waters cover the sea." Such is not Scripture. But in this ninth verse it is said, "The earth shall be full of the knowledge of the Lord, as the waters cover the sea." This relates to the coming of Christ, when not only the Jews shall have the Word of God and a knowledge of him, but every nation is granted the Bible and salvation.

One strong text for millennial teachers, as they suppose, is Acts 3:21: "Whom [Christ] the heavens must receive until the times of restitution of all things, which God hath spoken by the mouth of all his holy prophets since the world began." A text they use to teach there shall be a thousand years in which restitution is to be made, makes no such intimation. In fact, it teaches to the contrary. Let us carefully examine it. Christ was taken up to heaven. He will some day come again. Acts 1:11. The positive teaching of this text is that the heavens will retain the Lord Jesus until everything is restored to the Father. Christ came to restore all things. Mat. 17:11. Full restitution for sin was made by the Savior. The Holy Spirit all through this dispensation is leading men to the blood and restoring them to the Father. The day will soon come when the Holy Spirit has gleaned out the last one and all has been restored to the Father that will be restored. This then is the full restitution of all things. Then the heavens will retain the Son of God no longer. He will come to claim his own. Instead of this text teaching that restitution is to be made after Christ's second coming, it teaches that the restitution is to be made before he comes the second time.

We will now ask the reader to read the only text that speaks of a thousand years. This is found in Rev. 20:1-10. If you will open your Bible and read, we can by the help of the Lord show you that this can not possibly mean a thousand years of Christ's reign upon the earth after his second coming. This language is figurative. Satan is an evil spirit and can not be bound with a literal chain. After the thousand years have expired, Satan is to be loosed, and shall deceive the nations. After Christ reigns here a thousand years in righteousness shall Satan be loosed and deceive the nations? Who can look forward to such an end with joy? How do you know but you will be one that will be deceived? If you are building hopes upon a millennium you are already deceived, and this deception is among the deceptions which are to come after the thousand years. This thousand years is in the past. This may be a startling statement to one who has been educated to believe in a reign of Christ in person here upon the earth in some future age of a thousand years' duration. Reader, will you please notice that the devil and Satan, that was to be bound a thousand years, is also called the dragon? Now the Scriptures do not always mean Beelzebub when speaking of Satan. Jesus upon one occasion, because Peter was remonstrating with him concerning his death, said, "Get thee behind me, Satan." Christ did not mean to say that Peter was the devil, but he addressed him as Satan, because the devil was using him as an instrument to persuade the Savior to escape the death he came here to endure for all. So Satan and the devil spoken of in Rev. 20:2 does not refer to the personal devil, the prince of evil spirits, but to some great power antagonistical to gospel light and truth as revealed in the church of God.

Now we feel ourself under obligation to the reader to give him the correct interpretation of this binding of Satan a thousand years, and of his being loosed at the end of that period. The term "dragon" is used to represent a state power, which gives power to some religion antagonistical to the religion of the Bible. However the original and real fundamental dragon power was Rome, when she supported a heathen religion, and when the world on the whole was so under the seducing charms of idolatrous worship that it knew not the one true God and his relationship to man. The Syriac New Testament, in speaking of this dragon in verse two, says, "Who seduced the whole habitable world." The binding of Satan refers to some time when the delusive charms of heathenish worship were largely cleared away and there became a greater universal knowledge of the true God. At the end of that thousand years, or long period of time, which time we have reached, the true God and the pure religion will be lost or unknown to the generality of mankind, and heathenish rites and customs and ceremonies will be the universal religion. Do we not read that at the end of the thousand years Satan shall again deceive the nations? We understand by this that the world on the whole shall be reveling in the delusive seductions of a lewd, lustful, idolatrous religion, making the times like it was in the days of Noah. Let me again say we are now entering these times, and this world is swiftly passing under awful and blinding delusions. So great are the delusions that if possible the very elect should be deceived.

The religious teachers of to-day on the whole are in ignorance concerning the binding of Satan. We will give you a sample of the ignorance of these teachers. In the *Gospel Messenger* of March 25, 1899, the Querist Department in answer to a question asked concerning the binding of Satan, said: "Satan will then be bound, cast into the bottomless pit, and there will be a chance to convert the unrighteous and lead them to accept Christ as the Savior."

A subscriber in search of knowledge asked the

Querist Department to give a scripture to prove the last clause. He received this answer: "It seems to us that it is one of those self-evident views that needs no proof. If the Bible teaches otherwise let us have the chapter and verse. The Querist Department does not pretend to know everything."

There are many other chapters and verses that teach otherwise. "Now is the day of salvation." "How shall we escape if we neglect so great salvation?" The wicked shall be resurrected to damnation. John 5:29.

CONCLUSION OF PART SECOND.

We have now passed the noonday. The reader, no doubt, fully comprehends why it was dark. The morning was light because the whole Word of truth was taught and experienced by the church. All were under the immediate control of the infallible Holy Spirit.

The noonday was dark because the leadings and teachings of fallible man were substituted for the Holy Spirit and Word. A thousand errors were brought in, the Word of God rejected. The faith once delivered to the saints was lost, sin and iniquity abounded and their love waxed cold. The preachers divined for money, and sought places of affluence, and thus the day was dark over them. Sectism to-day is a mass of worldliness. Infidelity abounds and every abominable work. If you desire a perfect description of sectism as it appears upon the scene to-day, read that given by the angel in Rev. 18:2.

PART III.

THE EVENING;

or,

CHRISTIANITY IN THE CLOSING DAYS OF THIS GOSPEL ERA.

We have now come to consider the evening time of this gospel day. The morning was light because of the truth being experienced and taught. The noonday was dark because traditions and theories and vain philosophies of man became substitutes for the Word of God. This evening time was seen by prophetic eye. "But it shall be one day which shall be known to the Lord, not day, nor night: but it shall come to pass, that at evening time it shall be light." We are nearing the close of this gospel day. The sun of time hangs low in the western horizon. The gospel light is now shining in peaceful splendor like the clear setting of the sun after a dark and cloudy noonday.

"Misty fogs so long concealing
All the hills of mingled night
Vanish, all their sin revealing,
For the 'evening shall be light'"

"Lo, the ransomed are returning,
Robed in shining crystal white,
Leaping, shouting, home to Zion,
Happy in the ev'ning light."—*Sel.*

CHAPTER I.
THE APOSTASY IN TWO DAYS.

In our introduction we gave a number of texts which spoke of the whole of the gospel dispensation as one day; but any period of time distinguished by some extraordinary historic event may be and is also termed a day. The apostasy or dark noonday being under two forms is marked in Bible history as two days. The first form of the apostasy, namely, Catholicism, is called by the Scriptures a "dark day."

A CLOUDY DAY.

The second form of the apostasy was not such utter darkness as the first, and is therefore called a cloudy day. "For thus saith the Lord God; Behold, I, even I, will both search my sheep, and seek them out. As a shepherd seeketh out his flock in the day that he is among his sheep that are scattered; so will I seek out my sheep, and will deliver them out of all places where they have been scattered in the cloudy and dark day." Ezek. 34: 11, 12. The cloudy day was a day of the scattering of God's people. This has been true of Protestantism. God's own people have been divided and scattered among the various organizations of man. The time of the seeking out refers to the evening, when God is going to gather his children together that "were scattered abroad," and they shall be "one heart and one soul" as in the morning.

One more text refers to the cloudy day. "And it shall come to pass in that day that the light shall not be clear, nor dark: but it shall be one day which shall be known to the Lord, not day, nor night: but it shall come to pass, that at evening time it shall be light." Zech. 14: 6, 7. This day of Protestantism was neither "clear nor dark"; was neither "day, nor night." It was a mixture of light and darkness, truth and error, and therefore is fitly termed a cloudy day.

A REVIVAL.

After those two days there shall be a great revival caused by the outpouring of the Holy Spirit. "Come, and let us return unto the Lord: for he hath torn, and he will heal us; he hath smitten, and he will bind us up. After two days will he revive us: in the third day he will raise us up, and we shall live in his sight. Then shall we know, if we follow on to know the Lord: his going forth is prepared as the morning; and he shall come unto us as the rain, as the latter and former rain unto the earth." Hos. 6: 1-3.

The two days of beastly power come to an end. The time comes when they shall no longer govern God's true people. It was true of literal Babylon, that had taken captive the children of God, that the time came when they returned from their captivity. The same is true of spiritual Babylon. The children of God have long been taken captive in her. In the evening time, after two days, they shall say, 'Come, let us return unto the Lord: for he hath torn, and he will heal us; he will revive us in the third day, he will raise us up,' etc. Praise God! Then shall we know the Lord. "His going forth is prepared as the morning." Just as God was known in the morning in his holiness and power, just so he will be known in the evening. Throughout the "two days" (apostasy) the Lord in his power to save to the uttermost, to heal, and to exclusively control his church was unknown. Therefore he says: "Then shall the seers be ashamed, and the diviners confounded: yea, they shall all cover their lips; for there is no answer of God." Micah 3:7.

Such is the ignorance of the seers of Babylon. They are educated in the wisdom of the world, but know little of God. Their sermons are the theories of man, and not the pure Word of God. For this reason there is a great spiritual famine in Babylon.

The evening time is called the third day, when God shall send copious showers of rain. The first day is a "dark day," and relates to the reign of the Catholic power. The second or dark and cloudy day relates to the reign of Protestantism. The third day is the "time of the end," when there shall be a consumption of the beast powers. Dan. 7:26. Daniel was told that the fourth beast he saw in his vision was a fourth kingdom. This was the Roman kingdom. Three had preceded—the Babylonian, Medo-Persian and Grecian. This beast had ten horns. Ver. 7. These ten horns were ten kings, or kingdoms, which were created out of the Roman empire by the barbarians of the North. History records the overrunning of the Roman empire from A. D. 376 to A. D. 476 by the different "powerful and warlike nations of the North; namely, the Huns, Goths, Vandals," etc. Thus in one century of time the kingdom of the Cæsars gave rise to ten different minor kingdoms.

In verse twenty-four of Daniel seven the prophet was told that another horn should arise after these ten. From the description of this horn we at once learn it to represent the Roman hierarchy, or to be the same as the first beast of Rev. 13. In verse twenty-six the prophet says, "Judgment shall sit, and they shall take away his dominion, to consume and to destroy it unto the end." The apostasy is being consumed by the powerful and sharp judgments of God's Word being executed by the faithful and true who are proclaiming, "Fear God, and give glory to him, for the hour of his judgment is come." This is in the time of the end, this glorious evening hour.

The apostle Paul gives a description of the apostasy in 2 Thes. 2. In verse eight he speaks of its consumption, which is being effected in this evening of time. Babylon is being consumed. Hear her cries of pain. The prophet Isaiah foretells the consumption of the apostasy in these words: "And the destruction of the transgressors and of the sinners shall be together, and they that forsake the Lord shall be consumed." This is being accomplished in this present day. The gospel truth is being held up as a "lamp that burneth," and Babylon is consumed. The Lord is washing "away the filth of the daughter of Zion, . . . by the spirit of judgment, and by the spirit of burning." Isa. 4:4.

"Flee out of the midst of Babylon, and deliver every man his soul."

MORNING AND EVENING LIGHT COMPARED.

How light shall be the evening? Will God "revive us and raise us up" in the third day to the apostolic plane? The answer is, "His going forth is prepared as the morning." "Then shall thy light break forth as the morning, and thine health shall spring forth speedily: and thy righteousness shall go before thee; the glory of the Lord shall be thy rearward." Isa. 58:8.

By these two texts we are given to understand that in the evening the light shall shine as bright as in the morning. The church of God will be raised to the same plane from which it was dragged down by ecclesiastical lords. God's people shall enjoy the same degree of holiness in the evening as they did in the morning. They shall enjoy the same blessed unity— "one heart and one soul," "and all speak the same thing." They shall possess apostolic faith. They shall have power with God to heal the sick, to open blinded eyes, to cause the lame to walk and the deaf to hear, to cast out devils, and to raise the dead the same as did the saints in the morning. Why shall they be given such power? Because they believe, experience and practise the whole truth. They are free from all manism. God has absolute control in each and every heart. Every hindrance to faith is removed, every barrier between them and God is taken away, and the Lord works with them, "confirming the word with signs following." Glory to his name!

CHAPTER II.
THE TIME OF THE EVENING.

The morning was of 270 years' duration. The first form of the apostasy lasted, as we have shown, 1260 years, bringing us to the Lutheran reformation in 1530. Now when we ascertain the duration of the second beast power we will know the time the sun, moon and stars reappear in the evening. One especial text that gives us information on this subject is found in Revelation. In speaking of the two witnesses the Revelator says: "And they that dwell upon the earth shall rejoice over them, and make merry, and shall send gifts one to another; because these two prophets tormented them that dwelt on the earth. And after three days and a half the Spirit of life from God entered into them, and they stood upon their feet; and great fear fell upon them which saw them." Rev. 11:10, 11.

In this we learn the duration of the power of Protestantism and the breaking forth of the evening light. We have before proven that a day in Scripture is used to represent different lengths of time, sometimes the whole of the Christian era, sometimes a thousand years, sometimes a hundred years, and sometimes a year. In this text a day represents a century. Three days are three centuries, and a half day is a half century. After three days and a half, which are three centuries and a half, or 350 years, of the reign of Protestantism, the Spirit of life from God entered into them. This is the dawning of the evening, when the whole and entire Word of God is believed and experienced and the Holy Spirit has the same power in governing the church of God as he did in the days of the apostles. The downfall of the first beast, or Romanism, and the arising of the second beast, or Protestantism, was in the year 1530. The duration of Protestant power is 350 years, which added to 1530 brings us to the year 1880 A. D., at which time the dark noonday closes and we emerging hail with joy the peaceful glowing evening light.

Prior to the year 1880 it was, with rare exceptions, universally conceded that to gain heaven we needs must unite with some religious denomination. About this time God by his Holy Spirit gave to men everywhere (whose hearts were prepared) an intuitive knowledge that we could be saved and live a Christian life outside the walls of sectism. Just to lean upon

God alone and be guided solely by his Word and Spirit, they discovered to be their blessed privilege. We are not alone in thus interpreting Rev. 11: 11. We will quote from other authors. "Cloudy day (Protestantism). Length of period 350 years." Rev. 11: 9.—*S. L. Speck in Bible Readings*, p. 104.

"The two witnesses [Word and Spirit] lie dead three days and a half [three and one-half centuries]. Rev. 11: 7-9. The church dwells in a wilderness, which is neither dark nor light. Period 350 years. Time from 1530 to 1880."—*W. G. S. in Bible Readings*, p. 69.

"Time of reign of second beast, from the year 1530 to 1880, making 350 years."—*H. C. Wickersham in Holiness Bible Subjects*, p. 178.

This same author on page 244 in quoting Rev. 11: 11 encloses in brackets the words: "At the end of three hundred and fifty years of Protestant sectism the true children of God come out of Babylon and are sanctified."

"The three days and a half they were to lie dead is interpreted by the Holy Spirit to mean three centuries and a half. This gives us the length of the Protestant age."—*Biblical Trace of the Church*, p. 143.

In the few years prior to 1880 A. D., there was a great declension in the spirituality of Protestantism. Who can deny this fact? Quite a number of the leading denominations held revivals, where was witnessed the power of the Holy Spirit. People were genuinely converted. They loved and worshiped God in quite a degree of simplicity and equality. The ministry was of a humbler class and more devoted to its charges. In the decade preceding 1880 there was a great change. This change perhaps can be no better described than is done in the following words of Mr. Foster, bishop of the Methodist denomination:

"Worldly socials, fairs, festivals, concerts, and such like, have taken the place of the religious gatherings, revival meetings, class and prayer-meetings of earlier days. . . . Under such worldly performance spirituality is frozen to death. . . . The early Methodist ministers went forth to sacrifice and suffer for Christ. They sought not places of ease and affluence, but of privation and suffering. They gloried not in their big salaries, fine parsonages, and refined congregations, but in the souls that had been won for Jesus. Oh, how changed! A hireling ministry will be a feeble, a timid truckling, a time-serving ministry, without faith, endurance, and holy power. Methodism formerly dealt in the great central truth. Now the pulpits deal largely in generalities and in popular lectures. The glorious doctrine of entire sanctification is rarely heard and seldom witnessed in the pulpits."

There is not a Methodist minister but knows the truthfulness of these statements, however much they may deny it. In the quoted texts of Scripture from Revelation 11, the ninth and tenth verses say:

"And they of the people and kindreds and tongues and nations shall see their dead bodies three days and a half, and shall not suffer their dead bodies to be put in graves. And they that dwell upon the earth shall rejoice over them, and make merry, and shall send gifts one to another."

By the "dead bodies" is meant the two witnesses, the Word and Spirit. These throughout Protestantism were dead. While they professed to be led by the Spirit and to believe and practise the Word, they did neither. Thus they would not entirely and openly in words deny the power of the Holy Spirit and verity of God's Word, yet in works they did deny them. "They profess that they know God; but in works they deny him, being abominable, and disobedient, and unto every good work reprobate." Titus 1:16. These two witnesses were dead, yet they would not allow their dead bodies to be buried: they professed to receive them.

The tenth verse tells of the worldliness of sectism at the time the Spirit of life from God entered into the Word and Holy Spirit, after the 350 years or the ushering in of the evening light. They were making merry and sending gifts. Sectism is straining every nerve, and adopting most every scheme for money-getting. The fundamental object in the socials, fairs, concerts, etc., is to get money. They adopt these worldly, sensual amusements to rob men of their money. We have in possession a clipping from the *New York Sun* which is a fair sample of the present-day performances and merry making for money, and well explains the rejoicing, merry making and sending of gifts as mentioned in Rev. 11:10. It is as follows:

"*SAVED THE CHURCH.*

"Members Performed Many Services in Turning an Odd Penny.

"FROM NEW YORK SUN.

"Pittsburg, March 5.—The church edifice of the Coraopolis Methodist church was advertised to be sold by the sheriff this week, and the members of the congregation made a heroic attempt all last week to save it. Coraopolis is a few miles below here. One vivacious young woman won a wager by riding a spirited horse without a saddle; other good sisters and brethren cleaned shoes and peddled, while some pushed wheelbarrows in which were conveyed some very staid-looking business men. The whole church community was animated by the common desire to keep the sheriff from the church-door. Luxuries were denied, and many ludicrous situations were invented until enough money was raised to secure a postponement of the sale.

"Nobody seemed in the least disconcerted over these unusual exhibitions. If any one asked Samuel Marshall, the well-known station agent, what he was doing when he was shining the boots of the ex-Burgess, he would have replied: 'Raising money for our church. Don't you want a shine?' Among the most active in the work was Mr. Marshall, and his industry in turning in the most money won for him the prize of a gold watch. The following items from his statement show some of the methods adopted:

"February 20.—Delivered message to F. D. Stickney, 10 cents. H. S. Misseldine wanted me to stand on my head, but found I could not do this, so added up fifty columns of figures, for which I received 50 cents.

"February 21.—Carried can of milk to restaurant of J. G. Walters, 10 cents.

"February 22.—Delivered head of cabbage, which afterward on a 'banter' was thrown at Mr. Walters, 10 cents.

"February 23.—Young lady paid me 5 cents to call on her; polished shoes for George Arras, 5 cents.

February 24.—Swept pool-room of J. E. McKee, 10 cents; delivered hardware to Mr. Boyers, $2.00.

"February 26.—Wheeled M. W. Watson from store of J. C. Walters to shop, 25 cents.

"February 27.—Shaved Henry DeGrange, the barber, for which I charged him 10 cents.

"Mrs. Hamilton, a well-known society woman, sold bread and laundered the gentlemen's ties. She also presented a report in rhyme at the 'pledge meeting' on last Tuesday night. One item of the report was:

"First I peddled chestnuts and met with success,
And to-day I raked in nickels is the truth, you better gues
Say, I must tell a secret, those chestnuts were alive,
But what of that, when I realized one dollar thirty-five.

"Mrs Hamilton returned about forty dollars as the result of her labors. Miss Fannie Siebold, a vivacious young woman with auburn hair and with eyes that sparkle, was visiting friends in the place. She never lost an opportunity to show her interest in the little church. Her host, curious to see if she could not be made to retract from her offers, told her he would give her fifty cents if she would ride one of his spirited horses without a saddle.

"She was told that she might ride any fashion. Miss Siebold made all the male portion of the family promise to remain indoors, where they could not observe her during the performance. They agreed to this, but people passing along the road were surprised at the sight of a handsome young lady galloping over the fields on the flying charger in a manner that would do credit to any man.

"As a result of all the industry, $208.54 was raised, the sheriff's placard was taken down from the church-door, and a thirty days' extension secured on the $2,500 remaining to be paid."

The following article, recently published in a God-fearing, religious paper, contains weighty and powerful truths, and should awaken the reader to the present condition of things in this dark, seducing, and soul-deluding, sinful world.

"There has been for many years a rapid decline among the Protestant churches of the spirit of revivals and of the manifestations of the power of the Holy Spirit. Not only is there great ignorance on the doctrines of the Bible, but almost universally a positive antagonism to anything like the supernatural in religious experience.

"Just as Jesus was rejected and crucified by the professed church at the close of the Jewish age, so the Holy Spirit is being despised and crucified by the professed church at the close of the Gentile age. Just as Jesus was rejected from the nice homes of Bethlehem, and had to go into a stable to find a place to be born, and where he could utter his infant cries, so the Holy Spirit to-day is utterly rejected from thousands of Protestant churches, and he has to go into rented halls, slum missions, canvas tents, and woods meetings to find a place to utter his voice through the lips of those who know and feel him. Just as there were a few who had supernatural discernment to recognize and worship the infant God, so there are now a few who discern the personality and operation of the Holy Spirit, and pour out to him their gold and frankincense and myrrh. Just as the people of Bethlehem, who had turned the unborn Savior from their door were soon made to wail by the king's order of assassination, so the thousands of nominal churches which now reject the work of the Holy Spirit from their doors will soon wail under the awful tribulation that is rapidly coming on all the earth. Oh, if the Protestant churches could only see the day of their visitation, and that the history of the way the Jews treated Jesus is being exactly repeated over and over again in the way the modern churches treat the Holy

Spirit, and that the same doom that overtook the Jewish church for rejecting Christ, will speedily overtake the modern churches for rejecting the Holy Spirit!

"Another feature of the present crisis is, God is working mainly through individuals, and not so much through machinery. Thousands of individuals in Europe and America have been called of the Spirit to launch out into soul-saving work along lines of personal enterprise more than ever in past ages.

"There never was a time in the world's history when Christian men and women felt so led of God not to wait for committees nor the red tape of ecclesiastical authority, but to hurry forth under a personal call from God and do what they could with their individual means and talents for the saving of souls, the sanctifying of believers, and preparing the chosen few to meet Jesus. There never seemed a time when anything like church machinery would run to seed so quick as now. Even if an enterprise that is started definitely as a holiness work gets a few officers and committees in it, in a few days or months it gets just as churchly and high-headed and dictatorial as an old popish institution. For this reason God is utilizing individuality in his kingdom as never before.

"Another feature of the present crisis is, that God will test the faith of his waiting ones, and all those persons who are making almanacs for the Lord, and fixing dates for the fulfilling of certain prophecies, are going to be disappointed. We are living a life of faith in every particular, clear down to the last moment of his appearing in the sky. The Scriptures are very clear in setting forth two facts concerning Christ's coming. On the one hand we are told of the signs that would precede his coming, and we are told to watch those things, and they will indicate his coming as near; on the other hand we are expressly told that the day and hour of his appearing will never be made known beforehand, and our wisdom lies in not forgetting the signs on the one hand, nor in fixing dates on the other. Hence Jesus commands us to keep in the attitude of a watcher, always ready, always expecting, yet not knowing. In the parable of the ten virgins, our Savior clearly intimates that the bridegroom will tarry beyond the time that his people expected him. The picture is that of a crowd of passengers sitting in a station and waiting for a night train which is behind time, and while they are yet waiting they get drowsy and nod. The sentence, 'They all slumbered and slept,' should more properly be, they became 'drowsy and nodded.' This applies to the very elect, who will be taken into the wedding, and indicates a crisis of the trial of the faith of the sanctified ones.

"But the most significant of all things in the present crisis is the testing of true faith in all points of doctrine. There never was a time since the fall of Adam when the human race was so drenched with the muddy waters of heresy. Everything moves with lightning rapidity. The principles that lie hidden in every system of government, education, social life.

and manifold forms of religion, are swiftly pushing themselves to prestige and open manifestation. Sin is not only working out every species of wickedness that can be invented, but the intellect of the so-called Christianized world is showing signs of decay in its ability to grasp sturdy Bible truth, and is largely turning from the Bible to old worn-out heathen ideas. Every doctrine of the Bible is being twisted into fanciful theories. The scriptures teaching of sin and the need of broken-hearted repentance is practically ignored by thousands of ministers and church-members. The absolute divinity of Jesus is growing weaker in the faith of many who claim to teach his gospel, and some who profess to be very orthodox say they do not pray to Jesus. The literal resurrection of the body taught by the Scriptures is caricatured and treated lightly by professed theologians, ministers, and professed Christians. The immortality of the soul and its conscious existence, either in heaven or hell, during the sleep of the body in death, is being rejected for the old heathen notion. The experience of justifying and sanctifying grace, attested by the personal Holy Spirit, is rejected by millions of church-members. Everlasting reward and punishment is laughed at as an old tradition instead of a serious doctrine of the Bible.

"It is well nigh impossible to enter a single professed Christian family in Europe or America in which some member has not a new patent on Scripture truth and holds some fanciful notion concerning the serious teachings of the Bible. I find a great many passages in which the last form of testifying for God's saints will be that of their faith in the simple plain old doctrines of God's Word. Jesus warns us that just before his coming every possible heresy and every variety of false Christ will appear to deceive the people, and that if it were possible they should deceive the very elect. And John in Revelation tells us of an era of the going forth of frogs, which are evil spirits, to seduce the people from the true faith. We are living in the frog era. In nearly every city in the land there are from one to three persons who claim to be God, or an incarnation of Christ, or the Holy Spirit. Thousands of religious people think it is too tame and uninteresting to accept all of the plain old doctrines of the Scripture, so they want something original and startling."

In the past two years the popular religious bodies, including an aristocratic ministry, have turned to worldliness at a rapid and unprecedented rate, and what will be seen of proud formalism, socialism, and rejection of divine truth in the circles of denominationalism within the next ten years would now appear incredulous.

The following poem selected from a recent religious periodical is vividly descriptive of the present-day religious denominations, commonly known as churches. However the true church of God is an entirely different institution, and just as far separated from the world, and just as bitterly hated by her as when she imprisoned, stoned and martyred her devoted followers.

THE CHURCH WALKING WITH THE WORLD.

"The Church and the World walked far apart,
  On the changing shores of time;
The World was singing a giddy song,
  And the Church a hymn sublime.
'Come, give me your hand,' cried the merry World,
  'And walk with me this way;'
But the good Church hid her snowy hand,
  And solemnly answered, 'Nay,
I will not give you my hand at all,
  And I will not walk with you;
Your way is the way of endless death;
  Your words are all untrue.'

" 'Nay, walk with me but a little space,'
  Said the World with a kindly air;
'The road I walk is a pleasant road,
  And the sun shines always there.
Your path is thorny and rough and rude,
  And mine is broad and plain;
My road is paved with flowers and gems,
  And yours with tears and pain.
The sky above me is always blue:
  No want, no toil, I know;
The sky above you is always dark;
  Your lot is a lot of woe.
My path, you see, is a broad, fair path,
  And my gate is high and wide—
There is room enough for you and for me
  To travel side by side.'

"Half shyly the Church approached the World,
  And gave him her hand of snow:
The old World grasped it and walked along,
  Saying, in accents low,
'Your dress is too simple to please my taste;
  I will give you pearls to wear,
Rich velvet and silks for your graceful form,
  And diamonds to deck your hair.'
The Church looked down at her plain white robes,
  And then at the dazzling World,
And blushed as she saw his handsome lip
  With a smile contemptuous curled.
'I will change my dress for a costlier one,'
  Said the Church with a smile of grace;
Then her pure garments drifted away,
  And the World gave in their place,
Beautiful satins, and shining silks,
  And roses and gems and pearls;
And over her forehead her bright hair fell
  Crisped in a thousand curls.

" 'Your house is too plain,' said the proud old World,
  'I'll build you one like mine:
Carpets of Brussels, and curtains of lace,
  And furniture ever so fine.'
So he built her a costly and beautiful house—
  Splendid it was to behold;
Her sons and her beautiful daughters dwelt there,
  Gleaming in purple and gold;
And fairs and shows in the halls were held,
  And the World and his children were there;
And laughter and music and feasts were heard
  In the place that was meant for prayer.
She had cushioned pews for the rich and the great,
  To sit in their pomp and their pride,
While the poor folks, clad in their shabby suits,
  Sat meekly down outside.

THE LIGHT OF CHRISTIANITY.

"The angel of mercy flew over the Church,
    And whispered, 'I know thy sin.'
The Church looked back with a sigh, and longed
    To gather her children in;
But some were off in the midnight ball,
    And some were off at the play,
And some were drinking in gay saloons;
    So she quietly went her way.
The sly World gallantly said to her,
    'Your children mean no harm—
Merely indulging in innocent sports.'
    So she leaned on his proffered arm,
And smiled, and chatted, and gathered flowers,
    As she walked along with the World;
While millions and millions of deathless souls
    To the horrible pit were hurled.

"'Your preachers are all too old and plain,'
    Said the gay old World with a sneer;
'They frighten my children with dreadful tales,
    Which I like not for them to hear:
They talk of brimstone and fire and pain,
    And the horrors of endless night;
They talk of a place that should not be
    Mentioned to ears polite.
I will send you some of the better stamp,
    Brilliant and gay and fast,
Who will tell them that people may live as they list,
    And go to heaven at last.
The Father is merciful and great and good,
    Tender and true and kind;
Do you think he would take one child to heaven
    And leave the rest behind?'
So he filled her house with gay divines,
    Gifted and great and learned;
And the plain old men that preached the cross
    Were out of the pulpit turned.

" 'You give too much to the poor,' said the World;
  'Far more than you ought to do.
If the poor need shelter and food and clothes,
  Why need it trouble you?
Go, take your money and buy rich robes,
  And horses and carriages fine,
And pearls and jewels and dainty food,
  And the rarest and costliest wine.
My children they dote on all such things,
  And if you their love would win,
You must do as they do, and walk in the ways
  That they are walking in.'
The Church held tightly the strings of her purse,
  And gracefully lowered her hand,
And simpered, 'I've given too much away;
  I'll do, sir, as you have said.'

"So the poor were turned from her door in scorn,
  And she heard not the orphans' cry;
And she drew her beautiful robes aside,
  As the widows went weeping by.
The sons of the World and the sons of the Church
  Walked closely hand and heart,
And only the Master who knoweth all,
  Could tell the two apart.
Then the Church sat down at her ease and said,
  'I am rich, and in goods increased;
I have need of nothing, and naught to do
  But to laugh and dance and feast.'
The sly World heard her, and laughed in his sleeve,
  And mockingly said aside,
'The Church is fallen—the beautiful Church—
  And her shame is her boast and pride!'

"The angel drew near to the mercy-seat,
  And whispered, in sighs, her name;
And the saints their anthems of rapture hushed,

THE LIGHT OF CHRISTIANITY.

> And covered their heads with shame.
> And a voice came down, through the hush of heaven,
>   From Him who sat on the throne,
> 'I know thy work, and how thou hast said,
>   I am rich; and hast not known
> That thou art naked and poor and blind
>   And wretched before my face;
> Therefore, from my presence I cast thee out,
>   And blot thy name from its place!' "—*Sel.*

To-day the proud, fashionable sectarian churches are lovingly folded in the arms of the giddy world, and in her mad, drunken, lustful craze she is crying, "On with the dance, let joy be unconfined."

MYSTERIOUS PROPHECIES REVEALED.

The bringing in of the evening light by the Holy Spirit has been the clearing away of much mystery from prophetic texts. The voice of the angel said, in speaking to Daniel, "But thou, O Daniel, shut up the words, and seal the book, even to the time of the end." Dan. 12:4. We have reached the time of the end—the evening, and the book is unsealed and revealed and the "wise understand"; but "none of the wicked understand." Many texts of Revelation were fulfilled and understood when the evening light flashed across its pages. We will quote a few.

Revelation 14:6-8.

"And I saw another angel fly in the midst of heaven, having the everlasting gospel to preach unto them that dwell on the earth, and to every nation, and kindred, and tongue, and people, saying with a loud voice, Fear God, and give glory to him, for the hour of his judgment is come: and worship him that made heaven, and earth, and the sea, and the fountains of waters. And there followed another angel saying, Babylon is fallen, is fallen, that great city, because she made all nations drink of the wine of the wrath of her fornication."

Angel is from the Greek *anggelos,* and means agent or messenger. "Heaven" does not refer to the glory world above, but to the work of God and heaven here upon earth. This angel is a messenger or servant in the work of the Lord. He has the everlasting gospel to preach to the people. The burden of his ministry is, "Fear God, and give glory to him; for the hour of his judgment is come." The evening or time of the end is reached, the hour of God's judgment, the time of the bride's especial preparation for the coming of the bridegroom. This ministry is closely followed by another messenger declaring, "Babylon is fallen, is fallen, that great city, because she made all nations drink of the wine of the wrath of her fornication."

"Babylon is fallen." This is a prediction against mystery Babylon the great and her harlot daughters— Catholicism and Protestantism. This God's pure ministry has been preaching for the last two decades. Sectism is in a fallen condition. It is fallen into the depths of worldliness. She has opened her bosom and invited the world in to revel with her. She has prepared a potion of charming delusive spirits, by which she has intoxicated and inflamed the blood of nations. In the last few years the concerts, fairs and socials are frequented by both the professed Christians and non-professors, and in their dress, conversation, and general manner, they are undistinguishable. Sectism to-day in not enticing people to enter her fold by preaching the everlasting gospel, but she allures them by her seducing love decoction of lewdness, worldliness and licentiousness. Babylon is fallen.

Some of the Old Testament texts contain a spiritual import. "Flee out of the midst of Babylon, and deliver every man his soul: be not cut off in her iniquity; for this is the time of the Lord's vengeance; he will render unto her a recompense." Jer. 51:6. This language is especially forcible at this present day. We have reached the time of the Lord's vengeance.

"**Babylon hath** been a golden cup in the Lord's hand, that made all the earth drunken: the nations have drunken of her wine; therefore the nations are mad." Jer. 51:7. The woman (mystery Babylon and her daughters) sitting upon the scarlet-colored beast had a golden cup in her hand. Rev. 17:4. The day was, as we have before spoken, when God did save some souls in sectism and gave them the Holy Spirit's power. But Satan has succeeded in emptying the golden cup of that which was divine and filled it with intoxicating potions that have allured nations to commit fornication with her.

"Babylon is suddenly fallen and destroyed: howl for her; take balm for her pain, if so be she may be healed. We would have healed Babylon, but she is not healed: forsake her, and let us go every one into his own country: for her judgment reacheth unto heaven, and is lifted up even to the skies." Jer. 51: 8, 9. Babylon can never be healed. She will not be healed. She is irredeemable. Destruction is her doom. "Forsake her and let us go every one into his own country."

Hear the lamentation of the children of God in their captivity in Babylon: "By the rivers of Babylon, there we sat down, yea, we wept, when we remembered Zion. We hanged our harps upon the willows, in the midst thereof. For there they that carried us away captive required of us a song; and they that wasted us required of us mirth, saying, Sing us one of the songs of Zion. How shall we sing the Lord's song in a strange land?" Psa. 137: 1-4.

Perishing souls in sectism would love to serve God better, but in their captivity they can not sing the songs of praise and glory.

BABYLON.

By thy dark deceptive waters,
Sighing, moaning, troubled sea,
Captives sing their songs of sorrow,
Hoping, longing to be free.

> Who shall sing the songs of Zion
> On thy banks, O raging sea?
> The voice of bridegroom and the bride
> Is heard no more at all in thee.
>
> Golden days are gone forever,
> Days now dark and dreary be;
> Harps untuned and silent ever,
> Silent by the moaning sea.
>
> Sadly weeping stands the willow
> On thy shore, O surging sea;
> 'Neath its shade my steps shall never,
> Never, never more shall be.

"Zion" is a metaphor, signifying "Jerusalem, which is from above," or the church of God. It is the home of the saints, where they are cared for by the Lord. As the ancient literal city of Babylon typifies the great spiritual Babylon, so the literal city of Jerusalem typifies the spiritual Jerusalem or Zion or church of God. God does not want his people joined unto a sect and under the laws and creeds and authority of man. He wants the full care of them. However, many of God's children, through ignorance, have been induced to seek a home in Babylon. Here they have been taken captive. In this evening time God is leading them back to Zion. "The ransomed of the Lord shall return and come to Zion with songs and everlasting joy upon their heads." Isa. 35:10. The songs of Zion are not to be sung in the barren land of Babylon. Babylon has gone into Zion and captured God's devoted children, but God will be avenged. "And 1 will render unto Babylon and to all the inhabitants of Chaldea all their evil that they have done in Zion in your sight, saith the Lord." Jer. 51: 24.

Here is a prophecy relating to this evening time. "In those days, and that time, saith the Lord, the children of Israel shall come, they and the children of Judah together, going and weeping: they shall go, and seek the Lord their God. They shall ask the way to Zion with their faces thitherward, saying, Come and let us join ourselves to the Lord in a perpetual covenant that shall not be forgotten." Jer. 50: 4, 5. See them coming home to Zion with the glory of God risen upon them. Halleluiah!

ZION.

In thy clear, transparent water,
  Peaceful, cleansing, crystal sea,
In thy sparkling beauty flowing,
  Let me ever sail on thee.

There is music in the ripple
  Of thy wave, O purest sea;
Here we sing the songs of Zion,
  In a soft sweet melody.

Peaceful are thy streams forever,
  Gentle, calmest, tranquil sea;
Harps are tuned to heavenly music;
  Hear the pleasant melody.

Tree of life is blooming ever
  On thy shore, O crystal sea;
'Neath its shade my walk shall ever,
  Ever and forever be.

Revelation 18: 1-5, 16, 17, 23.

"And after these things I saw another angel come down from heaven, having great power; and the earth was lightened with his glory. And he cried mightily with a strong voice, saying, Babylon the great is fallen, is fallen, and is become the habitation of devils, and the hold of every foul spirit, and a cage of every unclean and hateful bird. For all nations have drunk of the wine of the wrath of her fornication, and the kings of the earth have committed fornication with her, and the merchants of the earth are waxed rich through the abundance of her delicacies. And I heard another voice from heaven, saying, *Come out of her, my people,* that ye be not partakers of her sins, and that ye receive not of her plagues, for her sins have reached unto heaven, and God hath remembered her iniquities."

"Alas, alas that great city, that was clothed in fine linen, and purple, and scarlet, and decked with gold, and precious stones, and pearls! For in one hour so great riches is come to nought." "And the light of a candle shall shine no more at all in thee; and the voice of the bridegroom and of the bride shall be heard no more at all in thee."

This holy messenger announces the fall of Babylon, and gives a description of it. All that is pure, holy and divine has been driven out of sect Babylon and leaves its subjects to be ravished by unclean, worldly spirits, devouring their souls, and leaving the whole an unclean cage. God has gone out of sectism. He works with them no more; his voice is heard no more in her, and his call to his people is to 'come out of her.' "Flee out of Babylon, and deliver every man his soul." God dwells in Zion, and there shines the beautiful light of the gospel. "Out of Zion the perfection of beauty God hath shined." "Arise, shine; for thy light is come, and the glory of the Lord is risen upon thee." Isa. 60:1.

Return and come to Zion, O captive daughter; unloose the bands of sectism from off thy neck; cast aside the creeds and tyranny of man; cease the cold forms and frozen conventionalities, and seek the green pasture fields of Zion, where there are songs and everlasting joy, and sighs and sorrow come no more.

Matthew 13th chapter.

The parable of the Savior in which he likens the kingdom of heaven unto a man which sowed good seed in his field is also illustrative of the gospel day. The field is the world. The Son of man sowing the good seed is the glorious gospel work of the morning. The enemy that sowed the tares is the apostasy, which destroyed much of the good seed and sowed discord, contention, strife and superstition. The harvest-time is the evening time. The angels are God's holy messengers.

In the evening of time the Son of man shall send

forth his angels or messengers, and they shall gather out of his kingdom all things that offend, and them which do iniquity. God is calling his people out of all confusion and darkness, separating them from sin and the works of man. Such is the work to be done in the end of the world.

Jeremiah 23d chapter.

In the fifth and sixth verses of this chapter is a beautiful prophecy of Christ. "Behold, the days come, saith the Lord, that I will raise unto David a righteous Branch, and a king shall reign and prosper, and shall execute judgment and justice in the earth. In his days Judah shall be saved, and Israel shall dwell safely: and this is his name whereby he shall be called, The Lord our Righteousness."

In the ninth verse the prophet tells of his broken heart because he foresees the dark apostasy. From verse nine to verse eighteen he speaks of the wicked doings of apostates.

In verse nineteen he describes the present holiness reformation that is sweeping over the land. "Behold, a whirlwind of the Lord is gone forth in fury, even a grievous whirlwind: it shall fall grievously upon the head of the wicked."

Matthew 24th chapter.

In the third verse of the twenty-fourth chapter of Matthew we read of the disciples questioning the Savior concerning the end of the world. They say, "Tell us, when shall these things be? and what shall be the sign of thy coming, and of the end of the world?" In answering, the Savior in the sixth and the following few verses speaks of political upheavals. In the eleventh and twelfth verses he predicts the apostasy of the noonday. "Many false prophets shall rise and shall deceive many. And because iniquity shall abound the love of many shall wax cold." That is why a child of God finds it so difficult to retain an experience of salvation in sectism. Iniquity abounds, and being yoked up with such evil companions he can not stem the tide of influence.

In the fourteenth verse the Savior says: "And this gospel of the kingdom shall be preached in all the world for a witness unto all nations; and then shall the end come." This preaching of the gospel of the kingdom is to be after the apostasy, and just prior to the end of the world. Throughout sectism theology and tradition have been substituted for the gospel, but in the evening time John beholds an angel flying in the midst of heaven having the everlasting gospel to preach to them that dwell on the earth. This is the same as the preaching of the gospel in the end of the world to which the Savior refers. He has now taken the disciples once down through the whole of the Christian dispensation to the end of the world.

In the fifteenth verse he begins with them again at the desolation spoken of by Daniel, which is the destruction of Jerusalem in the year 70 A. D. From the sixteenth to the twenty-second verse inclusive, he instructs them concerning this abomination. From the twenty-third to the twenty-sixth inclusive he again speaks of the apostasy. False Christs and false prophets shall arise. In the twenty-seventh and twenty-eighth verses he speaks of the end of the world. He has now taken them through the Christian era again down to the time of the end. In the twenty-ninth verse he leads them back again to the destruction of Jerusalem. "Immediately after the tribulation of those days [by this he refers to the destruction of Jerusalem] shall the sun be darkened, and the moon shall not give her light, and the stars shall fall from heaven." This is the obscuring of Christ and the church by the beast power in the noontime.

In the thirty-first verse he says, "And he shall send his angels with a great sound of a trumpet, and they shall gather together his elect from the four winds, from one end of heaven to the other." These are the angels that are shouting, "Come out of her, my people." They are gathering out of God's kingdom all things that do offend and them that do iniquity. This is the work of God in the time of the end. "Deliver thyself, O Zion, that dwellest with the daughter of Babylon." Zech. 2:7. "Behold, I will send for many fishers, saith the Lord, and they shall fish them; and after will I send for many hunters, and they shall hunt them from every mountain, and from every hill, and out of the holes of the rocks." Jer. 16:16.

"Woe be unto the pastors that destroy and scatter the sheep of my pasture! saith the Lord. Therefore thus saith the Lord God of Israel against the pastors that feed my people; Ye have scattered my flock, and driven them away, and have not visited them: behold, I will visit upon you the evils of your doings, saith the Lord. And I will gather the remnant of my flock out of all countries whither I have driven them, and will bring them again to their fold; and they shall be fruitful and increase." Jer. 23:1-3.

In the evening of time God will gather the scattered remnant of his people, but woe be to the pastors that scattered them. Let the proud lords of sectism repent of their evil doings ere God visits his woe upon them.

"For thus saith the Lord God; Behold, I, even I, will both search my sheep, and seek them out. As a shepherd seeketh out his flock in the day that he is among his sheep that are scattered; so will I seek out my sheep, and will deliver them out of all places where they have been scattered in the cloudy and dark day [sectism]. And I will bring them out from the people, and gather them from the countries, and will bring them to their own land, and feed them upon the mountains of Israel by the rivers, and in all the inhabited places of the country. I will feed them in a good pasture, and upon the high mountains of Israel shall their fold be: there shall they lie in a good fold, and in a fat pasture shall they feed upon the mountains of Israel. I will feed my flock, and I will cause them to lie down, saith the Lord God. I will seek that which was lost, and bring again that which was driven away, and will bind up that which was broken, and will strengthen that which was sick: but I will destroy the fat and the strong; I will feed them with judgment." Ezek. 34: 11-16.

God is gathering out his own into the beautiful light of Zion. We have now reached the time when the above promise is being fulfilled by the delivering hand of God. Amid the ruins of Babel confusion the Lord has a remnant which he is gathering home to their goodly fold, in the top of the mountains of Israel.

"Except the Lord of hosts had left unto us a very small remnant, we should have been as Sodom, and we should have been like unto Gomorrah." Isa. 1: 9. "Yet, behold, therein shall be left a remnant that *shall be brought forth.*" Ezek. 14: 22.

"'Have you heard the voice from heaven,
  Calling in a solemn tone,
'Come, my people, from confusion,
  This is not your native home?'

"Do you know, O ransomed brother,
  That we stand upon the verge,
Where old time fills up his ages,
  And the lost will mourn his dirge?

"Yes, I heard, and to my vision
Zion's glory brightly shone;
Then I rose and fled the ruin,
Taking not a Babel stone.

"Yes, my soul has come to Zion,
On the high and holy way,
And I've seen all darkness flying,
Driven by the light of day.

[Now the evening light is flashing,
God is gathering to their home
All the pure and holy remnant
Waiting for the Lord to come.]

"Oh, what myriad souls are sleeping,
Soon to wake in judgment-fires;
Help, O God, thy remnant gleaning,
Until time indeed expires."

I have cast each sectish idol
To the mole and to the bat; (Isa. 2: 20.)
I am feeding on the mountain,
And my soul is growing fat. (Ezek. 34: 14.)

THE SECOND COMING OF CHRIST.

When Jesus was taken up into heaven and a cloud had received him out of sight, two heavenly visitants appeared unto the men of Galilee and said, "This same Jesus, which is taken up from you into heaven, shall so come in like manner as ye have seen him go into heaven." Acts 1:11. Jesus went up in a cloud and he is to come again in like manner as he went up. "And then shall they see the Son of man coming in the clouds with great power and glory." Mark 13: 26.

No one knows the exact time of his coming. "But of that day and hour knoweth no man, no, not the angels of heaven, but my Father only." Mat. 24: 36. We can know, however, when his coming is near. "So likewise ye, when ye shall see all these things, know that it is near, even at the door." Mat. 24: 33. The things spoken of here by which we may know that the coming of the Lord is near, is the gathering together of God's elect from out the ruins of Babylon and the world. The work of gathering is now in rapid progress. The messengers are flying with the everlasting gospel. Soon it will reach all nations. They are calling, 'Come out of her, my people, for the hour of her judgment is come.' Thus we now see the Savior's coming is near, even at the door. Even so, come, O Lord Jesus!

He sounds a warning to all to be ready. "Therefore be ye also ready: for in such an hour as ye think not the Son of man cometh." Mat. 24: 44. What will be the condition of this world when Jesus comes? "But as the days of Noe were, so shall also the coming of the Son of man be. For as in the days that were before the flood they were eating and drinking, marrying and giving in marriage, until the day that Noe entered into the ark, and knew not until the flood came, and took them all away; so shall also the coming of the Son of man be." Mat.

24: 37-39. Who is not able to fully understand this? In the end of the world wickedness and revelry shall be as it was in the days of Noah. "In the last days perilous times shall come." "But evil men and seducers shall wax worse and worse, deceiving and being deceived." 2 Tim. 3:13. The very deepest deceptions shall be upon the people in the time of the end. They shall be saying, "Peace and safety," then sudden destruction cometh upon them.

Just before the second coming of the Savior, and while God is gathering together the scattered fold of Israel, Satan "shall go out to deceive the nations which are in the four quarters of the earth, Gog and Magog [both forms of the apostasy], to gather them together to battle: the number of whom is as the sand of the sea. And they went upon the breadth of the earth, and compassed the camp of the saints about, and the beloved city [Zion]." Rev. 20:8, 9.

We are now living in the time when the sixth angel is pouring his vial upon the great river Euphrates, and the waters are being dried up. The time when the unclean spirits (the state power, ecclesiastical power, and the Babylon ministry) are going out unto the whole earth to gather them to the battle of that great day of God Almighty. Rev. 16:12-14. Even at this day the state power is favorably inclined toward the beast power. The candidate for office is upheld and defends the corrupt city for advantage. The kings of the earth are committing fornication with her. The state officials are so infatuated with her delicacies and intoxicated upon her wines that a true child of God can scarcely get a hearing of justice to-day in the courts. The prophet (ministry), church (so-called), and state, are the powers engaged in battle against God.

We are living in the time when the sixth angel is sounding. Rev. 9:13. Soon the seventh angel will stand upon the land and sea and with hand uplifted to heaven swear by him that liveth forever and ever, that time shall be no longer. Rev. 10:5-7. That day shall not come unawares upon the children of light. They will be watching for their Lord to come, when they shall be caught up to meet him in the air and forever be with him. Amen. 1 Thes. 4:17.

What shall be the doom of the wicked when that great and notable day of the Lord shall come? "And to you who are troubled rest with us, when the Lord Jesus shall be revealed from heaven with his mighty angels, in flaming fire taking vengeance on them that know not God, and that obey not the gospel of our Lord Jesus Christ: who shall be punished with everlasting destruction from the presence of the Lord, and from the glory of his power." 2 Thes. 1:7-9.

This flaming fire in which the Lord shall be revealed from heaven is the fire that shall come down from God out of heaven and devour Gog and Magog as they are compassing the camp of the saints and the beloved city. Rev. 20:9.

Dear saint, our God is able to deliver thee. "Wherefore, beloved, seeing that ye look for such things, be diligent that ye may be found of him in peace, without spot and blameless." 2 Pet. 3:14. The Holy Spirit is in the world searching out and bringing to the light every one that can be persuaded to accept salvation. Soon he will have gone over the world and gleaned out every one that is disposed to serve God. The world at large will reject him. His mission will be ended. He will ascend to the Father. Then as Christ went into heaven he will come again, taking vengeance on them that know not God, and receiving his own unto himself. Then the Savior's mission will be ended. He will turn all over to the Father, and the three shall be but one.

"Be ye therefore also ready; for in such an hour as ye think not the Son of man cometh." "Prepare to meet thy God."

THE LAST DAY.

This gospel day is the last day. There never will be another age of time. An age-to-come teacher is branded by the Word of God and the Holy Spirit, as a false teacher. We need no other age in which to prepare for eternity. This is the day of salvation. "Now is the accepted time." Now is the day and this is the time for us to accept Christ, and to be accepted of him. The Word of God holds no promise to you of another day of salvation. How can man, unless he be wholly subverted, teach another age to come when so many immutable and infallible texts declare this is the last day and last time? We will quote a few texts on this subject, and that alone will convince every one that is candid.*

"That in the dispensation of the fulness of times he might gather together in one all things in Christ, both which are in heaven, and which are on earth; even in him." Eph. 1:10. Are we not to understand that with this dispensation time is full? Then it will be the end, and as the seventh angel declares, "Time shall be no more."

"This know also, that in the last days perilous times shall come." 2 Tim. 3:1. These are declared to be the last days, hence there is no other day to come. Only eternity lies before us when this present time is ended.

"God, who at sundry times and in divers manners spake in time past unto the fathers by the prophets, hath in these last days spoken unto us by his Son." Heb. 1:1, 2. Here again it is declared that the day of Christ, this Christian dispensation, is the last day, and that "there should be mockers in the last time, who should walk after their own ungodly lusts." Jude 18. How can you expect another time when this is declared to be the last time? "Who verily was foreordained before the foundation of the world, but was

*See "The Last Dispensation." Gospel Trumpet Co., Moundsville, W. Va.

manifest in these last times for you." 1 Pet. 1:20. "Knowing this first, that there shall come in the last days scoffers." 2 Pet. 3:3. "Little children, it is the last time." 1 John 2:18.

How does John know it is the last time? Because the antichrists that Paul says should come in the last days have come, therefore John says in the same verse, "We know that it is the last time."

Many more texts from both Testaments could be quoted, but surely the reader will not ask for any more to help him believe it is the last time.

> "While false prophets are confiding
> In a foolish, erring dream,
> Of millennial enjoyments,
> They neglect the cleansing stream.
>
> "O poor sinner, don't believe them,
> There will be no age to come;
> If in life you find not Jesus,
> Death will seal your awful doom."

CONCLUSION OF PART THIRD.

We have placed before the reader in the best manner we could, considering our limited time, the beautiful light and wonderful accomplishments of redeeming grace in the morning of this gospel day. In the apostolic period, we again repeat, the church was the light of the world. The Christians believed the whole Word of God. They taught the whole truth and no more. They lived a pure, holy life just as Jesus lived and just as the Bible declares that Christians must live. They were fully consecrated to God. They counted not their lives dear unto themselves. They forsook all to follow Jesus and lived wholly unto him. They had faith in God and power with him. They were of one heart and of one soul. They all spake the same thing. They were humble and equal. They healed the sick, cast out devils, and raised the dead in Jesus' name. Thus they were the light of the world.

Now the evening shall be as light as the morning. Man, as a Christian, shall live as pure and holy and as deeply consecrated in this evening of time as did the Christian in the morning time. At this present time God is raising up a people who believe, experience and teach the whole Word of truth. They have fled the ruins of Babylon and are proclaiming the everlasting gospel in the fear of God and the clear light of heaven. God is working with his pure and consecrated ministry, confirming the Word with signs and deeds and wonders, the same as he did with the early ministry.

There are thousands to-day who gladly bear testimony to the wonderful healing power of God. The blind have been made to see, the lame to walk; broken bones have been united, cancers removed, consumption cured. The deaf have been made to hear, the dumb to speak, and devils have been cast out. All these wonders, and many more, have been wrought in the name of the holy child Jesus in God's pure church within the last few years. God is increasing his church in faith, purity, power, and glory, and in the immediate coming years much greater things than these shall ye hear and see. Amen.

A PERSONAL EXPERIENCE.

It is recorded in the Bible that God will not hear sinners. While this is true it has its modifications. Those who are in wilful and stubborn rebellion against God he will not hear, even though in a day of trouble and fear they should call upon him. But when in the more sober moments of life man's heart feels the influence of the Holy Spirit inclining his desires toward a better life, arousing the nobler aspirations of his soul, enkindling to a brighter flame the spark of humanity; when, though he be not in possession of God's saving grace, under such an influence he, in sincerity of heart, calls upon God, he will hear and answer his call as far as consistent with the divine mind, and thus encourage his soul on to the Christian goal.

Our boyhood days and the early days of our manhood were spent amid the gay scenes and pleasures of life. When in the whirl of society-life we had no serious thoughts. There would, however, in our more secluded hours, when naught stood between us and the whisperings of our soul, arise thoughts of futurity. The Holy Spirit would speak to our heart of God, of heaven, of Christ and the blood; he would hold before us in a beautiful picture the life of a Christian journeying onward to a glory world. He would also disclose to our view the hideousness and awfulness of sin, and the uneasiness, discontentments, trouble and fear attending the wicked as they journey onward to the eternal region of woe.

In these more sober hours we would seek God for his protection with sincere, heartfelt pledges that some day we would serve him. God heard these prayers and gave his protection. We now in reviewing the scenes of those early days see the many snares and dangers Satan had arranged for our destruction, but out of them all the Lord delivered us. Bless his name! There was one instance of God hearing our prayer, though in what may be considered a trivial matter, yet made a deep impression upon us and went far to enforce upon us the reality of God and his Word.

One night we had a journey of several miles to make on horseback. It was nine o'clock when we started. After traveling about two miles our horse became very lame. In our pity for him we dismounted and throwing the reins over the saddle started the horse on before us. After some two or three miles of traveling thus, our horse seemed much improved. For the purpose of faster travel, we concluded to again ride. Our attempts to catch the horse seemed in vain. Repeatedly we tried to come up with him, but when we had come near he would trot on before. After many unsuccessful trials it occurred to our mind that we should ask God to aid us. Accordingly the Father was implored to cause the horse to stand that we might come up with him. Although not a Christian we believed there was help in God, and trusting in him we approached the animal, speaking to him as we had before, when he stopped and we mounting continued our lonely journey in deep and solemn thought of the verity of God.

In the winter of 1886-87 we became very much concerned about our soul. A revival meeting was in progress in the little village in which we lived. They did not teach salvation by grace through faith as was taught by the apostles, but we, knowing no better, and wanting to escape the damnation of hell, and hoping for an avenue of escape, concluded to take this. Accordingly we gave the minister our hand one night, and answered in the affirmative his few questions concerning our belief in God. On our way home we were baptized, for we were taught that the water washed away sins. During the days following we kept a close watch upon our heart and life to learn if there was any change. We were disappointed. We found that sin held the same power over us. There remained the same uncertainty of our eternal state. The thoughts of death had lost none of their fear, and the grave none of its terror. We were troubled. Here we had entered, as we hoped, a path that led to heaven, but yet all was dark and uncertain. O God, is this all of thy kingdom upon the earth?

I would question the older members of our congregation about their experience. Should you be called for to-night to depart this life are you fully assured that your home will be in heaven? Have you no fear to meet God? They would answer me thus: "We can never know in this life just what the decision of the Great Judge will be until we come before his awful tribunal. In this world we can only go on the best we can, and hope for the most in the judgment."

This was sad news to my soul. Is this all there is in a Christian life? Where is the great peace, the joy, the bright hope and positiveness promised in the Bible? But thinking these old heads knew all about the Christian life, I endeavored to console myself and calm my fears. I very poorly succeeded, for which I now praise God.

One instance occurred at this time that troubled me very greatly. One night after retiring we heard a shout of "Fire! fire!" upon the street. On rushing to the door and looking up the whole heavens above us seemed to be one burning flame. All was on fire. The first thought that came to our mind was, It is the last night of this world. The earth, and all its works, is burning up. A great fear came upon me. Whither shall I go, and whither shall I flee from His presence? The cause of alarm proved to be a burning building over a hill, casting the reflection on the dark clouds over us. We read in the Bible of a class unfit and unprepared for heaven, that would in that day call for the mountains and the hills to fall upon them to hide them from God's presence. Here we, trying and claiming to be a Christian, experienced just what was said should be the experience of the wicked, and my soul was alarmed. Earnest became our efforts to live a better life. Fierce was our struggle against sin, deep and firm would be the resolutions, but sin was a hard, strong master, who ground us beneath his iron heel. We sought every known means for relief, walking for miles to hear a sermon to learn of a more successful life.

Often in these days of struggle would I become unpleasant in my home. Should my children be a little trying, I would speak to them in a cross, snappish way. I would see them stand back in fear before my harsh voice, and this would sting my conscience. A child in fear of its father! how unchristianlike! When my wife, whom I had vowed to love always, would not do according to my judgment I would hastily reprove in strong language. We would see the tears start from her eyes, and again our conscience would be heavily smitten. Resolve after resolve was made to be more tender and kind to our dear ones, only to be broken by the power of impatience.

In our efforts to become more gentle and tender we often would read an article in an old schoolreader entitled "Sorrow for the Dead." In this the writer said words like these, to the best of our remembrance: "As we look upon the cold, lifeless form of some dear, departed friend, there will come rushing to our memory, the unkind acts and deeds and thoughts we have had toward them. This remorse of conscience," he said, "should cause us to be more true to the living." We often would read this, and did receive some benefit from it for the time, but we found it powerless to conquer an irritable disposition. We can not forbear telling the reader here, although it is a little in the advance, that the day came when we found the Savior in the wonders of his redeeming love and he broke the power of sin, and by his grace did strengthen and help us to be "true to the living." Glory, glory to his name!

It was in the summer of 1890 that the struggle became very desperate. The convicting hand of God lay heavily upon me. The burden of sin lay heavily upon my soul, especially the sin of tobacco using. We had no man to teach us. None seemed to care, nor pity. God, however, was humbling us down to a final decision. One late October morning on our way to the schoolroom, as we were teaching at that time, all alone upon the road, God spoke peace to our soul. Where is the pen to describe the experience of that hour! Mine, it seems, is utterly helpless. We were conscious of a life, power and glory, not terrestrial, filling our entire being. The earth was lit up with a splendor never seen before. In our days of deepest conviction we would picture to our mind the happiness of angels, but here we had come to the realization of something that far surpassed all we had imagined of the heavenly host. We felt like we wanted to sing and praise God forever. Wife had received a similar experience in her home a few days before. Our home at once became a heaven. We remembered in pity those who had endeavored to comfort us in our fears and tell us there was no better way.

Two weeks passed of uninterrupted glory. However, one morning after about two weeks, when doing some work which went wrong, we were strongly tempted to speak as we had formerly done on such occasions, but we overcame. The second time the work went wrong as previously, when the temptation came stronger than before. We felt something unpleasant within us; however, God helped us to overcome, and we set to doing the work over, when it went wrong the third time. This time we were overcome and gave utterance to a word that brought a sense of guilt. No sooner had we spoken than we fell upon our knees and did not arise until we knew we were forgiven. By this experience we became conscious of a foe within us that was going to give us trouble in the Christian life.

About this time we providentially received a copy of a holiness paper, *The Gospel Trumpet*, which taught a higher life, namely, entire sanctification. This came as a light from heaven. We began to earnestly seek this experience. Before we reached this experience there were a few other occurrences in our Christian life of which we wish to speak. At this time we were very ignorant of the Bible. It was our custom to have prayer at the schoolroom after the children were all gone to their homes. We would then go to our home with a heavenly glory resting upon us. One evening on our way home, we met a company of our former worldly associates. They accosted us in their customary worldly way. We replied somewhat under the influence of their worldly spirit. I felt the glory depart, and an emptiness instead. I went on my way hastily, asking God to smile upon me again. He taught me by this that he had chosen me out of the world and its witticisms, and that slang phrases were foreign to his salvation.

Soon after this, one morning in November when laboring in my garden a transparent glory shone all around me, and my soul was filled with peace. It was on election day. After working a few hours amid rapturous bliss, we went to the place of voting and cast our ballot along with political men. A shade came over my spirit, and for the remainder of the day it appeared that God had forsaken me and would never smile on me again. He taught me once more that he had chosen me out of the world and that politics in civil government was foreign to the kingdom of heaven.

The Christmas-time drew near, and great preparations were being made by the people for their festivities. In these we found nothing congenial to our spirit. We had decided to remain at home on the night of these festivities and have a protracted Bible reading and prayers. We looked forward to the evening with pleasure, expecting great blessings from God. Just before we were ready to begin our Bible reading wife was taken with a severe aching in the head, that threatened to mar the enjoyment of the evening. We wondered why it was that God permitted us to be thus interrupted, when the Holy Spirit whispered, "If you will ask God, he will heal her." Accordingly we fell upon our knees and petitioned God for his healing virtue, and instantly she was healed. This was our first experience in divine healing.

In the following February a Holy Ghost minister came to our place and held a short series of meetings. He taught us the way of God more perfectly. We entered the glorious experience of entire sanctification during this meeting. We also beheld the body of Christ, the one true church, and saw in a clear light the monstrous beast religion in all her evils. God soon after called us into his work. We sold our little home, all we had of this world, and used the means in the work of the Lord. Our work for God has been independent of the creeds of men, teaching a full salvation and trusting God for everything. We have held meetings in over twelve of the different states, and have never asked for money. Not on one single occasion have we taken up a collection. It would require volumes to tell of the many times the Lord has blessedly answered our prayers. God has never called us to any conspicuous position in this world. The great faith for the building of orphanages and homes, and establishing missions has been entrusted to other men. Our faith has been only for our daily bread and needs. Oh, what an assurance our heavenly Father gives us that he will never forsake us. We do not want the riches of this world. We would rather not have them. There is a blessedness in taking our every want to Jesus. To look unto him daily for your temporal as well as spiritual support has a strong tendency to draw one very near to him.

We would take pleasure in telling you of many of the instances in which God has heard and answered our prayers, but fearing you will take less pleasure in reading we will forbear, only saying that God has been petitioned for corn for our horse, and the prayer answered in a marvelous way before the day was over. We have asked God for a spool of thread, and our prayer has been answered at once. One time wife was on her knees asking God for soap, when there was a rap at the door, and upon opening it a lady presented her with a bar of soap. Almost daily the Lord is petitioned for flour, meat, sugar, or clothes, and he always gives us what we need. It is wonderful and just as glorious as it is wonderful. In fact, such a life is made up of glory.

Some one may wonder if we ever have any tests of our faith. Oh, yes; there is where the greatest glory is. Not long since we were much in need of a dollar. In searching through my vest pocket for a match I found a dollar bill all neatly rolled up. Where it came from, and how, I never knew, only that the Lord sent it. Just last night, our twelve-year-old daughter said, "This is the last Sunday I can wear these shoes. Unless I get a new pair I shall have to stay at home." We asked her if she had been asking the Lord for a pair. She answered, "Yes, sir." This morning in our family devotions we made especial mention, amid some other things, of the shoes. In less than two hours a Christian man came to the door and presented her with a pair. Yes, we would rather have a faith and trust in God than the wealth of a world. We feel more secure.

The times God has healed different ones of our family we are unable to number. For the past eight years he, and he only, has been our physician. We have not in that time spent one cent for medicine. We have three children, aged four, six, and eight years, who have never tasted medicine. They never were given a dose of any kind of soothing syrups or "teas." God has always healed from the toothache to a broken limb. It does not take much of the Lord's means to provide for us. We wear no superfluous clothing. Our daily fare is plain and common. We use no stimulants, narcotics, nor medicines, and consequently just a few pennies a day is all we need. God in his great goodness supplies all these, while we go telling the world of the wonderful blessings of salvation.

We are at present engaged in ministerial work without salary. In all our meetings we take up no collection, we ask for no money in any way of man, and we have no other source of support but in God alone. Just as the apostles lived in the morning light, so we live in the evening light. Just what they enjoyed, we enjoy. In their preaching they gave God's people warning of the apostasy. In our ministry we preach, "Come out of her, my people."

We enjoy more of the love of God than ever before. His very life and power and glory fills our soul to the full. We are led exclusively by his Spirit and are fed and clothed by his bountiful hand. Our life is one of blessed contentment. Our home is a heaven and our happiness is complete. Even as we write, the waves of glory roll over our soul until we are made to shout praises to our God. We have never a care nor a sorrow, but a faith and trust in God that keeps us above every wave of trouble. We are dead to the world and living alone for his glory. His great heart's love sweetens and tenders every fiber of our soul, and bids us wait in brighter hope the happy day when he shall call us to our home.

> O home of my soul,
> In that far away goal;
> Each day brings me nearer to thee,
> The great throne so white,

And my crown shining bright,
　　Mine eyes ever longing to see.

There's a musical strain
From that far away plain;
　　Its melody sweeps o'er my soul,
While a wave of sweet peace
In my heart shall increase,
　　While the years of eternity roll.

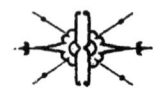